Educonomy

A volume in
Innovation in Human Centered Sustainability
Maria-Teresa Lepeley, *Series Editor*

Educonomy

Unleashing Wellbeing and Human Centered Sustainable Development

Maria-Teresa Lepeley

IAP

INFORMATION AGE PUBLISHING, INC.
Charlotte, NC • www.infoagepub.com

Library of Congress Cataloging-in-Publication Data

A CIP record for this book is available from the Library of Congress
http://www.loc.gov

ISBN: 978-1-64113-492-7 (Paperback)
978-1-64113-493-4 (Hardcover)
978-1-64113-494-1 (ebook)

Printed and bound by CPI Group (UK) Ltd, Croydon, CR0 4YY

Contents

PART III

The Educonomy and Its Three Pillars

Introduction

There is only one good, knowledge. And one evil, ignorance.
—Socrates

Educated people are much superior to uneducated people as the living are to the dead.
—Aristotle

The Human Centered Approach. Nothing New. But Economics Needs a Review

In 2001, I wrote a book where I argued that in the Era of Knowledge nations unable to improve the quality of education were mortgaging economic growth, people's wellbeing and sustainable development. In 2018, I coedited the book *Wellbeing for Sustainability in the Workforce* where scholars from five continents participated in the discussion of the challenges humankind is facing to gain productive work as a necessary condition to attain wellbeing. The authors addressed wellbeing from different dimensions, disciplines, management, economics, psychology, education, women, but all aiming at the same target: how to improve wellbeing in the workforce. Which strategies have succeeded and which ones have failed? The book you are reading now is aimed to advance wellbeing within a new framework of human centered economics. I consider this a critical discipline that is long overdue.

Educonomy, pages vii–xxv

I am also coediting a book on wellbeing on entrepreneurship to be published in 2019. Three decades of research and experience have shown me that wellbeing is the common denominator across disciplines and professions aimed to promote progress and growth to attain sustainability. Yet, even if at first sight wellbeing may seem obvious and natural to all human endeavors, it is not. Indeed, it is still more the exception than the norm.

Why is it taking so long for sciences and the professions to secure human wellbeing and sustainability? Why is wellbeing not an imperative to increase performance and productivity in the workplace and worldwide in spite of surmounting evidence that confirms this? And why has wellbeing not been at the core of the workplace given that employment and work are fundamental for people to survive, essential to meet needs, to build a life, for the individual, the economy, and society at large? As we will see next, quantities and numbers show little when quality is overlooked.

But there are great challenges to attain wellbeing. Often these challenges are so close that many people take them for granted. Probably that is what makes it most difficult to find solutions.

Another challenge is confusing happiness for wellbeing. While many seek the panacea of happiness, that is immediate pleasure and absence of pain; few are aware that it takes a great deal of individual hard work and effort and collective perseverance and responsibility to attain wellbeing. wellbeing is sustainable, builds human capital, increases performance and productivity that leads to economic growth, sustainable development, and inclusive societies. Transient happiness does not.

One of the main challenges to secure work as a necessary condition to advance wellbeing is correlated with education. But in the "Knowledge Economy," it needs to be emphasized that it is not the quantity of schooling but the quality of education learners receive.

The quality of education affects the outcome of all students to attain a better life, but the impact is significantly deeper amongst most vulnerable learners in low income cohorts with greater need to have access to good jobs.

Challenges in education are surmounting, as I discuss throughout the book, because education is entrenched in stubbornly rigid structures—a lack of agility and innovation to adjust to a world where continuous change is the only constant. The queries are intense and deep and prospects for solutions are mixed.

Good Jobs Are Scarce Worldwide

The Gallup organization recently released the 2018 Global Great Jobs Briefing titled *3 Billion Still Looking for Great Jobs* (Gallup, 2018). Jon Clifton, Gallup Global managing partner introduced the report confirming something I reiterate in this book, "What the world wants is a good job." He emphasized that in the last decade this is the recurrent, most important finding of a longitudinal study conducted by Gallup in 140 countries.

In this report, Gallup (2018) unveils a common problem of multilevel models that this organization, scholars, and researchers face that hinder the search for solutions to the most pressing challenges that affect humanity. It is based on inconsistent interpretations and discrepancies between different data sources. With employment being one among the most critical discrepancies due to human, economic, and social implications.

World's official statistics are helpful, but not unreservedly because of the use of specific measurement standards. The International Labor Organization (ILO) reported global unemployment at 5.6% or 260 million people in the world. This number is extremely low considering the entire world population. Gallup (2018) points out to a much higher number and explains that the problem is the metrics official agencies use to measure unemployment are different from Gallup's. ILO, as do many other world official agencies, uses a broad framework of labor force statistics collected from national statistics offices worldwide.

It is important to clarify that to work with global data bases is a complex task. The disparity in efficiency of data collection and analysis in nations around the world varies widely and specially between sophisticated methods used in developed and high income developing countries compared with low income nations that lack infrastructure and resources necessary to collect and process big data. To normalize global data, most countries collect job data using simple surveys that ask people questions like: "Did you work 30 or more hours in the past week?" "Did you work for an employer or for yourself?" If respondents are not employed, they are asked whether they are looking for work. Then the data collected become the official employment statistics for the country (Gallup, 2018).

Although it is rational to think that low income developing countries have higher unemployment than high income developed countries, according to official unemployment figures this is not the case. For instance, low income countries like Cambodia or Belarus appear to have the lowest rates of unemployment in the world, while France and other countries in the European Union show three times higher rates of unemployment.

When looking across all countries, results show no statistical relationship between GDP or income per capita and unemployment. This leads to the misconception that the countries in need of more assistance to reduce unemployment are developed countries; while low income developing countries, showing low unemployment rates, are progressing fine.

Here is the explanation. When subsistence farmers in Africa or women selling charms and ornaments on the street in India are asked if they worked 30 or more hours last week, they reply affirmatively. They worked many hours although their work barely provides income to cover basic survival needs, but for global agencies this is considered *work*. In official records these people appear as self-employed, which means they are not unemployed.

The reason why official unemployment appears so low in low income countries is because a significant percentage of unemployed are counted as self-employed. Self-employment is about 30% of the workforce. But this statistic is misleading because self-employed includes small-business owners and entrepreneurs; both economic activities that are admired buzzwords and increasingly popular sources of employment in the new global economy in developed and some high income developing countries with market economies.

The disparity in unemployment rises because official global agencies classify self-employed in low income developing countries as small-business owners or entrepreneurs, but in reality their work allows these workers to live on less than US$ 2 a day.

What is then a real job or a good job? What is the kind of job the whole world wants? Gallup (2018) argues that based on at least 30 hours per week of consistent work with a paycheck from an employer only 28% or 1.4 billion out of the world's 5 billion adult population has a *good job*. Among the rest of the 3.6 billion people, 1 billion are self-employed; 300 million work part time and do not want full-time work; 400 million work part time but want full-time work; 260 million are unemployed; and the rest are out of the workforce.

Among the self-employed, not all are despairingly unemployed and Gallup's conservative estimates is that one half of them are. These are about 500 million that added to the 400 million part-time workers who want full-time work, plus the unemployed total, resulting in about 1 billion people globally who are truly unemployed. This is one-third of the entire world's adult workforce of 3.3 billion. Gallup estimates global unemployment closer to 33% compared to ILO's 5.6% estimate.

But the most critical shortcoming of official jobs metrics is that it does not measure the quality of jobs. Gallup, a world pioneer in measurement of wellbeing in the workforce, uses additional metrics to assess quality of jobs: pay and benefits to assess whether people love or hate their work.

Gallup (2018) surveys show consistently that when people have a job they hate, they rate their lives as poorly as people who are unemployed. But these findings are ignored in the world's official metrics.

Gallup (2018) further investigates the problem asking people about jobs and work using metrics of levels of *employee engagement*. In the surveys, Gallup asks workers to mark one of these three categories: engaged, not engaged, or actively disengaged with work. People who are engaged at work or those who have a *great job*, do what they do best, have the equipment they need to do their jobs, and have a strong sense of mission and purpose with their work.

Gallup (2018) asked the engagement questions worldwide and found that between 2015 and 2016 only 16% of the people with good jobs felt engaged with work. In other words, 16% of people in the world have *great jobs*.

Among the 5 billion adults in the world, 1.4 billion or 28% have a good job but only 16% of these workers felt engaged with their work. In the global workforce, an estimated 3.3 billion adults are working or looking for work; 7% or 214 million people have a great job, but 3 billion people who want a great job don't have one.

The dream of men and women around the world is to have a good job and ultimately a great job. Yet only 214 million people are realizing this dream. The Gallup (2018) report provides clear evidence that the main responsibility of global leaders in all sectors, scientists and policy makers, is to stimulate the creation of *great jobs*.

A word of caution is necessary about the use of multilevel models to present results from different data sources. They facilitate comparisons significantly to discuss broader views of a problem, but different models use different hierarchical or clustered structures that may show discrepancies in longitudinal studies where individual responses are correlated. In this data, the comparison is between big data analysis of world official agencies and data collected by the Gallup studies. The subject is multidimensional and the risk justifies the need to increase knowledge about world labor markets.

There is growing evidence that to advance it is imperative to use relevant and representative human centered metrics. Keeping in mind that focusing on wellbeing humanizes the workplace emphasizing the importance of making workers happy but it is essential to improve organizational culture that leads to high performance and productivity. Since the industrial revolution the oversight of human centered approaches has opened deep gaps between education and the workplace that must be bridged as a condition for sustainability.

In this book, I focus on wellbeing as the central key to return the world to levels of performance and productivity required to foster economic growth and sustainable development. I make special emphasis on quality education as a critical factor for progress and I explain the human and economic costs of deviating from this critical path in the Knowledge Economy.

I argue that the causes and effects of unemployment and lack of engagement affecting workers worldwide reported by Gallup (2018) are largely rooted in disengagement between education and the economy, between educational systems and productive sectors, and a growing mistrust of people with formal education and schooling. The level of dissatisfaction is reaching limits creating a massive exodus from formal schooling to informal education among adult learners and homeschooling among children and youth. These findings can only be identified and solved using human centered, multidisciplinary methodologies.

A similar apocalyptic view of the workplace is presented by Jeffrey Pfeffer (2018), professor of Organizational Behavior at the Graduate School of Business in Stanford University in his book *Dying for a Paycheck: How Modern Management Harms Employee Health and Company Performance and What We Can Do About It.* Pfeffer argues that the workplace can inflict dangerous levels of stress on employees. He warns that these practices hurt companies and governments are ignoring an emerging public health crisis. He starts his book identifying the following results of a survey:

- 61% of employees said that workplace stress had made them sick,
- 7% report been hospitalized because of stress,
- job stress costs U.S. employers over $300 billion annually,
- job stress is related to 120,000 deaths each year, and
- in China, 1 million people a year are estimated to die from overwork. (n.p.)

Pfeffer (2018) asserts that people are literally dying for a paycheck and he warns this has to stop.

Regrettably, Pfeffer (2018) blames modern management practices for the malaise. I agree with the harmful practices he identifies: long work hours, work–family conflict, and economic insecurity that hurt employees resulting in lack of engagement with work, increasing turnover, negative effects on physical and emotional health, and organizational culture hindering performance, but I contend that his perspective shows nothing new.

On the contrary these harmful work practices have perpetuated from the resource-centered, money-oriented work frameworks of the industrial age. His arguments arise when human-centered approaches to management, economics, and organization development are ignored or overlooked.

Pfeffer's (2018) analysis is focused on the old resource-centered model of the industrial past. Overlooking studies and efforts in human centered management, scholars undermine the impact of a paradigm shift that started last century. The Academy of Management has recognized their management books as the most influential of the 20th century. Namely Drucker (1954), *The Practice of Management*; McGregor (1960), *The Human Side of the Enterprise*; Simon (1947), *Administrative Behavior: A Study of Decision-Making Processes in Administrative Organizations*; Maslow (1954), *Motivation and Personality*; Argyris (1957), *Personality and Organizations: The Conflict Between the System and the Individual*; Mayo (1933), *The Human Problems of an Industrial Civilization*; and Deming (1982b), *Quality, Productivity and Competitive Positions*. More recently, human centered management, a concept I coined in 2015, has evolved with a series I launched on the subject that includes the following books: *Human Centered Management in Executive Education* (Lepeley, von Kimakovitz, & Bardy, 2016), *Human Centered Management: The 5 Pillars of Organizational Quality and Sustainability* (Lepeley, 2017a), *Wellbeing for Sustainability in the Global Workplace* (Ochoa, Lepeley, & Essens, 2018), *Rethinking Leadership: A Human Centered Approach to Work Ethics* (Bardy, 2018).

Pfeffer is right to emphasize that the harmful resource centered–money oriented work frameworks of the industrial age must stop. But I warn that the harmful practices he identifies will not stop unless there is significantly higher awareness about the imperative of a universal paradigm shift from resource centered–money oriented work frameworks to a human wellbeing centered management as a top priority for companies, governments, scientists, and workers worldwide. This change is not only urgent, but long overdue. It is no longer a need, it is an imperative for wellbeing and human, organizational, national, and global sustainability.

Enlightening Now

On the bright side of a gloomy workplace scenario, I insert Steven Pinker's book *Enlightenment Now: The Case for Reason, Science, Humanism, and Progress*. Pinker (2018) is a Canadian-American cognitive psychologist, linguist, popular science author, and a Harvard professor who has taught at MIT and Stanford Universities. I include this book because it deploys a balanced human centered approach that is necessary to advance management, economies, and societies to new heights.

There is no doubt that human life, organizations, and the world permanently go through high and low stages. Problems and disruptions are unavoidable. Of course it is necessary to identify problem areas to correct and improve them. But it is critical to recognize the good to build upon as a condition for continuous improvement and to reach quality standards. In the 21st century, progress is built with talent, agility, and innovation, as essential elements to attain sustainability (David & Congleton, 2013). Somber and rigid structures and strategies deviate from this objective (Lepeley, 2017a; Essens & Lepeley, 2018).

Bill Gates said that Pinker's (2018) *Enlightenment Now* book is his favorite of all time. I trust Gates' opinions. He is one of the most innovative human beings alive and conducting, in addition to his commendable technology business enterprise, an outstanding number of human centered initiatives and programs to improve the wellbeing of people worldwide focusing on two fundamental fields: health and education. Gates created Microsoft in the mid-seventies. In 2015 Microsoft had 124,000 employees worldwide. The number of employees more than doubled between 2005 and 2015. In year 2000, he and his wife created the Bill & Melinda Gates Foundation that gives employment to approximately 1,400 people. The Foundation

> is guided by the belief that every life has equal value... in developing countries, [the Foundation work] focuses on improving people's health and giving them [opportunity to lift] out of hunger and extreme poverty. In the United States, it seeks to ensure that all people—especially those with the fewest resources—have access to the opportunities they need to succeed in school, [higher education], and life." (Bill & Melinda Gates Foundation, n.d., para. 1)

Gates is a Harvard dropout. He left the university to develop his business venture. He became the quintessence of the entrepreneur that the Austrian economist and Harvard Professor Joseph Schumpeter envisioned would save the world. Gates developed fundamental bright spots that have indeed changed the world.

In retrospect, in the mid-20th century, Schumpeter (1934) enunciated two prominent insights of human ingenuity that would change and improve the world: (a) innovation as the driving force of economic progress and (b) entrepreneurs as agents of innovation. He voiced that entrepreneurs are possessed by "the dream and the will to find a private kingdom" (n.p.). To achieve their dreams entrepreneurs have to face all sorts of obstacles that leave winners and losers, because innovation is hard to produce and harder to sustain.

Pinker (2018) asks enticing queries to make us rethink and re-assess the world we live in. If you think the world is coming to an end, think again: people are living longer, healthier, freer, and happier lives, and while problems are formidable, solutions lie in the enlightenment ideal using reason, science, and humanism. This is coherent with the human centered approach in this book and faith in the potential to turn the world to a higher stage.

Pinker's (2018) statements are supported by data showing that the world is not falling apart. The ideal of progress is not obsolete, but actually, I think it should be a daily pursuit for every human being, as I discuss later. Pinker recommends objective judgment using scientific data to assess gory headlines and prophecies of doom with potential to induce psychological biases and harming effects. Because every human being is free to choose, whether to sink in the dooms or rise and thrive. This is a personal choice. And according to my experience as economist and educator it is not related only to money or resources, but it is anchored in the human courage we have the option to develop, or discard.

To accentuate the positive, Pinker (2018) reports in his book that life, health, prosperity, safety, peace, knowledge, and happiness are on the rise worldwide, and now not exclusively in developed countries. Something I confirm based on extended experience. He argues that this progress is not the result of fate. On the contrary it is the outcome of reason and rigorous sciences that have connected and integrated to enhance human flourishing. This integrative approach needs vigorous defense more than ever. Enlightenment and the human centered axiom go against currents of tribalism, authoritarianism, demonization, and demagogues that pervade life and work environments and hinder the pursuit of knowledge, wellbeing, and human thriving.

Socrates and His Disciple Aristotle Were Right

Beyond the transitory state of happiness, all human beings long for wellbeing, indeed for sustainable wellbeing. Wellbeing is embedded in human nature. It is the conjunction and collusion of "well" and "being." Although some hyphenate and separate *well* from *being*, I consider them inseparable. I unite wellbeing in one word as a unified and irreplaceable: wellbeing.

Wellbeing is the core pursuit of a well-balanced life for individuals, high performing organizations, growing economies, and inclusive societies. Yet after thousands of years, humankind is still marginally patting the concept and have not reach consensus about how to reach one of the most critical imperatives of life. We remain querying and quarreling what is wellbeing and what to do to get it.

This inquiry is not unfounded because the concept of wellbeing is often blurred by pressing needs that postpone it by immediate goals or wants. But there is surmounting evidence that in contrast to happiness, which is a transient state of pleasure and absence of pain, wellbeing is not a passing mood but a transformation of the self. And the transformation of the self is essential to transform organizations and attain sustainability.

Historically, since ancient Greece, the instrument to facilitate the transformation from happiness to wellbeing has been knowledge and education. The same pursuit moves nations today and worldwide to invest a significant proportion of the national income in education of its citizens, aiming to improve wellbeing and create better societies.

After 2,000 years, in the quest for wellbeing today, it is not only necessary but it is an imperative to evaluate the causes and effects that induce advances or backtracks to the universal dream: knowledge and how to use it properly to improve wellbeing.

In the Knowledge Economy, a concept coined by Peter Drucker more than a half century ago, education, is a critical factor that impacts wellbeing, therefore education deserves special scrutiny. This is education that is effective and useful to improve the quality of life, not mere years of schooling that take people nowhere. I am talking about education that stimulate students' knowledge, education that enthuses people to be creative and entrepreneurial to create jobs or to get a good job. That is productive work where workers feel engaged, committed, and proud of, instead of work forced to perform.

In the previous section we saw that a good job is one of the fundamental elements for people to attain wellbeing in life. But the world is far from achieving this important objective. To provide jobs that fulfil basic human needs as the first step to advance quality of life in a rapidly changing world, where change is the only constant and the workplace is in constant evolution, and even in turmoil with disruptive technologies that affect all workers.

Why is it taking humankind so long to advance human wellbeing? What are we, as individuals and society, doing wrong that is leading to such detrimental results and the surmounting level of disengagement with work revealed in the 2018 Gallup Jobs Report, or the harmful management practices highlighted in Pfeffer's (2018) book *Dying for a Paycheck*? What do we need to learn and do differently to build on the good humanity has achieved unveiled by Pinker (2018) and unleashed by Gates' business acumen and philanthropic achievements?

In the 21st century the instrument for personal transformation is knowledge. I am not inventing this reasoning. I am just citing Socrates and Aristotle who said this more than 2,000 years ago. Things have not changed much with respect to the knowledge imperative, and neither about ignorance as evil.

But the knowledge inquiry I am exploding and exploiting in this book is the link between knowledge and wellbeing using economics and education as mechanisms that foster or hinder wellbeing with a closer attention in needed multidisciplinary approaches.

The argument I post is that in the 21st century most of the problems humankind face are not for lack of knowledge but for inefficient use of knowledge. To a large extent people are not optimizing the use of knowledge because of lack of quality standards in education for all.

In reality, schooling without quality standards for all has high potential to be an obstacle instead of a stimulus for learners. In the 19th century, Hölderlin, a German poet influenced by Goethe, Schiller, and Greek philosophers said that children are divine creative human beings until schooling transforms them into adults. I use this quote in my books.

Knowledge: From Socrates to Drucker

Knowledge is critically important today because the wellbeing of humankind depends on knowledge more than ever before. Socrates and Aristotle uncovered the importance of knowledge and the evil of ignorance in 400 B.C. A modern recreation of knowledge evolved with Peter Drucker, the visionary Father of Management, when in 1967, anticipating big changes in economies, societies, organizations, and workers introduced the concept of the Knowledge Economy in his book *The Effective Executive.* In this book, written during the period of the post industrial revolution, he described deep differences emerging between manual workers and what he coined *knowledge workers.* Drucker (1967) described manual workers as those who work with their hands to produce goods or services and knowledge workers as those who work with their heads, more than with their hands, to produce ideas, knowledge, and information.

I have to add to Drucker's notable and influential idea of the knowledge workers that has transformed management since then, that the need for knowledge is now universal. The pursuit of knowledge is the reason why most people go through schooling for many years and why nations invest in education.

Today manual workers are no longer excluded from providing ideas, on the contrary, workers who do not provide ideas are failing. Manual workers need to gain knowledge and use it effectively to do manual tasks, not to be substituted by artificial intelligence and robotics. This requires human ingenuity and the creativity that Hölderlin referred to in the 19th century. In the 21st century we cannot think that knowledge is a privilege for some people, knowledge must be open to all those who want it and education's responsibility is to motivate all learners to gain and optimize the use of knowledge to preserve the value of freedom and make wellbeing reachable and sustainable.

Everything that is sustainable is the result of knowledge, effort, dedication, and cultivation. Wellbeing is associated with acquisition of knowledge (education) on one hand and with optimal use of knowledge (economics) on the other.

The natural questions that arise are: How much aware are world leaders and societies about human wellbeing as the focus of national sustainable development and progress? To what extent are leaders and societies assuming responsibility to answer the inquiry about the importance of knowledge and the harm of ignorance posted 2,000 years ago by Socrates and Aristotle? Is there an urgency to open equal access of knowledge to all people?

To Advance Knowledge Avoid Disciplinary Silos: Wellbeing Is Built in Multidisciplinary Solutions

When I studied my first academic degree in education I was totally unaware of the hazards of disciplinary silos. Overall, because university studies worldwide for most of the 20th century, were structured strictly by disciplinary divisions. The first university degree I completed in Chile in the late 60s was in education. Although I did not intend to pursue education as a career, I chased opportunity over preference and I was extremely fortunate that it was the best decision. When one is young and inexperienced it is very difficult and close to impossible to make such an important life decision. My parents emphasized I had to get a university degree, but the rest was left to me, and given my school records and grades, which were not the best, I must admit. So my choices were not unlimited, as for most high school graduates. But when I started teaching I realized that education was my passion and my destiny. I realized that education allowed me to really help other people. I educated myself because when I learned something new I could share it with my students, who then benefited from what I had learned and the knowledge I had gained.

But it was not until I completed a graduate degree in higher education management and leadership and after I switched and completed a graduate degree in economics and wrote a thesis on the impact of higher education in economic development, that I grasped the real shortcomings of binding disciplines and scientific segmentation. Since then this has been one of the most critical human development concerns impressing me to bring change.

In the last 3 decades I have collected the knowledge I share in this book. And overall, the way I have used this knowledge to understand the complex, convoluted, and irrevocable connection that exists between education and economic development—and today, between education quality and sustainable development embedded in the theories I deploy here.

Today problems are increasingly complex and solutions are always multidisciplinary. Knowledge evolves and grows from the cross fertilization of disciplines and decays with segmentation. Challenges are huge because humanity is the product of explosive development in disciplinary sciences that often combat for territorial rights at the expense of knowledge integration.

I only know that I know nothing.
—Socrates

Socrates was also right when he uttered the quote above. The more we collect, assimilate, and use knowledge to understand the world and try to solve challenges, the more we realize that we know so little. The more we learn of different disciplines results in a new vision, broader and deeper. On the other hand it makes us more aware that increased knowledge shows how much we still have to learn. It is a never-ending endeavor. Lifelong learning is the imperative for every person today. The mission of education is no longer and not only to transmit information that many students fail to transform in useful knowledge to advance wellbeing, but it should be: to help students advance capacity for lifelong learning. This should be education's priority in the 21st century. Information and knowledge change fast and lifelong learning is the key to wellbeing.

Main Problem Is Not Income Inequality It Is Education Inequality

I close this chapter with an argument that will resonate throughout this book and will become increasingly clear: The main problem societies face today to attain sustainable development and human wellbeing is not income inequality, it is lack of quality in education for all. This is an inefficient use of resources spent in education.

Putting Capital as Master at the Expense of Knowledge and Education

In the last 5 years, after the French economist Thomas Piketty (2013) published his book *Capital in the 21st Century* which focused on wealth and income inequality in Europe and the United States, the debate on income inequality exploded with great force and unforeseen menacing consequences (Delsol, Lecausin, & Martin, 2017). Not only because Piketty (2013) argued that income accumulation is the result of the rate of return on capital greater than the rate of economic growth, which he later retracted as inaccurate; but for his delusional proposal of a global system of progressive wealth tax to a few rich to reduce income inequality to billions of poor people. Piketty (2013) once again bluntly ignored that imposing exorbitant tax rates on the productive sector, as the main job creator in countries worldwide, would significantly reduce workforce expansion leaving more workers unemployed. But even more questionable is his proposal to confiscate wealth from the few rich and productive and give it to inefficient government bureaucrats to manage income redistribution. Piketty (2013) should have provided at least one example where his proposal has worked showing that all the people are better off than they were in 19th century Europe or the United States. Until now I have not seen any.

There is no doubt that the debate on *income parity* is important and must continue.

But the key issue here is to objectively recognize, aside from political interests, that income inequality cannot possibly be solved unless societies are capable, highly efficient, and productive to educate all people as producers of capital, instead of recipients of governments' aid and spenders of other people's money.

Much more attention should be given to the other side of Piketty's coin (or capital), that is leading nations to deeper problems. Piketty fails to acknowledge that these levels of income inequality expose the high inefficiency of world leaders, governments, and world developing agencies that for ages have failed to achieve their principal responsibility: provide quality education to all to foster growth in the economy and inclusive societies protecting freedom, fairness, and most of all, using cost effective and optimizing ways and means to open opportunity for all people to access a good job and a better life. All are essential conditions to attain human wellbeing and sustainability.

Realistic efforts must be directed to find solutions to improve *income parity*—over income inequality—as an essential focus at the top of the development agenda in all nations. This is crucial looking at the results of government administrations in some of the most developed countries in the world. Not to mention their peer developing countries.

Bureaucracies Facts and Failure: A Doom Scenario

As the baby boom generation retires, there is a growing number of pensioners and fewer workers to support them in all world regions except Africa. Contrast these statistics with a 25% unemployment rate among younger workers who don't have a job to cover their expenses and are neither contributing to public retirement programs.

The European retirement system presents a doom picture. The population of pensioners, already the largest in the world, continues to grow. Europeans 65 and older who retired are 42 for every 100 workers. The prognosis: This proportion is estimated to rise to 65 per 100 by 2060 (Samuel, 2016). Public pension plans in the pay-as-you-go countries would replace about 60% of retirees' salaries. The problem increases faster because several of these countries let people retire at less than 60 years old. Therefore, fewer than 25% of workers would be contributing to the pension plans. Unfunded retirement government programs are surmounting given the low performance, lack of cost controls, and inefficient administration in numerous countries. Among the most critical are Greece, Spain, Italy, and France.

But this does not clear the younger U.S. nation of all faults. In 2017, 61 million retirees were supported by 171 million workers. In 2014 the Social Security main program (Old-Age and Survivors Insurance [OASI]) ran a $39 billion deficit, with 5 years of consecutive cash-flow deficits and unfunded obligations that continue to grow. It is projected that OASI will reach insolvency in 2035 (Boccia, 2015). Entitlement programs uncontrolled for efficient performance and rates of returns to expenditure continue increasing the U.S. federal deficit of US$ 19 trillion in 2017 or 104% of GDP. In 2001 President George W. Bush said: "Today's young workers who pay into social security might as well be saving their money in their mattress" (n.p.). The UN's Population Division: World Population Projects, 2015 Revision in Figure I.1 shows he was not kidding.

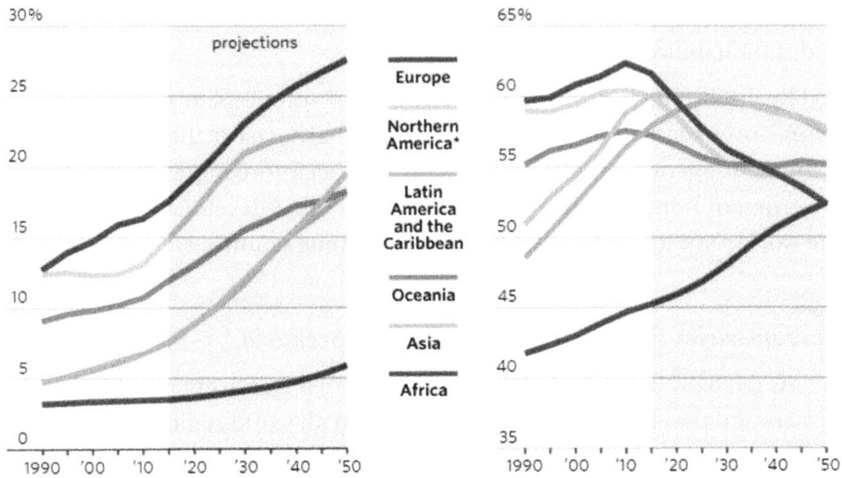

Figure I.1 A growing mismatch. The share of Europe's population 65 years and older is and will be larger than in any other region (left) and the share of Europe's population 20–64 years old is shrinking (right).

* U.S., Canada, Bermuda, Greenland and Saint Pierre and Miquelon.
Source: UN Population Division, World Population Prospects, 2015 revision.

Young Facebook Co-Founder Proposes Universal Guaranteed Basic Income, to Increase Deficit and Decrease Efficiency

Chris Hughes (Steverman, 2018), a Harvard cofounder of Facebook Inc., age 34, is devoting his time to evangelizing for higher taxes on the rich, such as him. And he is proposing that the government pays a guaranteed income of $500 a month to every person and working American earning less than $50,000 a year. This would add US$ 290 billion each year to the already sizable deficit. Hughes admits that this is a staggering number but points out that it would tackle inequality that is destabilizing the nation. He said that he worked hard for 3 years at Facebook and the financial rewards he received were substantial and disproportionate with the work he put in. He called his business experience *a lucky break.*

Hughes (Steverman, 2018) stated that his case is extreme but said lots of people are getting lucky because of the way the economy is structured. Oddly he confirms that the janitors, who work hard to clean up Facebook offices at the end of the day, had not had a wage raise in many years. Although he recognized this unfairness with workers who are struggling to make ends meet, he shows no empathy for low income workers. Actually, instead of helping his workers and giving janitors a substantial raise, Hughes blames the way the economy is structured.

Hughes is one of the clearest examples that the problem is not the economic system but the lucky and greedy business individuals who fail to help their own workers, but instead create a philanthropy organization to show off his questionable charitable arguments.

The real problem is people who neglect their own low skilled workers, but publically utter to be compelled by "a moral obligation to eradicate poverty and restore opportunity to the middle class" (Steverman, 2018, para. 8).

Hughes's proposal is to pay every person in the United States a guaranteed cash income of $500 including workers earning less than $50,000 a year. He proposed to cover this expenditure imposing a 50% tax rate on income and capital gains for all Americans earning more than $250,000. He believes that there are many ways to pay for a guaranteed income and the resources can and should come from people who most benefit from the structure of the economy. He claims that people are craving for great ideas with potential to push the boundaries of what is possible. He pointed out to the challenges of the skills gap and jobs of the future that require job training, expressing concerns that in the long history of jobs training some programs have worked but many have not.

Since 2013, Hughes is no longer with Facebook and since then he has diversified his investments. He mentioned that people frequently ask him for financial advice, and he replied to one of them: You should ask an entrepreneur. He said he is not good at calculating taxes. He states he has more money than he ever dreamed. He feels fortunate and he and his husband have made a commitment to give away their money over the course of their lifetimes.

He confirms the wealthiest have more information and knowledge and more access to investment advisers and sophisticated investment strategies than other people, this enables them to get higher returns on capital. He emphasized that there are lots of people selling snake oils to rich people and poor people alike. The difference is that while rich people can recognize the trick or can afford to buy gadgets and make mistakes here and there, everybody else with less knowledge and limited means cannot (Steverman, 2018).

But overall, technology and connectivity have unleashed the voice of the people and the growth of populism in countries around the world, and not as a reaction against the rich and wealthy, because although people in general and workers in particular know the rich have advantages and privileges, they also create millions of jobs and are the main source of employment. What populists aim is to counteract power concentration in politics and irresponsible and corrupt government bureaucracies that use the money of the people but deprive citizens of the quality services they are called to provide. Naturally, populists are against unscrupulous and ruthless employers who, in spite of rising to the top of the wealthy, neglect the wellbeing of their employees and fail to raise them in synch. For further reference on this subject see *Human Centered Management in Executive Education* (Lepeley, von Kimakowitz, & Bardy, 2016), *Human Centered Management: 5 Pillars of Organizational Quality and Global Sustainability* (Lepeley & Human, 2017a); *Rethinking Leadership: A Human Centered Approach to Management Ethics* (Bardy, 2018); *Wellbeing for Sustainability in the Global Workplace* (Ochoa, Lepeley, & Essens, 2018).

Overall, one of the most critical issues of contention of the people against governments and bureaucracies worldwide is the historic failure to provide quality education for all. In spite of spiking investments in education in nations worldwide students and graduates are failing to find good jobs because they lack the skills needed in the workforce in a highly dynamic Knowledge Economy where static educational systems are lagging far behind. Educational systems are wasting billions financing inefficient programs, unproductive educators, and low performing institutions at all levels impairing millions of learners eager to achieve a good job and thrill in life. Educators and education shape a sector that is most critical to help—or harm—human wellbeing and sustainable development. Until now education has been deprived of this important recognition and it is about time to reposition. This book takes the side of education and the urgency to heighten education at the helm of progress with world recognized quality standards that are imperative in the human centered Educonomy.

This book is divided in three parts. Part I is an introduction to human centered economics and discusses the most critical microeconomic and multidisciplinary human development themes of the construct that conditions people to thrive. Part II inserts the microeconomic underpinnings of the human centered model into the macroeconomic framework I call *balanced sustainable development ESTE* (economic, social, technology, environment) which is essential to systematically promote wellbeing as a condition for progress and sustainable growth in the Knowledge Economy. Part III deploys the arguments and explains the needs that call for the Educonomy as the missing link and essential component to optimize benefits and minimize costs in the Knowledge Economy. The Educonomy is strengthened by three critical pillars: the *talent economy*, the *agile economy*, and the *quality economy* that sets the quality parameters of an Educonomy anchored on people's wellbeing and sustainable development.

PART I

The Wellbeing Pursuit: People Are the DNA of Sustainable Development

1

Human Centered Economics

In the knowledge—human centered—economy the talent of people is the most important asset to foster innovation and continuous improvement essential for sustainability

Is Economics the Mother of All Sciences? Good Deeds Not Greed: An Unbiased View

In the early 1980s, just after I had transferred from education to economics, I read that economics was the mother of social sciences. I thought this was the most arrogant and voracious slogan and I was committed to demonstrate it wasn't. To do that, I had to learn economics in depth and thoroughly. After graduation I not only realized that I could not refute this claim, but I started to acclaim economics as one of the best professional decisions I had ever made. And I affirm this today. Moreover, I regret that more people don't study economics. And I lament that economics is not taught to every student from kindergarten through grad school. Since very early ages, children, free from misconceptions, can learn fundamental economic

Educonomy, pages 3–13

principles as they enjoy the company of parents and small friends. I have tried it with my five grandchildren and their friends. And it works!

I understood that economics deals with activities of daily life, not exclusively with stock exchange markets (although I became much better at this too). Economics deals with problems of scarcity and trade aimed to improve human and national wellbeing. Economics is about how we use the knowledge we have to optimize decisions we make with limited resources we have at our disposal. I learned that the professional responsibility of economists is to make sure that the limited resources available on earth are optimally transformed, traded, and distributed in equitable ways. I realized that as economists we are responsible to maximize the utility of people to make everybody happy. Yes! This is not a joke or a fairy tale. This is economics! That is one of the reasons why I regret that many people misunderstand the benefits of learning fundamental principles of economic "freedom and fairness."

Although traditionally other social sciences are closely associated with the development of human beings, like psychology, health, education, political sciences, sociology, ethics, history, to name a few; economics has to deal with some of the most pressing aspects of human beings, organizations, and society. This was clearly discussed in the Introduction showing that less than a quarter of the workers feel engaged, enjoying their work and thrill in life, while a gross majority are detached or suffer doing every day a job they dislike or are unemployed. Globally, the workplace is not optimizing human talent, and unsatisfied workers are unable to optimize resources essential in production, consumption, and distribution to satisfy human needs and increase sustainability.

Too often economics is associated with money and capital, which are only instruments to facilitate human transactions. After the fundamental need and utility of money to satisfy basic and essential human needs, every person decides if money, capital, and monetary wealth are instruments to facilitate trade or are icons that make them subordinates to its mandate. We are all aware that money cannot buy happiness and capital does create more wisdom. As instruments they are useful, and people need money and income to trade and satisfy needs. But to become subordinate to money or measure wellbeing in monetary terms is a shortcoming in the Knowledge Economy.

Many people are scared of economics and particularly of its math and statistical components. And I understand why. I was also scared and had to overcome many fears with great effort when I studied economics. But I think it is unfortunate that in many departments/schools of economics, math prevails over the nature of economics as a core social science. This needs to change. Economics needs to rely more on its human roots and less on regression analysis. Economics has to emphasize the importance to its social essence with capital in a marginal role as a facilitator. There is no doubt that classical economics, free markets, and the price system are among the most important social discoveries that have significantly improved the quality of life of people around the world. Since Adam Smith until today, money and capital have had marginal roles not central stakes, especially in the era of knowledge, when returns to investment in human capital surpass returns to physical capital.

An Urgent Discussion to Optimize Potential for Progress

This discussion is urgent to advance human center economics because businesses and the productive sector globally are forecasting incomparable options to advance that have not been seen since the last recession. But increases in performance and productivity, necessary to foster growth and inclusive societies, depend on human decisions that will move the world in the direction of development or decay.

In 2018, global leaders in business, governments, and international development organizations for the first time show consensus that world economic and financial balances are better aligned and the interfaces between developed and developing has higher potential to advance global progress. This coincidence could reverse decades of low productivity.

But global leaders and decision makers who envision surmounting economic opportunities are also cautious and warn that recovery will only be possible if countries around the world realize the importance of an economic approach that benefits all people. In other words, the positive effects of current global balances can benefit societies worldwide only if the wellbeing of people is at center stage. Otherwise, this potentially good economic period could be wasted (World Economic Forum, 2017).

Klaus Schwab, founder and chairman of the World Economic Forum, has emphasized that the Fourth Industrial Revolution will drastically alter how we produce, consume, educate, communicate, and live. The disruptions that societies worldwide will face will deeply modify relationships between people, between producers and customers, and between citizens and the state. And we have already seen these developments.

Leaders agree that change will open extraordinary opportunities for people to enhance their lives and improve societies. But, Schwab (2016) reiterates, change will offer more benefits than costs to society only if we, all of us, *get it right.* He emphasizes that progress is a shared responsibility.

Every person needs to find and use their talents to be able, willing, and prepared to assume responsibility to advance the human potential to improve collective wellbeing and inclusive societies.

In this environment, more than ever in the past, the quality of education is the most critical element for social progress and economic sustainability (Lepeley, 2017a). This is the fundamental principle of human progress that gives origin to a new economy called the *Educonomy* that I formulate in the rest of the book.

The Fourth Industrial Revolution is anchored in technology. But the main consideration is that technology is useful only if people can use it. Here again, quality education, education centered on the needs of the learner, not on the regulations of the system, is essential to unleash human growth supported by technology. Technology, like money and capital discussed above, is a means to improve human wellbeing, not a master to overwhelm people.

Rajeev Suri, president and CEO of Nokia Corporation (Suri, 2017), states that technology serves its purpose when it gives people more time to do things that are uniquely human, enjoyable, creative, and productive. He emphasizes that in the workplace, in nations and societies, the benefits of technology are often associated with economic variables like productivity, competitiveness, and business growth, but rarely with people's wellbeing, as it should be.

As the world moves deeper into the Fourth Industrial Revolution, the need for a human centered economy increases in sync with the digital transformation of work and life. The potential benefits and costs associated with the new digital era are central to the ongoing humane discussion.

Suri accurately questions if the Fourth Industrial Revolution will deliver the promise of driving productivity gains to come out of sluggish decades and promote business outcome to foster economic growth is well synchronized with the wellbeing of all people. My response is that to a large extent it will depend, again, on quality education and the capacity to develop, spread, and consolidate the human core of the economic science.

The Human at the Center Is Not New, but Economics Needs a Review

Adam Smith: The Theory of Moral Sentiments: Two Decades Before the Wealth of Nations

Human centered economics started with Adam Smith two centuries ago. But although most people recognize Adam Smith (1723–1790) as the father of modern economics, few are aware that the human focus and concern for people's wellbeing was central to all his endeavours. This is explicit because Smith's book *The Theory of Moral Sentiments* was published in 1759, almost 2 decades before he wrote his economic masterpiece *The Wealth of Nations* (1776). The full title is *An Inquiry into the Nature and Causes of the Wealth of Nations* and here it is important to clarify that the wellbeing of people was and is central to Smith's inquiry of the causes and effects that promote and hinder individual and national wealth.

Smith was a Scottish professor of moral philosophy whose concern for the wellbeing of people led him to develop a revolutionary doctrine built on people and freedom as the essence of human development and economic progress. In the 17th century the freedom of people was uncommon and a treasure as the ultimate human achievement. Probably comparable to those of us who have been exposed to highly controlled socialist regimes and closed economies that suppress freedom and control all aspects of people's lives.

For Smith, the freedom of people and their free will to choose were essential to produce goods, to trade and distribute them for consumption in free markets, and to foster inclusive economic and social systems. Smith theories provide the foundations for contemporary human centered economics.

While in the *Wealth of Nations,* Smith (1776) combines philosophy with economic history and political theory, his main concern was the solution of practical problems that affected the wellbeing of people. Smith's writings focused on the importance of integrity, virtues, and respect. He emphasized human attributes and ethics as fundamental principles to foster economic and social progress in a sustainable way, and essential to avoid entropy and regression. He warned that without values no nation could attain the wellbeing all people need and constantly seek. The same principles apply to human centered economics today.

Smith's major work as chair at the University of Glasgow, concentrated in theology, ethics, and jurisprudence, while he was developing the fundamental principles of his human centered economics. In *The Theory of Moral Sentiments* (Smith, 1759), he developed the intellectual and ethical framework for his later work including the *Wealth of Nations.*

For Smith, the selfish nature of man refers to the need for self-cultivation and improvement that he considered fundamental to be able to appreciate and help others. Smith's "selfish motive" has been widely misinterpreted and confused with vanity, conceit, and human insensitivity, which profoundly contradicts the meaning that Smith and other human centered economists that follow him, imply.

To a large extent, Smith's assumption of human being and behavior can be traced to the Aristotelian eudaimonic principle: The human being has to cultivate self as a precondition to help others and make a better contribution to society. Although this fundamental principle seems to be common sense, it is often misinterpreted as selfishness, conceit, and egoism. Humanly speaking nobody who is unhappy and has unsatisfied needs is able to help others. This is a critical concern in human centered economic principles developed in this book supporting the argument behind the importance of quality education for all and the emergence of the Educonomy.

Where Economics Deviated From Its Human Core

Unlike other social sciences, that induce smoother reactions in the general public, economics is often considered an elite science polarized between avid supporters from crude dissidents. This split is not surprising when we think that economics is the most criticized and the most glorified among the social sciences.

Economics has been coined from *the mother of all sciences* to the *dismal science.* These labels come with a history that some people know but most do not. Unfortunately, bad names perpetuate deeper and faster in a void of ignorance and an ocean of disdain. And economists do not do much to adjust, correct, or reverse.

Economics: The Dismal Science

The origin of dismal science comes from Thomas Carlyle (1795–1881), a Scottish philosopher, historian, satirical writer, and influential social commentator of the Victorian Age. Carlyle gave this detrimental label not because he despised economics, but on the contrary, his satirical purpose was to discredit the lugubrious theories and economic predictions of Thomas Malthus (1766–1834). Malthus was an English cleric and political economist who claimed that humanity would be trapped in a vicious circle of increasing consumption and decreasing natural resources that in turn would create widespread land degradation and human misery. Malthusian theories argued that growth and development would ignite increasing demand for food leading people to unlimited consumption. This life in abundance, instead of just maintaining the same standard of living, would irrevocably deplete food production leading to starvation. This vicious circle became known as the *Malthusian trap.* Malthus harshly disputed the 18th-century views that European societies were improving and were perfectible. In opposition he professed that "the power of population growth is indefinitely greater than the power of earth to produce subsistence food for men " (Malthus, 1798, n.p.). His critics said that as a cleric, Malthus realized this impending human problem divinely imposed him to teach virtuous behavior.

Malthus did not envision or trust in the potential of human ingenuity and creativity that were unleashed during the Industrial Revolution (1780–1840) deeply changing methods of production, distribution, and consumption—first in developed countries, and slowly but surely also in developing nations that were then in a very precarious state.

Although some people align with the Carlyle's dismal connotation and Malthusian trap, an inescapable element of his economics was the constant pursuit for human wellbeing.

Economics: The Mother of All Sciences

While some have criticized economics as a dismal science, throughout economics history and across economic extremes—from those who propose human freedom as an essential economic engine aligned with the classical theory and free market systems to those who promote central controls of resources like Marxism—all agree that economics is the mother of all social sciences (Samuelson, 1980).

Since Adam Smith to the Austrian School of Economics, and Nobel laurates who pioneered people's freedom and responsibility, including F. A. Hayek, Theodore Schultz, Gary Becker, and Milton Friedman, promoting free markets to optimize production, consumption and distribution of resources, the economic science has made crucial contribution to development and sustainability of human wellbeing.

For Karl Marx economics was the mother of all science. Doctrines of central control of national resources anchored in economic controls of capital, production, consumption, and distribution managed by workers were essential economics for social and political order.

Economics and Multidisciplinary Human Approaches in the 21st Century

Economics is the study of why and how people and society freely choose—with or without the use of money—to optimize limited resources and alternatives available to increase human wellbeing. Economics deploys human imperative constantly assessing how goods and services are distributed to optimize consumption for people and society. Economics investigates the cost and benefits of alternative options and opportunities to constantly improve the wellbeing of people.

The function of money in the economy and how it affects human wellbeing is discussed later. In the human centered economy, money is a manageable utensil that facilitates understanding of economic problems. It is not the master, as commonly assumed in theories focused on capital as a doctrine not an instrument to facilitate transactions.

Capital—physical capital—is understood as an accumulation of money to be distributed for different uses aimed to advance the human activities and conditions through different frameworks such as wealth, income, wages, prices, consumption, and investment as tools to facilitate understanding of micro and macroeconomic concepts that affect organizations, the economy, and people's wellbeing.

Economics and Psychology... One New Discipline

Professor Jonathan Cohen, a psychologist and director at Princeton Neuroscience Institute (https://pni.princeton.edu/), has described neuroeconomics as a discipline bridging economics, psychology, and neuroscience. He has asserted, "I think of economics and psychology as really, in some sense, one discipline. [...] They really are siblings separated at birth. [...] complementary disciplines, in many cases studying the same phenomena" (as quoted in Torkington, 2016, para. 2).

Advances in Neuroscience and the Advent of Neuroeconomics

Historically, rationality has been a central issue in economics. Largely based on theories that economics, more than any other social science, is closely related to exact sciences like mathematics and statistics. Therefore, enhancing its forecasting and predictive capacity consolidates its meaning. Economic theories are entrenched in rational expectations of people's preferences, decisions and actions, and multivariate analysis subject to the ceteris paribus condition.

Ceteris paribus is a Latin phase common in economics that means *all other things being equal* or constant. This assumption rules out probabilities that other factors can influence variables under study. Nonetheless it remains active in the economic lexicon, it sure made more sense one or two centuries ago, when change was slow, but it is disputable today given that change is the only constant. Given the disruptions of the VUCA (volatile, uncertain, complex, ambiguous) environment, today's world is mutatis mutandis (constant change) rather than ceteris paribus.

An erratic economic debate between rational decision-making and contending behavioral models framing irrational behavior in psychological constructs of risk has followed. The irrational loss aversion and irrational human preferences aimed at immediate rewards unleashed by psychologist and 2002 Nobel Prize award in Economics, Daniel Kahneman and his colleague Tversky (1979), have been refuted by rational heuristic expectations proposed by Todd and Gigerenzer (2000) based on new developments in neuroscience.

Technology is facilitating new developments in neuroscience that help understand the mind and how human beings make decisions, support rational traits, and increasingly dismantle irrational behaviors. In addition to the traditional subjective analysis of human behavior, objective observations of brain activity are possible and elucidating previously identified empirical anomalies that are giving birth to the new science of *neuroeconomics* (Frey, 2010; Frey & Stutzer, 2007).

Watch the Brain: Making Rational Decisions

Professor Michael Platt, an expert in neuroeconomics and psychologist at University of Pennsylvania Wharton School of Business, in the 2016 Conference of World Economic Forum explained how neuroscience makes it possible to observe the brain make decisions (Torkington, 2016). He stated that it is possible to measure how much value a person assigns to an object or situation monitoring brain functions and without uttering a word. Human preferences can be measured using an MRI machine by taking snapshots of the brain in action and predicting decisions.

In reality the brain weighs evidence and assigns value separately to make a decision. Platt (Torkington, 2016) gives a graphic example using a simple decision a driver does to either hit the gas or the brakes in specific situations. Platt states that values assigned to similar decisions can change over time and even from moment to moment depending on the level of information the person has. In the driver's case, the time variable, if the driver is running on time or late for work, can influence a decision to pass a traffic signal changing from green to red.

Platt (Torkington, 2016) says that there is always an economic decision when the brain turns an emotion into a mathematical way of solving a problem that always optimizes personal benefit.

In the "hit the gas or the brake" case, a drawing would look like the driver has two buckets in the brain, and each time the brain gets more evidence it fills one of the buckets. The bucket that fills first will be the decision the driver will make. In the case of the traffic light, the more evidence supporting the yellow light is on and the driver is late for work, the decision will be to run a yellow light and assume the risk. If there is evidence that the light is red, the driver will stop. Platt emphasizes that seemingly simple neuroeconomic techniques are applied to areas much more complex in economics, including scanning the brains of a sample of people in a laboratory to predict effectiveness of marketing and micro-lending campaigns on the Internet.

The New Rational Side of Emotions

Northeastern University's Interdisciplinary Affective Science Laboratory (IASL; see http://www.affective-science.org) is dedicated to the study of emotions and conducts research on psychology and neuroscience to understand how the brain creates the mind. Theories are constructed on emotion hypotheses and long-term mental events that result from the interplay between brain networks and neural connections. IASL developed the *theory of constructed emotion* that integrates principles of neuroconstruction with psychological construction and social construction that uncovers fundamental roles of the brain that affect emotions. Findings show that human beings are not at the mercy of emotions, but the inverse is true. The brain creates emotions based on a continuous unconscientious capacity to predict events as a genetic survival mechanism. Studies show that emotions are agile (David, 2013, 2016), and that people can manage emotions (Barrett, 2017) and cultivate knowledge, develop abilities and skills conducive to improved life, and work leading to wellbeing.

Humans are emotional beings genetically predisposed to manage emotional states and to advance from emotional to cognitive-rational states (Barter, 2007). This is confirmed because human beings can learn new things and given opportunities, can increase capacity to cultivate themselves and optimize decision-making according to their talents and the education they receive (Lepeley, 2017a).

Human Beings Act **Irrational** *Only When They Lack Knowledge and Information to Act Rationally*

To the largest extent, irrational behavior is not embedded in human nature, as some tend to believe. It is due to lack of information, it is exposure to years of neglect and deficient schooling that hinders options for self-cultivation and self-improvement. The situation is particularly painful for low income learners who have the most critical need for quality education but are forced to confront the most unfavorable schooling conditions.

To clarify, quality education means personalized education focused on the learner's holistic development, talent identification, and opportunities for continuous learning to advance to a better life with unobstructed access to education and the workforce. Not merely a good grade in a course or to pass a test.

From the economic dimension, the 2007 book *Economics and Psychology: A Promising New Cross-Disciplinary Field*, written by Economists Bruno Frey and Alois Stutzer, presents one of the best introductions to the subject.

2

Economics of Wellbeing

In spite of limitations of the applicability of the neoclassical theory to the educational field, still this theoretical framework is the most reliable to analyze process optimization and resource allocation comparing costs and benefits of different distributions.

Utility Theory: The Forgotten Human Side of Economics

Human beings are constantly—consciously or unconsciously—making economic decisions and choosing among multiple alternatives. The way the reader is sitting at this moment is in reality an economic decision, because, unconsciously, you are optimizing a comfortable position. Optimizing utility. Utility is one of the most basic and important concepts in economic theory and indeed the human side of the economic science.

All human beings make decisions based on the "utility" they accrue from something—that may be buying something or sitting comfortably. Nobody can fake utility. This optimization decision is based on the information the person has available and it positions utility as a monumental and

Educonomy, pages 15–23

fundamental principle supporting the only law[1] that exists in economics, the law of supply and demand.

Paradoxically, economics books, surpassed by other theories, underscore the value of utility and its implications probably because the human nature behind utility is more complex to deal with than mathematical formulas or regressions. When utility is cited, it is marginally to emphasize causes and effects of the concepts of total or marginal utility, but overlooking the central role of utility in decision-making.

Paul Samuelson's (1980) economics textbook has 826 pages and only two pages are related to issues of marginal and total utility. It needs to be emphasized that this occurrence was not unusual in the 20th century because economics was focused on predicting—with as much certainty as possible—future outcome relying on regressions of past experiences and ceteris paribus. Therefore, limited knowledge of human behavior—per neuroeconomics—persistently avoided discussion and ignored ramifications of a cross fertilization between economics and psychology. Utility was out of consideration in the economic realm, until very recently and associated with neuroeconomics.

To ignore that human beings are by nature irrational and that's why people make bad decisions, or decisions that can hurt more than help, is to ignore the fundamental developments in neuroscience previously described. Human beings make decisions based on the information they store in their brains. Neuroscience shows that the level of effectiveness or rationality (to use a traditional economic term) of human decisions is closely related to the amount of information or knowledge a person has. Neuroscience is showing that people act irrationally only when they lack information and knowledge.

The Utility Behind Human Preferences and the Price System

Since people's needs and wants cannot be measured directly for all people, the price system was an astonishing coincidence that led to an efficient forecasting instrument allowing indirect measurement of the social phenomenon of human preferences. Prices came about as a result of money used in transactions instead of bags of salt, as in antique times, and heavy metals that were replaced with coins and bills to expedite transactions of goods and services. Without direct influence of anybody, the price system moves large markets, and collects and synchronizes sizable amounts of information about people's preferences for goods and services. Furthermore it synchronizes the producers' capacity to offer goods and services with people's demands. Adam Smith paraphrased the price system as the *invisible hand* that balances supply and demand for goods and services which in turn became the core of the economic science based on human preferences and utility theory.

Utility: Precursor of Wellbeing

In economics utility is the degrees of satisfaction, preference, or value a person derives when making a decision to choose among a number of alternatives. In classical economics utility is associated with the price system that represents objective personal choices easy to account for.

Utility theory is aligned with the rational theory of choice assuming that people are free to choose from alternatives available in a market system. Economics builds theoretic models to compare customers' utility observing economic choices. In its simplest form they reveal people's willingness to pay different prices for different goods that satisfy individual needs and wants.

Utility and Rational Choices: Not Only Theories but Evidence

Rational choice theory is a framework to understand individual and social behavior in economics. The basic assumption is that free market systems work as an instrument to collect information about individual behavior. The sum of the behaviors of every person making individual decisions about preferences among many alternative choices provides the market price information. A rational person uses all available information to calculate, in the best possible way, the probabilities of an event, the potential benefits and costs, and acts consistently choosing the best action or the best price that optimize a personal budget.

Rational assumptions are extensively used in economic theories and in most economic textbooks on decision-making. Milton Friedman and Gary Becker, both professors at the University of Chicago and Nobel Prize recipients in Economics in 1976 and 1992, respectively, are recognized as instrumental pioneers of the *rational choice theory*.

Although the rational choice theory was harshly criticized at the end of the 20th century, and even today by psychologists who profess that human beings act irrationally, neuroscience studies previously discussed enhance the validity of rational choice in economics, and naturally, the growing importance of utility and the utility theory as the human core of economics. To a large extent, this is the result of critics of freedom to choose theory, who have overrated irrational behavior as a natural human trait over and above the importance of knowledge and information to optimize decision-making.

Utility is the basic information economic theory uses in the construction of the *indifference curves*. This is a fundamental microeconomic construct to plot optimal combinations of goods or commodities based on individual preferences to optimize the level of satisfaction and wellbeing.

Utility and the Transition From Welfare to Wellbeing

In the human centered economic model utility functions and rational choice theories provide the analytical framework to transform individual utility into collective wellbeing. For instance, at the micro level, student's exposure to quality education helps to advance knowledge, self-cultivation, and holistic development central to improve performance, to find a good job in turn contributing to increase workforce productivity, foster economic growth, sustainable development, and inclusive wellbeing-based societies. At the macro level, benefits accrued by individuals from schooling and quality education—as opposed to deprivation from lack of schooling or deficient education—create individual talent and add human capital to the pool of collective and social wellbeing built on the sum of individual efforts. It is important to highlight that in the long run, lack of access to formal schooling or exposure to deficient education have similarly negative effects on individuals curtailing possibilities to achieve a better life.

At the micro level, individual wellbeing is at the center of sustainability. It refers to the results of personal efforts and free choices aimed to the fulfillment of human needs, including basic food to room and board, from love and affection to social affiliations, attainment of financial security, intellectual needs, and spiritual fulfilment (Maslow, 1943) necessary to attain wellbeing in life. A life of wellbeing focus helps people find purpose in life complementing the physical, financial, social, and community dimensions (Rath & Harper, 2010) as shown in Table 2.1.

At the macro level, although wellbeing and welfare are sometimes used as synonyms, they are different concepts. Wellbeing is built from individual efforts and escalates to higher dimensions in organizations and the nation based on freedom to choose and opportunity available to all in market systems that provide a higher degree of financial independence. In market systems, welfare is associated with financial or other kinds of assistance to

TABLE 2.1 Dimensions of Wellbeing

Wellbeing dimension	Conditions	Outcome
Individual (a) Maslow *Human Needs*[a]	• Food, room, board • Love, affection, affiliation • Economic, financial • Self-actualization • Spiritual	Quality of life
Individual (b) Rath & Harter *Wellbeing*[b]	• Purpose • Physical • Financial • Social • Community	Quality of life
Organizational McGregor *Theory "Y"*[c]	• People like to work and engage with work when their needs are satisfied • People like to assume responsibilities • People feel proud of work well done • People value to be trusted to assume responsibility • Leaders need to provide clear guidelines and fast feedback to stimulate high performance • Workers are encouraged to fulfill the organizational mission when they value its culture, work in teams, are supported by fluid and transparent information, and receive effective and *affective* support from leaders and supervisors.	High performance culture Global sustainable quality standards
National	Balanced Sustainable Development ESTE (economic, social, technology, environment):[d] • The Educonomy[e] – The Talent Economy – The Agile Economy – The Quality Economy	Sustainable development and inclusive societies
Global	• Free trade FT • Fair trade agreements FTA • Developed countries expedite trade with developing countries to help them grow to stabilize global economy	Global sustainability

[a] Maslow, A. (1943). The Theory of Human Motivation. *Psychological Review, 50*(4), 370–396.
[b] Rath, T., Harter, J. (2010). *Well-being. The Five Essential Elements.* Gallup Press.
[c] McGregor, D. (1966). *The Human Side of the Enterprise.* McGraw-Hill.
[d] Author. Presented in Part II
[e] Author. Presented in Part III

individuals or families with special needs provided by city, state, or national government.

In contrast, welfare is embedded in a higher protectionist role of the state in the production, administration, and supply of services to citizens in exchange for higher taxes. German Chancellor Otto von Bismarck (1815—1989) created the welfare state that extended through Europe in the 19th century to protect people from detrimental economic and social conditions that prevailed 2 centuries ago. The welfare state has perpetuated to the 21st century based on the argument that it provide services to all citizens regardless of condition and protects nations from income inequality. In Europe, the welfare state is more prevalent in Germany, France, Belgium, the Netherlands, and the Nordic countries of Iceland, Sweden, Norway, Denmark, and Finland. The welfare state is funded through higher taxation of citizens with a progressive tax system. People transfer to the state a much higher proportion of freedom to choose provisions for services such as education, healthcare, and pension systems than in nations with market economies.

In the 21st century, welfare states are confronting growing challenges pressed by changes in demographics affecting population structure and workforce participation. In the European Union the population is aging due to the combination of increasing longevity and low birth rates. The over 65 group is increasing fast while the 15–64 age group is shrinking. As a result the EU projects to move from four working-age (15–64) people for every person aged over 65 years to just two by 2060 (Eatock, 2015). According to Forbes, France, Belgium, Germany, Austria, and Spain are in deeper trouble with pay-as-you-go systems (PAYG) meaning that there are no savings in public coffers for future pension obligations requiring governments to pay pension obligations by withdrawing from the general budget. Crises are forecasted as fiscal funds are falling (Mauldin, 2017). The global migrations challenges are a contributing factor to fiscal perils.

In his 2017 article *The Future of the European Welfare State: The Intriguing Role of Demographics,* Juhana Vartiainen, a member of the Finnish Parliament said that the aging problem and transition to a new demographic pattern presents a feasibility test for European *social economies.* Although many voters liked the welfare state and public pension system in the 1960s and 1970s, when they were easy to finance and neither demanded much sacrifice, today stringent government policies plus increased work-based immigration are drastically altering its political feasibility. Vartiainen forecasts that if this policy challenge is not adequately dealt with, historians will conclude that the much-celebrated European welfare state was a temporary arrangement made possible by special and provisional demographic structure of that time. Although he looks at the situation improving and accents that in the long run fast growing populism and nativist movements will not succeed because they do not provide solutions, he argues that the sustainability of European welfare states has no alternative but responsible economic management and policies that may be politically painful (Vartiainen, 2017).

The challenges European countries with welfare states face are a confirmation that welfare policies deployed in the 19th century no longer work and actually curtail potential for economic growth and development. In the Knowledge Economy empowered by technology and global connectivity, a much better educated population is pressing to have more voice to make choices that increasingly challenge welfare states, questioning efficiency of bureaucracies and benefits versus costs. The rise of populism is just one sign among many of discontent with underperforming systems struggling to finance entitlements and pension funds that curtail capacity to stimulate economic growth. On the other hand, growing obstruction of the productive sector with taxes, rules, and regulations hinder growth. Furthermore, corporate social responsibility, rooted in values anchored in individual responsibility and organizational cultures that prioritize wellbeing and ethics, need clear signs of optimism and trust to produce and to increase productivity in an increasingly competitive global economy that European social democracies may not be providing.

Government administered welfare systems, identified as pay-as-you-go, perpetuate old retirement funding formulas pushing countries into financial insolvency and growing social unrest. To counterbalance effects of the growing aging population and inefficient administration of national retirement fund programs, countries around the world are liberalizing social security systems, deploying individual retirement accounts or mixed private–public systems. The pension privatizations movement started in Chile in 1981 with the reform of the underperforming and insolvent national pension system that had become a significant burden for economic growth (Kritzer, 2005). Today, 30 developed and developing countries around the world have advanced pension privatization (Kritzer, 2005).

In the delivery of educational services, European social democracies have been notably more successful in the provision of better standards of education in early childhood, primary, and secondary education. I consider that this has been the principal contributor to higher income parity and high levels of wellbeing in the region in comparison with other regions. This is an important discussion that I will expand next.

Human Centered Development, Technology, and Connectivity

In human centered economics wellbeing is a multidimensional framework that integrates individual, organizational, national, and global dimensions. Given the importance of freedom and individual choice, all these dimensions share equal responsibility for the optimization of limited resources available based on quality outcome, operationalized through continuous improvement at all levels—the individual, organizations, government, market systems, and global commerce and trade aiming for sustainable development.

In the model, individual wellbeing is aligned with the Aristotelian eudaimonic principle that a person has to cultivate and consolidate self-improvement in a sustainable way as a necessary condition to make a better contribution to improve organizations and society. In turn, the wellbeing of society is a responsibility shared by all people to attain inclusiveness.

Organizations have the same responsibility as individuals for continuous assessment and improvement and quality standards to optimize their contribution to the economy and society. Nonetheless, organizations are inert instruments moved by human beings. So this is the main reason why this wellbeing model is scalable from the individual to the upper dimensions of organizations, markets, the economy, and society. To attain sustainability is a human decision (Lepeley, 2017a).

Table 2.1 presents the dimensions of wellbeing escalating from the individual to the global dimension. Given the importance of individual responsibility for wellbeing in the other dimensions, Table 2.1 includes two complementary theories that shape individual wellbeing which are the satisfaction of human needs (Maslow) as a condition to attain the five wellbeing essentials (Rath and Harper, 2010) that define quality of life.

Organizational wellbeing is defined in terms of McGregor's Theory *Y* which is the positive view of people in the modern organizations that he contrasts and compares with workers in the hierarchical and authoritarian organization described in Theory *X*.

At the macro-national level the human center economic model is built on the Balanced Sustainable Development ESTE (economic, social, technology, environment) that is explained in the next chapter. The construct is anchored in the assumption that in the Knowledge Economy, sustainable development is embedded in the Educonomy built on three fundamental pillars: the talent economy, the agile economy, the quality economy. These three economies are complementary and advance in tandem to strengthen the Educonomy. The Educonomy and the talent, agile, and quality economies are discussed in Part II and Part III.

I close this chapter with a forecast of the International Monetary Fund's (IMF) *World Economic Outlook* (2018). IMF forecasts that the global economic upswing that began in mid-2016 has become broader and stronger. The April 2018 Cyclical Upswing, Structural Change report projects that advanced economies will continue to expand above their potential growth rates in 2018 and 2019 before decelerating, while growth in emerging market and developing economies will rise before leveling off. For most countries, IMF states current favorable growth rates will not last and policymakers should seize this opportunity to bolster growth, make it more durable, and equip their governments better to counter the next downturn (International Monetary Fund, 2018).

I would add a line to this IMF report: Policymakers should seize opportunity to foster and deploy human centered management to advance consolidation of the Educonomy supported by the talent, the agile and the quality economies to attain the quality education all countries need to prepare human capital to bolster growth as a condition to make it sustainable, and equip their governments better to optimize benefits and minimize costs of human wellbeing and progress in the Knowledge Economy. Monetary systems should be the first to lead with the human centered approach to make monetary policies sustainable.

Note

1. Here the reference to a scientific law is description of the same observed phenomenon which reiterates the same results. In contrast, the explanation of a phenomenon is called scientific theory. Scientific theories may or may not turn into laws.

PART II

Balanced Sustainable Development ESTE (Economic, Social, Technology, Environment)

3

ESTE Human Centered Balanced Sustainable Develop (Economics, Social, Technology, Environment)

The educated differ from the uneducated as much as the living differ from the dead.
—Aristotle

A New Human Centered Development Paradigm ESTE HC BSD

The balanced sustainable development (BSD) ESTE is built on the four dimensions of the wellbeing construct deployed in Chapter 2 and aligned and integrated with economic, social, technological, and environmental development as necessary conditions to attain sustainability and inclusive societies.

This chapter is divided into two parts. The first part presents the characteristics of the human centered BSD ESTE. The characteristics are later

Educonomy, pages 27–54

illustrated with a presentation of the development strategies of three developed and three developing countries on three continents that have attained top global rankings in global competitiveness, economic freedom, transparency, and national happiness that serve as a basis for comparison. The following official rankings were used to identify characteristics of BSD complementing economic, social, technological, and environmental dimensions: the Global Competitive Index (GCI, 2018) of the World Economic Forum, Index of Economic Freedom, Transparency International (perceptions of corruption), and the World Happiness Index (Helliwell et al., 2017).

These six countries confirm that economic and social development are complements, not substitutes, and a balance of both are needed to attain human centered development sustainable in the long run.

To close the chapter, I compare positions and proposals of international organizations to advance global development and how they coincide or deviate from ESTE Human Centered Balanced Sustainable Development (ESTE HC BSD). The purpose here is to get a better understanding of where the world is going and to consider the disruption that nations worldwide are facing in relation to sustainable development strategies.

The contents in this chapter support the argument that in the Knowledge Economy the quality of education and the need to focus on the continuous improvement of education are necessary conditions to attain sustainable development goals. Nations failing to strengthen the quality education imperative, or confusing causes with effects, will continue to impair development efforts.

An Agile View of Human Centered Sustainable Development

Until now development strategies have focused on factors that impact growth but have marginalized people and displaced human wellbeing. Human wellbeing has been a by-product in development formulas, not the center of attention. In the 21st century segmented formulas that persist to focus on resources at the expense of the importance of human beings will increasingly fail to achieve development objectives—to a large extent because those strategies are anchored in priorities of the 19th century industrial revolution that are short of meeting the new challenges of the Knowledge Economy and the fourth technology driven revolution of the 21st century.

To attain sustainable development today it is imperative to bring human wellbeing to the center of the equation. Otherwise neither technological nor environmental components of development will reach continuous improvement of human wellbeing. Development potential will be curtailed unless human wellbeing is aligned, synchronized, and shared by individual and collective efforts.

In the era of knowledge and information, development formulas must be focused on people's wellbeing and aligned with people's responsibility to attain sustainable societies—with high awareness that people are unable to assume responsibility when they lack a sense of direction and accomplishment or lack knowledge and information to optimize decisions, as described in previous chapter.

Broad base human centered development strategies extend beyond the transitory feature of happiness as a development strategy but concentrate on wellbeing. This kind of wellbeing is not a given, or a human right, but is the result of personal effort and social responsibility. To this end, it is necessary to consider that only educated people have capacity to optimize decisions that benefit self and project to the whole society. In this environment the importance of continuous improvement and quality education for each and every learner who participate in schooling becomes a development imperative. Moreover, access not only to education but to quality education is fundamental for learners in the most vulnerable groups in society that need special support for upper mobility.

Given the challenges and demands of the knowledge and information age, persistence of obsolete development formulas that ignore the central importance of human wellbeing on one hand, and omit the crucial relevance of quality education for all, on the other, are failing but most of all hurting many generations. These are the fundamental principles of the human centered ESTE BSD in the context of the global VUCA (volatile, uncertain, complex, ambiguous) environment.

Once again sustainable wellbeing evolves from the responsibility driven Aristotelian eudaimonic philosophy to build a better life by cultivating oneself as a condition to make better contributions to society. To advance self-cultivation the impact of quality education on the individual and society requires special attention. And clarity that the wellbeing principle contrasts with the self-indulgent, immediate rewards and pain avoidance characteristics of Epicurean hedonic philosophy, commonly associated with happiness, which is a transitory state. Individuals must assume responsibility and make special efforts to transform temporary happiness into sustainable wellbeing. It is necessary to understand the difference between wellbeing and happiness to manage causes and effects of the human centered sustainable development model.

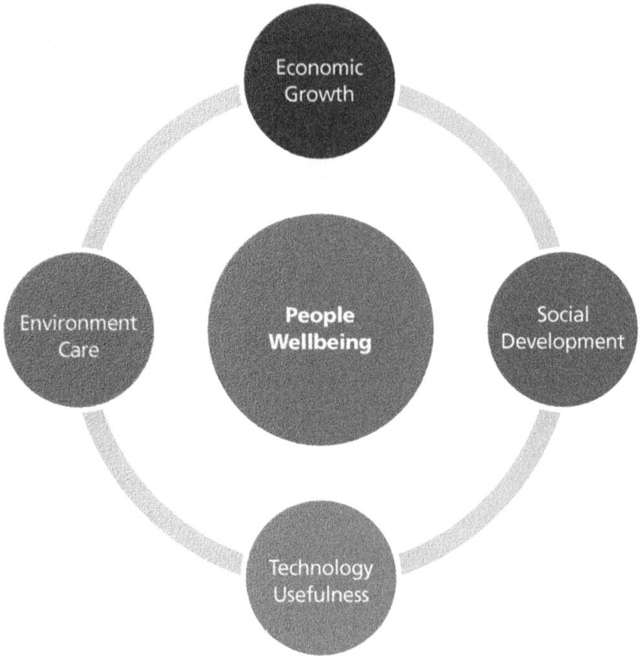

Figure 3.1 The human centered ESTE (economic, social, technical, environment) balanced sustainable development BSD model.

The human centered ESTE BSD model implies a paradigm shift that reverses the marginal role of the human being and positions wellbeing at the center of SD as shown in Figure 3.1.

A Paradigm Shift

The human centered paradigm shift is strengthened by forces driving societies worldwide that include technology, free information flow, instant world communications, and connectivity that to a large extent contribute to promote freedom and deter barriers transforming nation states into stateless regions. And the same principles apply to developed and developing countries with consequences that are still unforeseeable.

In terms of freedom, today two-thirds of the nations around the world have attained economic freedom that expedite development, growth, and improve the condition of people. But constant efforts need to be done to secure freedom in all countries as a most critical element of human wellbeing. The 2018 Freedom Report shows that among 195 countries 45% are free,

30% are partly free, and 25% are not free. In population percentages, 39% is considered free, 24% part free, and 37% of the world population is not free (Freedom Report, 2018). In free societies, attainment of sustainability is consistent with individual responsibility for continuous self-improvement and the continuous pursuit of a growing economy to build inclusive societies (Lepeley, 2017a; 2018 Index of Economic Freedom). Sustainable development is anchored in the wellbeing of people at work and in organizations (Ochoa, Lepeley, & Essens, 2018).

The Human Centered Balanced Sustainable Development ESTE HC BSD model is built on: (a) the importance that all people have equal opportunity to improve themselves through formal and informal education, (b) all have equal access to quality education (relevant education for a better life), and (c) self-improvement in all aspects of life is a personal responsibility and a precondition to help and improve society. Contrary to axioms that uphold capitalism as doctrine and ideology, and money and capital as the master and humans as slaves, and income inequality as the most critical problem for societies, ESTE HC BSD positions people, human capital, and talent as the engine of growth and development and quality education for all as the operating system to attain sustainability. This new paradigm establishes the bases for the new education based economy called Educonomy with learners, educators, and education at the center of sustainable development.

In the ESTE HC BSD framework, personal responsibility for sustainable human wellbeing transcends the temporal connotation of happiness. ESTE HC BSD conjugates personal responsibility for self-improvement and wellbeing as condition for improvement of the wellbeing of society (Ryff and Keyes, 1995).

The Foundations of ESTE HC BSD

The original gross domestic product (GNP) formula is based on the aggregate accounting of factors of production of goods and services produced in an economy as follow:

$$GDP = C + Lb + La$$

where

GDP = gross national product
C = capital investment
Lb = labor and wages
La = use of land and resources

In an open international economy trading with the world the formula becomes:

$$GDPxi = C + Lb + La + X - I$$

where

X = exports
I = Imports

There is an inverse relation between exports and imports.

- *Exports:* A nation benefits from trading and selling national products and services to other countries. This is a benefit of international trade.
- *Imports:* A nation benefits from imports because citizens have access to products and services produced in other countries at lower prices than if they were produced nationally. Hence, this exchange and imports benefit consumers giving them access to a significantly larger pool of options to choose from. Expansion of the national offer and consumption are among the benefits of trade.

A country has to pay for imports. In the ideal case exports or sales to other nations equal imports, or purchases from other countries. When this happens we talk about a *trade balance*. When exports are higher than imports, a nation has a *trade surplus*, and these international sales add positively to the national income account and the GDP. When a nation imports and purchases more from other nations than sells abroad, this creates a *trade deficit* in national income.

Nations export products and services where they have comparative advantages. That is, the country can produce at a lower cost than importing nations.

This summary conveys the basics in international trade in a highly interconnected world and the irrevocable global economy that affects growth and trade balances within and among countries. Although these terms should be understood by all people, formal education fails to inform all learners about important economic facts that affect them.

ESTE HC BSD

The human centered sustainable development model is anchored in the formula and the balance described as follows:

$$HC\ BSD = E\ (GDP) + S\ (Educonomy: TE + AE + QE) + T + E$$

where

HC BSD = Human centered balanced sustainable development
E = economic growth GDP
S = social development anchored in the Educonomy supported in three pillars: the talent economy, the agile economy, and the quality economy.

- *Educonomy:* In the Knowledge Economy the Educonomy is central to the support of economic growth, social progress, and inclusiveness assuming responsibility to help all students who go through the educational system develop optimal capacity to find jobs, attain a better life, and cooperate to foster social development to advance income parity.
- The Educonomy is deployed through three main optimization components:
  - *Talent economy* (TE) aimed to optimize the discovery and development of talent of all students.
  - *Agile economy* (AE) adjusts fast and efficiently to changes in labor markets and society to help learners of all ages advance in the rapidly changing global VUCA environment.
  - *Quality economy* (QE) responsible to systematically assess continuous improvement required to secure world recognized quality standards.

T = technology's effect in human development
E = human centered environmental development.

To identify parameters that foster ESTE HC BSD in the 21st century, I selected six countries that represent appropriate comparison standards to understand sustainable development strategies in developed and developing countries with market economies (4) and social welfare states (2).

Only People Can Change Their Nation, for Better or for Worse

I start this section with this subtitle because decades of experience show me that only people are able to change the world, for better or for worse. Although every country is different and cultures may have different values, human history shows that certain development principles hold across national, regional, and continental borders but people are the same everywhere, and this evidence is increasingly demonstrated by the latest developments in neuroscience.

At the microeconomic level, I maintain that the capacity every person can develop to optimize life potential has direct relationship with the quality of education they receive at every stage of life.

At the macroeconomic level, I emphasize that although money, capital, and GDP growth cannot warrant human development, there are no examples of countries that have improved human wellbeing in a sustainable fashion without economic growth.

Case Studies to Illustrate HC ESTE BSD

To illustrate HC ESTE BSD, I selected six countries in different world regions that in the 20th century went through different stages of transformation and in the 21st century are ranked among the best among developed (Norway, The Netherlands, United States) and developing nations (Chile, Singapore, Hong Kong) in terms of economic and social transformation leading to sustainability and wellbeing.

To provide broader analysis of development strategies I use multilevel models and a series of explanatory metrics including rankings of 2017 GCI of the World Economic Forum, that integrate economic variables such as GDP, GDP per capita, production, labor, and financial markets with social variables that impact development, like education, health, institutions, and infrastructure. But primarily because GCI associates development stages with education levels, which complements highly with topics of Educonomy.

GCI enhances the importance of economic growth as a condition to generate new resources required to improve education, health, security, infrastructure, job markets, and to increase people's income. Economic growth is critical to advance social progress and inclusion attuned with the Educonomy.

I contend the position of nihilists in high income developed countries or in high paid jobs and positions who accept and feel complacent with low or nil levels of economic growth claiming growth is unnecessary. It may be for the rich. This assumption is deeply unrealistic and misleading in both developed and developing countries, as I will demonstrate in relation with sustainable wellbeing. I take this detrimental assumption seriously and disclaim it throughout the book. Most proponents of *growth-does-not-matter* enjoy high living standards and know little about sustainable development. This is the equivalent of the Carlyle paradox I discussed in the previous chapter.

Opposing the benefits of economic growth is a damaging proposition for *people* and all nations. But it does not hurt—as much—rich countries where proponents of the "growth-does-not-matter mantra" came from.

Stages of Economic Development and What to Do to Advance

Table 3.1 shows the GCI framework and factors that drive economic progress in the three stages of development: (a) factor-driven economies (low income), (b) efficiency-driven economies (medium income), and (c) innovation driven economies (high income).

Each development stage of GCI is supported by the following 12 pillars that lead performance and global competitiveness: (a) institutions, (b) infrastructure, (c) macroeconomics, (d) health and primary education, (e) higher education and training, (f) goods market efficiency, (g) labor market efficiency, (h) financial market development, (i) technical readiness, (j) market size, (k) business sophistication, and (l) innovation.

While the 12 pillars empower all economies, economies in higher development stages are supported by all the pillars but the development strategy is driven primarily by the upper pillars.

Factor-driven economies focus on the development of strategy strengthening institutions and infrastructure, improvement of macroeconomic environment, and the broad base consolidation of health and primary education. The majority of factor-driven economies are in Africa.

Efficiency-driven economies are led by expansion and strengthening of higher education and training essential to support labor markets, goods markets, and financial markets in countries that are technology ready and have access to international trade to expand local/national markets of small size. These economies are primarily in Asia and Latin America.

Innovation-driven economies promote increased participation of the private sector for support and innovation and business sophistication to

TABLE 3.1 Global Competitive Index: Economic Categories and the 12 Empowering Pillars

Factor-Driven Economies	Efficiency-Driven Economies	Innovation-Driven Economies
Basic Requirements	*Efficiency Enhancements*	*Innovation & Sophistication*
1. Institutions 2. Infrastructure 3. Macroeconomic environment 4. Health & primary education	5. Higher education & training 6. Goods market efficiency 7. Labor market efficiency 8. Financial market development 9. Technological readiness 10. Market size	11. Business sophistication 12. Innovation

Source: Based on 2017–2018 Global Competitive Index, p. 12

foster sustainable growth and development. Most innovation-driven economies are in North America, Europe, and Asia Pacific.

Within the 137 economies that participated in the 2017–2018 GCI, 25.5% (35) were factor-driven, 11% (15) were in transition from factor-driven to efficiency driven, 23% (31) were efficiency-driven, 15% (20) are in transition from efficiency-driven to innovation-driven, and 26% (36) were innovation-driven.

Global Examples of Human Centered Sustainable Development

Table 3.2 shows details of the six countries that show a better complement between economic and social development promoted in ESTE HC BSD. These countries were selected because they have reached the top stages in their respective developmental stage and are in top places in economic freedom, transparency (lowest levels of corruption), and in the world happiness index—important promoters to sustainable development. Rankings of economic freedom and transparency are highly associated with human centered sustainable development. There is growing evidence in nations worldwide that lack of freedom and transparency significantly hinders economic growth and harms social development and inclusive societies.

The six countries include two top nations in Europe (Norway and the Netherlands), two in the Americas (United States and Chile), and two in Asia Pacific (Singapore and Hong Kong). The two European countries have different economic systems. Norway is ranked 1st in the 2017 World Happiness Index (WHI) and 11th in the GCI. It is an independent Northern European economy with a constitutional monarchy. It does not belong to the European Union (EU), but supports the EU. It has its own currency and monetary system based on the krone.[1] The Netherlands is 4th in the GCI ranking and 6th in the WHI. It has a constitutional monarchy, belongs to the EU, its currency is the euro, its monetary system is pegged to the European financial system. Norway and the Netherlands are considered *mostly free* according to the 2018 Index of Economic Freedom of the Heritage Foundation (180 countries). These countries have more centralized government and managed economies than the other four freer market economies in the cohort.

The United States, Chile, Singapore, and Hong Kong have the most consolidated market economies in the world and rank higher in GCI in their respective categories. The United States ranks 2nd, Singapore 3rd, Hong Kong 6th, and Chile in 33rd place and is the most competitive economy in

TABLE 3.2 Countries Comparison Based on 12 Pillars of the Global Competitive Index (137 countries)

	Norway	The Netherlands	United States	Chile	Singapore	Hong Kong
GCI ranking place (137 countries)	11	4	2	33	3	6
Population (millions)	5.3	17	323	18	5.6	7.4
GDP per capita (US dollars) 2016 World Bank	$ 58.790	$50.538	$57.638	$23.194	$87.832	$58.618
Institutions	6	7	20	35	2	9
Infrastructure	34	3	9	41	2	1
Macroeconomics	1	14	83	36	18	6
Health & primary education	9	4	29	66	3	26
Higher education & training	8	4	3	26	1	14
Goods market efficiency	22	5	7	39	1	2
Labor market efficiency	12	13	3	49	2	4
Financial market development	9	28	2	17	3	5
Technical readiness	11	3	6	38	14	9
Market size	49	23	2	44	35	33
Business sophistication	12	4	2	50	18	11
Innovation	14	6	2	52	9	26

(continued)

TABLE 3.2 Countries Comparison Based on 12 Pillars of the Global Competitive Index (137 countries) (cont.)

	Norway	The Netherlands	United States	Chile	Singapore	Hong Kong
Main areas of improvement						
1	Tax rates	Restrictive labor regulation	Tax rates	Restrictive labor regulation	Restrictive labor regulation	Insufficient innovation
2	Insufficient innovation	Inefficient government bureaucracy	Tax regulation	Inefficient government bureaucracy	Insufficient innovation	Inefficient government bureaucracy
3	Restrictive labor regulation	Tax rates	Inflation	Policy instability	Inflation	Inflation
2017 Unemployment rate (World Bank)	4.2 (2017)	4.9 (2017)	4.1	6.9 (2017)	3.2	3.1
Poverty rate (World Bank)	9.3[a]	8.8[b]	12.7 (2016)[c]	7.9 (2015)[d]	N/A	19.2 (2012)[e]

Source: Author prepared from 2017–2018 Global Competitive Index

[a] The Nordic Page. Nov 15, 2017. https://www.tnp.no/norway/economy/poverty-income-inequality-increase-norway.

[b] CIA The Fact Book https://www.cia.gov/library/publications/the-world-factbook/fields/2046.html
12.7% and 16.8% Eurostat 2016 Poverty rate The Netherlands. http://ec.europa.eu/eurostat/news/themes-in-the-spotlight/poverty-day-2017

[c] U.S. Census. Poverty rate in US remained constant between 2007 and 2016 during the Obama administration. https://www.census.gov/library/publications/2017/demo/p60-259.html

[d] Chile. World Bank Profile http://www.worldbank.org/en/country/chile

[e] Hong Kong. CIA The Fact Book

Latin America. It is worth mentioning that Chile was the 13th most competitive country in the world in 1995, but due to government economic policies that deviated from the successful market system that the country had deployed since the mid 1970s the national productivity and competitiveness have decreased in the last decades. The rankings of these four countries confirm that high performance market economies provide the best conditions for sustainable development and human wellbeing when nations promote economic freedom, performance efficiency, and transparency that deters corruption leading to high employment and lower poverty rates.

These results reject the argument that income inequality is the major problem for societies because these high performing market economies have lower levels of poverty rate. In high performing market economies, income inequality is the outcome increasing the number of opportunities open to people with capacity to fill those jobs. The problem is that income inequality is exacerbated when educational systems fail to prepare students and graduates for job openings in the labor force. Income inequality is embedded in a history of misalignment between education and labor markers. I discuss this in detail in the next chapter. Income inequality is increased when educated skilled people have access to more and better jobs than people with less education and low skills. The worse drama is when people in the low income range have attended schooling but have learned little or have not developed skills demanded in labor markets. They have been deprived of job opportunities by failing educational policies, systems, schools, and educators unable to meet the responsibility to provide quality education to all students.

Moreover, a lack of quality standards in education for all is the most significant obstacle learners in the most vulnerable groups face, because it hinders opportunities to attain a better life. Underperforming schools and educational systems perpetuate a vicious circle by failing to develop talent and human capital the workforce needs to advance agile economies and inclusive societies to attain sustainability in the 21st century.

Income inequality is not the problem, it's the result of failing government policies that rob learners' access to a better life and better jobs. The only solution is the continuous improvement of offering quality education to all and relevant education necessary to attain human wellbeing.

In the group of selected countries, income per capita fluctuates between US$ 70.392 in Norway and US$ 23.194 in Chile, which is a high income developing country.[2]

Table 3.2 shows rankings in the GCI in the first row followed by rankings in the 12 pillars of development, the areas of improvement these countries

TABLE 3.3 Selected Country Comparison: Happiness Index, Economic Freedom, Transparency

Region/country	Happiness Index[a]	Economic Freedom[b]	Transparency International[c]
Europe			
Norway	1	23 mostly free	6
The Netherlands	6	17 mostly free	8
The Americas			
United States	14	18 mostly free	18
Chile	20	20 mostly free	24
Asia Pacific			
Singapore	26	2 free	7
Hong Kong	71	1 free	15

[a] 2017 World Happiness Index (176 countries)
[b] 2018 Index Economic Freedom. Heritage Foundation (180 countries)
[c] 2016 Corruption Perception. Transparency International (176 countries)

need to pay attention to according to the World Economic Forum, unemployment rates, and poverty rates. The unemployment rate was lowest in Hong Kong (3.1%), highest in Chile (6.9%). The poverty rate was lowest in Chile (7.9%) and highest in Hong Kong (19.2%). Chile is among the countries with the lowest poverty rates, in spite of a 2015 Gini coefficient of 47.70. Gini increased in Chile from 47.30 in 2013 to 2015 during the socialist government of Michelle Bachelet.

The United States tops with 323 million people and Norway has the lowest population of 5.3 million. Population size is important because the complexity of development policies is correlated with population size, education level, and the time it takes to reach expected targets in the 12 development pillars that impact economic growth and social development.

Table 3.3 shows a country comparison based on the 2017 WHI, 2018 Index of Economic Freedom, and the ranking of 2016 Transparency International and perception of corruption. The two European countries that have the highest rankings on happiness among 176 countries were Norway 1st and the Netherlands 4th followed by the two countries in the Americas, the United States ranked 14th and Chile in 20th place in the world—ranking 2nd happiest in Latin America. According to a UN report, Chile is the happiest country in South America in 2018.[3]

In terms of economic freedom, Hong Kong has the freest economy in the world among 180 countries, followed by Singapore in 2nd place. In 17th place is the Netherlands, the United States is in 18th place, Chile in 20th, and Norway is in 23rd place. In terms of transparency and lower levels of corruption, Norway is ranked in 6th place among 176 countries, followed by Singapore in 7th, the Netherlands in 8th, the United States in 18th, and Chile in 24th—with one of the lowest levels of corruption in Latin America.

Characteristics of Top HC Sustainable Development Countries in the World

The following section presents a description of the economic, social, and government conditions of the six selected countries with the purpose to clarify why these countries were chosen and to facilitate understanding of the ESTE HC BSD model.

Norway: The Happiest Country

The 2017 World Happiness Report ranked Norway the world's happiest country, displacing Denmark this year. According to World Happiness Report (Helliwell, Layard, & Sachs, 2017), Nordic nations easily switch the highest places in this ranking because their development stage allows them to share the following characteristics: balance economic prosperity with social capital, higher proportion of income equality anchored in high degree of social trust, confidence in government, and low or no corruption. The WHR index measures happiness according to six factors of development: per capita gross domestic product, healthy life expectancy, freedom, generosity, social support, and absence of corruption in government and business.

Norway ranked in 11th place as the most competitive economy. In terms of the 12 development pillars it is among the top 10 in macroeconomics (1/137), higher education and training (8/137), health and primary education (9/137), and financial market development (9/137). In freedom, it is ranked 23rd and is considered a *mostly free* economy (among 180 countries). It is 6th in the world in transparency and perception of corruption. It has 4.2% unemployment and 9.3% poverty rate.

Norway is a stable economy with a vibrant private sector, a large state sector, and an extensive social safety net. It opted out of the EU in a 1994 referendum but it is a member of the European Economic Area and contributes sizably to the EU budget. The country is endowed with natural resources, oil and gas, hydropower, fish, forests, and minerals. It is the world's 2nd largest exporter of seafood and petroleum, an industry that provides 9% of jobs, 12% of GDP, 13% of the state's revenue, and 37% of exports. Norway saves state revenue from the petroleum sector activities in the world's largest sovereign wealth fund to help balance the federal budget each year. After solid GDP growth in the 2004–2007 period, the economy slowed in 2008 and contracted in 2009 and has had modest to positive growth from 2010 to 2017.[4]

Norway, a 5.3 million population nation, tops the 2017 World Economic Forum report in inclusive economies. This is a study that ranks the best countries in the world that provide sustainable economic growth over decades anchored in a broad variety of productive sectors with high capacity to create jobs and provide work opportunities for the majority of the population as an essential condition to reduce poverty. Norway has achieved this standard showing the lowest income inequality in the world focusing on policies that support education and innovation (Corrigan, 2017).

According to the World Economic Forum (WEF), Norway has managed economic policies to attain sustainable growth and rising standards of living. WEF reports Norway's GDP per capita as $89,741,[5] it is among the highest in the world and well above the $44,656 average of the 30 most advanced economies. The cost of living is high but adjusted for purchasing power parity it has the highest median income at $60.4 per person per day.

How Does Norway Achieve These Standards?

Quality Education

Norway is 2nd for quality of schooling. It tops in OECD Programme for International Student Assessment (PISA) in the Social Inclusion Index, a measure of socioeconomical school diversity.

Early childhood education: For children from zero to 5 years of age. The state subsidizes childcare, capping fees and using means-testing so that places are affordable—although according to parents, there are some areas of improvement to find available places. Parents are legally entitled to place their children in kindergartens from the age of one.

Diversified learning. Kindergarten education focuses on areas of learning that include language, numbers, creativity, nature, and ethics.

Education and economic diversification. The government prioritizes education as an instrument to diversify the economy and foster inclusive growth promoting science, technology, engineering and mathematics (STEM) with special development of vocational and entrepreneurial education and skills across the population.

Training quality teachers. In 2017 Norway launched a "five-year masters course" for teachers aimed at raising quality of teaching and raising the status of the profession.

Wellbeing in the workplace. Like the other Nordic countries and Switzerland, Norway does not have a statutory minimum wage.

70% of workers have some form of collective agreements with specific wage floors.

Norway tops GCI in accessible and stable employment and how well workers are paid. Since 2013, Norway provides 49 weeks of parental leave at full pay (or 59 weeks at 80% of earnings) when a child is born.

Policies that support parenthood are key to increase gender parity and support inclusive growth.

Inclusiveness. Inclusiveness goes beyond employment and it is linked to the key factors education and gender parity.

Gender parity. Norway tops in gender parity on access to education, labor force participation, or income.

0.95 ratio of women to men in the job market.

0.79 ratio of female to male earned income,

Ranks 4th out of 30 advanced economies on women's job market and income in GCI.

Since 2003 Norway has a gender quota obliging companies to ensure 40% of board members are women (Corrigan, 2017).

Norway Promotes Business Expansion

Norway runs a research based innovation program to support growth of the sector allowing companies to apply for research and development (R&D) grants aimed to add equitable value to companies committed with social responsibility.

It also offers companies tax incentives and tax credit to encourage R&D spending.

Environment care. Norway has historically benefitted from selling fossil fuel reserves, but today approximately 98% of its current energy production comes from renewable sources, mainly from hydropower and electric vehicles.

Half of all new cars in Norway are electric or hybrid.

Areas of improvement. GCI identifies the following areas of improvement to promote business and expand markets and growth in Norway: tax rates, insufficient innovation, and restrictive labor regulations. Norway receives lower GCI ratings in market size (49/137), infrastructure (34/137), and goods market efficiency (22/137). Given its natural resources, Norway is more fortunate than most nations. But the nation shows awareness that its economy is exposed to oil price shocks needing constant monitoring to harness natural strengths and growth to sustain high employment ratios and high living standards for all. Norway can offer valuable lessons to policy-makers worldwide showing that a strong economy and sustainable growth are essential for inclusive development that benefits all people.

The Netherlands

The Netherlands: Education and Technology Advantages

The Netherlands is in 4th place among the most competitive nations in the world. It is ranked among the top 10 pillars of development in: infrastructure (3/137), technical readiness (3/137), higher education and training (4/137), health and primary education (4/137), business sophistication (4/137), goods market efficiency (5/137), innovation (6/137), and institutions (7/137).

The Netherlands ranked in 6th place in the World Happiness Report (among 176). In the freedom ranking it is in 17th place, considered a *mostly free economy* (among 180). It ranks 8th in transparency and perception of corruption (among 176).

In 2017 The Netherlands had a 4.9% unemployment and 8.8% poverty rate.

The Dutch Economy

The Netherlands is the 6th largest economy in the EU and plays an important role as a European transportation hub. It shows consistent high trade surplus, stable industrial relations, and low unemployment. Main industries are focused in food processing, chemicals, petroleum refining, and electrical machinery. It has a highly mechanized agricultural sector that employs 2% of the labor force but provides large surpluses of food-processing as the world's 2nd largest agricultural exporter.

The Netherlands is part of the euro zone and its monetary policy is controlled by the European Central Bank. Following a recession from 2009 to 2013 with unemployment close to 7.4%, economic growth began to increase in 2014. Since 2010 the government has implemented significant austerity measures to improve public finances and broad structural reforms in key policy areas, including labor markets, housing sector, energy markets, and the pension system (The World Factbook, 2018).

OECD's Better Life Index[6] ranks countries on how successfully households mix work, family commitments, and personal life and reports that the Netherlands is the country with the best work–life balance (Smith, 2018). Dutch employees work the lowest rate among OECD countries, devote about 16 hours per day to eating, sleeping, and leisurely pursuits, a rate surpassed only by the French, who spend 16.4 hours per day on leisure and personal care.

Life Satisfaction

Dutch people are more satisfied with life and rate 7.4 (max 10), which is higher than the OECD average of 6.5. Ninety-three percent of the 11- to 15-year-old cohort reports above average life satisfaction. The level of child income poverty is below average and youth unemployment is very low. Work responsibilities are shared among Dutch families. The number of women in paid employment doubled from 35% in 1980s to 69.9% in 2017, above OECD average of 57.5%. The Netherlands has a strong sense of community. Ninety percent of people say they know a friend or family member they could count on in times of trouble. This is better than 89% across OECD countries. The Dutch are highly engaged in the political process with voter turnout at 82% in the last elections and far higher than the OECD average of 69%. Among the top 20% of earners, voter turnout was 92%. Among the 20% who are worst-off, voter turnout drops to 71%, pointing to shortcomings in the political mobilization of low income groups, OECD says.

Areas of Improvement

GCI identifies the following areas that restrict business expansion in The Netherlands: restrictive labor regulations, inefficient government bureaucracy, and tax rates. The following are the lower scoring development pillars in the Dutch economy financial market size (28/137) and market size (23/137).

United States: Second in Global Competitiveness, Top Innovation, and Sophistication

GCI ranks the United States in 2nd place as the most competitive economy in the world. The United States gets the highest ranking in the following development pillars: financial market development (2/137), market size (2/137), business sophistication (2/137), innovation (2/137), higher education and training (3/137), labor market efficiency (3/137), technical readiness (6/137), goods market efficiency (7/137), and infrastructure (9/137).

WHR ranks the United States in 14th place on the happiest countries in the world index. Although the U.S. society has low tolerance for corruption, the country ranks in 18th place showing considerable deterioration in perceptions of corruption in the last decade, which has also affected economic freedom. The Untied States ranked 18th place and is considered a *mostly free* economy. In 2017, the United States had a 4.1% unemployment rate and a 12.7% poverty level.

The United States' economic freedom score is 75.7 points, making it the 18th freest economy in the 2018 Index.[7] Its score increased with significant improvement in financial freedom offsetting a decrease in government integrity. The decline in government integrity reflects a growing perception of special treatment, elite privilege, and corruption in the last administrations.

The United States' economic freedom has dropped compared with improvements in other countries, but the 2017 increase in the overall score indicates that a decade-long decline in economic freedom is reversing. There are signs of renewed labor market dynamism and increased growth based on less regulations and tax reforms that are increasing business confidence and investment.

The United States has one of the world's largest and most diversified economies. Services account for about 80% of GDP but the United States remains the world's second-largest producer of manufactured goods and the leader in research and development.

Property rights are guaranteed, judiciary sector functions are independent and predictable. Protection of property rights has improved rolling back various acts of federal regulatory areas in environmental protection, education, and health care. American society has had a tradition of intolerance toward government corruption that in 2018 has been tested.

Areas of Continuous Assessment and Improvement

GCI identifies the following areas of improvement for the U.S. economy: tax rates, tax regulation (both reformed in the Trump administration), and inflation. The lowest ranking development pillars for the United States are macroeconomics (83/137), health and primary education (29/137), and institutions (20/137). Investment in human capital and talent development, congruent with changes in the economy and global disruptions, are crucial for the United States to maintain its top competitive position. The country needs to reverse macroeconomic policies that have weakened economic confidence in the last decade including tax and regulation reform to stimulate the economy and continue in top places in global competitiveness.

Chile: The Most Competitive Economy in Latin America

In 2017 Chile was ranked in 33rd place in global competitiveness. GCI ranked the following as the strongest development pillars in Chile's high-income, efficiency-driven economy: financial market development (17/137), higher education and training (26/137), institutions (35/137), and macroeconomics (36/137). Chile's level of poverty is 7.9% and unemployment 6.9%. It is in 20th place in the freedom ranking and its economy today is considered mostly free, and in 24th place in transparency and perception of corruption. WHR ranks Chile in 20th place among the happiest countries in the world and the happiest in South America. Among developing countries, Chile is ranked the best places in these rankings.

The Chilean Economy: From Worst to Best in Latin America

Although the country remains the most stable and competitive economy in the region, its competitiveness has declined significantly since 1995 when it was ranked 13th most competitive in the world with the deployment of a high performing free market economy for two decades. In the 1970s Chile was the first country in Latin America to go through the deepest economic transformations in Latin America from a highly centralized underperforming socialist regime characterized by growing depletion of national resources and scarcity that led to intense social turmoil. A new regime conducted deep economic transformation to a market system led by some of the best and most recognized free market economists of the time and a group of Chilean economists who became known as the *Chicago boys* after studying economics in that American university. In the 1980's, the country became known as *the Chilean economic miracle.* The Chilean economic transformation from central to market compared highly at that time with similar economic transformations in Singapore, Hong Kong, and Taiwan, that following Japan's success became known the *Asian economic tigers.* Singapore and Hong Kong have remained among the most competitive high performing market economies in the world until today. Chile's economic performance has declined, influenced by government administrations that have unsuccessfully tried to deviate, introducing reforms that conflict with market economies resulting in deteriorating global competitiveness and economic performance. The deployment of free market allowed Chile to have the largest decrease in poverty in the region from 49% in the early 1970s to 8% in the mid 2010 decade. Chile is among the countries with the lowest poverty rates in the world.

Chile's economic freedom score is 75.2, making its economy the 20th freest among 176 counties in the 2018 Index.[8] Its overall score has declined by 1.3 points due to lower scores for government integrity, fiscal health, and labor freedom overriding improvement in trade freedom. Chile is ranked 3rd among 32 countries in the Americas after Canada and the United States, 9th and 18th, respectively, it is 1st in Latin America and its overall score is above the regional and world averages of economic freedom.

The Chilean government has followed a countercyclical fiscal policy accumulating surpluses in sovereign funds during periods of high copper prices and economic growth and allowing deficit spending only during periods of low copper prices and slow growth. Chile's openness to global trade and investment, transparent regulatory environment, and strong rule of law continue to provide a solid basis for economic dynamism.

According to the World Bank's overview of Chile[9] it has been one of Latin America's fastest-growing economies enabling the country to significantly reduce poverty. Between 2000 and 2015 the population living in poverty decreased from 26% to 7.9%, a record achievement for a developing country, attributable to the efficient performance of a market system and an open economy. GDP fell from a high of 6.1% in 2011 to 1.6% in 2016 negatively affecting private investment and exports. Unemployment rate has remained relatively stable due to rising self-employment in response to stagnation. During a socialist administration the central government's fiscal balance shifted from a surplus of 0.6% of GDP in 2012 to a deficit of 2.8% in 2016. Sluggish economic growth had negative impact on fiscal income due to increased spending on a higher centralization education reform and countercyclical fiscal policy. On the external front, the current deficit declined from 4.2% of GDP in 2013 to 1.4% in 2016 due to reduced private investment and lower returns on foreign investments. Growth is expected to recover gradually from 2018 under a new center-right administration elected in December 2017. Fiscal income is expected to benefit from economic recovery, higher copper prices, and private investment. Responsible macroeconomic and fiscal management provides a solid base for inclusive growth in Chile. To achieve this potential the country needs to improve the quality of the educational systems and revert ineffective reforms that have harmed the system. In the short term, Chile needs to recover the trust of the private sector to stimulate investment in all sectors that have been hindered in previous administrations. In the long term, the country must address structural challenges to increase productivity, to recuperate the competitive standards Chile has had in the past.

Between 2011 and 2016, World Bank financing supported Chile in the following program:

To the education sector[10] aimed to improve quality and performance of higher education (Lepeley, 1996, 2002). Today over 50% of students in technical and professional degrees benefit from redesigned curricula, retention rates have increased, 74% of first year undergraduate students remain at the institution in the 2nd year; and the number of full-time-equivalent faculty members with PhDs increased between 2011 and 2016. Chile made changes in legislation to improve the accreditation of quality and institutional accountability, following experiences from OECD countries.

Chile is among the world's leading copper producer, which with other exports like minerals, wood, fruit, seafood, and wine drive GDP growth. Solid economic fundamentals support growth prospects. Chile retains the Pacific Alliance's best investment profile based on multiple free-trade agreements with countries in the region and worldwide and high connections with countries in the Pacific. Although Chile remains as South America's least corrupt country some political-financing scandals shook the last socialist administration. Most legal, regulatory, and accounting systems are transparent and encourage competition for businesses. Chile has laws and regulations that are enforced in accordance with internationally recognized labor rights. Trade is significant for Chile's economy; the combined value of exports and imports equals 56% of GDP. The average applied tariff rate is 0.6%. In general, government policies do not deter foreign investment. The financial system facilitates efficient access to financing. Reforms to improve access to financial services for small companies have progressed gradually.[11]

GCI identifies the following areas of improvement in Chile: restrictive labor regulation, inefficiency of government bureaucracies, and policy instability during the last administration. The lowest ranking development pillars are: health and primary education (66/137), innovation (52/137), business sophistication (50/137), and labor market efficiency (49/137).

OECD on Education in Chile

Angel Gurría, the Secretary General of OECD,[12] in a recent visit to Chile emphasized that the country, as well as all the countries in Latin America need to pay special attention to education quality that result in enhanced productivity. Gurría highlighted that productivity growth in Europe is very slow, but their productivity today is double that in Latin America per work hour. He states that this must change fast to make Latin American countries more competitive regionally and globally.

Singapore[13] the Freest Economy and Third Most Competitive

The city-state of Singapore is the 2nd economically free country in the world. GCI ranks Singapore as the 3rd most competitive economy, just after the United States. Its unemployment rate is 3.2% and it is ranked 7th in transparency internationally and in perception of corruption.

GCI identifies the following development pillars with the highest scores: higher education and training (1/137), goods market efficiency (1/137), labor market efficiency (2/137), institutions (2/137), infrastructure (2/137), health and primary education (3/137), financial market development (3/137), and innovation (9/137).

After 144 years under the British crown, Singapore became part of Malaysia in 1963 and became independent as the Republic of Singapore in 1965.

The World Bank[14] ranked Singapore as a high-income economy with one of the world's most business friendly environments for local entrepreneurs. After its independence, Singapore deployed a market system that rapidly developed from a low-income to a high-income economy with the highest GDP growth at an average of 7.7% since independence topping 9.2% in the first 25 years. After rapid industrialization in the sixties this island nation's development in manufacturing became a main driver of growth. In the seventies it reached full employment, joining the emerging market economies of Hong Kong, South Korea, and Taiwan in Asia and Chile in Latin America, which were coined in the early eighties as "the economic miracles" (Lepeley & Albornoz, 2013). Manufacturing and the service sector remain the pillars of Singapore's high value-added economy. In 2017, Singapore became the regional trading hub as "Asia's Infrastructure Exchange, [. . .] where infrastructure demand and supply can connect, infrastructure expertise and financing can be obtained and infrastructure needs are met."[15] Singapore has a strong ecosystem that integrates infrastructure along the value chain of multilateral banks, private financiers, lawyers, accountants, engineers, and other professional services. The program includes the World Bank Group Singapore Hub as the first overseas "One Bank Group" office to service the full project financing value chain in the region.

WHR ranks Singapore in 26th place among the 176 happiest countries in the world.

Singapore's economic freedom scores the 2nd freest economy in the world. Economic freedom has increased with improvements in government integrity, labor freedom, and property rights that outweigh decreases in business freedom and fiscal health recently. Singapore ranks 2nd among 43 countries in the Asia-Pacific region and its overall score is above the world average. Singapore's highly developed free-market economy owes its success to its remarkably open and corruption-free business environment, prudent monetary and fiscal policies, and a transparent legal framework. The government is prudent in its implementation of active industrial policy to promote economic development and diversification and addressing business concerns with significant public investments and fiscal incentives. Well-secured property rights promote entrepreneurship and productivity growth. Social intolerance for corruption strongly supports the rule of law. [16]

Singapore is one of the world's most prosperous nations. Despite an active parliamentary opposition, it has been ruled by one party, the People's Action Party (PAP) for the last 50 years. Services dominate the economy but Singapore is a major manufacturer of electronics and chemicals and operates one of the world's largest ports. Principal exports include integrated circuits, refined petroleum, and computers. Rights to moveable and real state property are protected, contracts are enforced, and property registration procedures are efficient. Singapore has one of the strongest intellectual property rights regimes in the world. The judicial system is efficient and independent. Singapore is one of the world's least corrupt countries nonetheless power entrenched in political elites raises concern.[17] The entrepreneurial environment is efficient and transparent, labor laws allow for relatively free hiring and firing practices. The government funds housing, transport, and health care programs. Trade is extremely important to Singapore's economy and the combined value of exports and imports equals 318% of GDP. More than 95% of banks operating in Singapore are foreign owned.

GCI identifies the following areas of improvement for Singapore: restrictive labor regulations, insufficient innovation, and inflation. The lowest ranked development pillars are: market size (35/137), business sophistication (18/137), and macroeconomics (18/137).

Hong Kong: The Freest Economy in the World

Hong Kong is ranked 1st in the world's 1st freest economic system, the 6th most competitive economy in the world, and the 15th most transparent nation in perception of corruption.

GCI ranks the following development pillars the highest in Hong Kong: infrastructure (1/137), market efficiency (2/137), labor market efficiency (4/137), financial market development (5/137), macroeconomics (6/137), technical readiness (9/137), institutions (9/137), business sophistication (11/137), and higher education and training (14/137).

Hong Kong's economic freedom is based on government integrity, business freedom, and monetary freedom. It is ranked 1st among 43 countries in the Asia-Pacific region and its overall score is well over regional and world averages. Hong Kong is an exceptionally competitive financial and business hub and one of the world's most resilient economies. A strong legal system provides effective protection of property rights rules of law, there is no tolerance for corruption and a high degree of transparency enhances government integrity. Regulatory efficiency and openness to global commerce drive a vibrant entrepreneurial climate. Hong Kong's economic linkage with mainland China is most evident in the finance and trading sectors.[18]

Hong Kong became part of the People's Republic of China in 1997. Under the "one country, two systems" agreement China does not impose its socialist policies on Hong Kong and allows a high degree of autonomy in all matters, except in foreign and defense policy for 50 years. In spite of some interference, Hong Kong's open and market-driven economy continues to flourish integrated with the mainland through trade, tourism, and financial links. Corruption rate is low and business operates within an efficient and transparent regulatory framework. In 2016, Hong Kong expedited business starts reducing the business registration fee. The labor code is strictly enforced but it is not burdensome.

Hong Kong is the world's most services-oriented economy. It has few price controls but the government subsidizes and regulates some services.[19] International trade is extremely important to Hong Kong's economy. The combined value of exports and imports reaches 373% of its GDP. There is no general screening of foreign investment. The financial sector remains highly competitive and well capitalized serving as a leading global hub.

GCI identifies the following main areas of improvement for Hong Kong: insufficient innovation, inefficient government bureaucracy, and inflation. The development pillars that rank lower are: market size (33/137), innovation (26/137), and health and primary education (26/137).

WHR ranks Hong Kong in 71st place, in the midrange of happiness among 176 countries. This ranking does not surprise me because my studies on Bhutan, another nation in Asia, in spite of the fact that this is the country that "invented happiness" and has deployed the Gross National

Happiness survey as its development strategy for decades, was ranked in 77th place in the WHR (Helliwell et al., 2017).

Quality Is Education: The Common Denominator of Sustainable Development

The most evident common features among this selected group of countries chosen to illustrate the characteristics of ESTE HC BSD model is a consistent concern for the quality of education at all levels. This is the evidence that led me to invent the Educonomy as the most essential element for sustainability in the global VUCA environment.

The economic and social standards used to assess development in this country comparison, such as competitiveness, happiness, freedom, and transparency, all converge in an important common denominator: education. At lower or higher levels, education is the main pillar and essential to support all other development pillars. In the above comparison the countries with better development rankings show highest levels of concerns for education and have some of the best educational systems in the world in their cohorts.

Quality Education: Condition for Human Centered Sustainability

But the results also reveal critical consequences of the education component of development. The main problem that affects development today is no longer the quantity of education or access to education, but it is the quality of education. At all levels and in all countries student centered education demonstrating quality standards is a fundamental element for human centered sustainability. Until now the main problem to improve quality in education is a surmounting amount of partial and segmented solutions that fail to provide comprehensive proof of continuous improvement in education. This subject is central in my complementary book *Eduquality. Human Centered Quality Management in Education. A Model for Deployment, Assessment and Sustainability.*

The quantity–quality deliberation in education is generating increasing debate, but it is not providing solutions because of a lack of fundamental understanding between quality as just a qualifying adjective and quality management as a systematic methodology of continuous improvement of people, processes, and organizations that is the core of sustainable quality. In the Knowledge Economy this clash is leading to surmounting misallocations and deviating from the urgency to increase education quality aimed to optimize the wellbeing of students, performance, and productivity of the workforce, and to foster inclusive societies. The economic foundations of the quality concerns in education are discussed throughout this book, in particular in the quality economy, which is an important pillar of the Educonomy, and the management fundamentals to attain systematic quality in education are analyzed in my book *Eduquality. Human Centered Quality Management in Education. A Model for Deployment, Assessment and Sustainability.*

Notes

1. Not to be confused with the Danish krone or Sweden krona.
2. UN Country classification 2012 http://www.un.org/en/development/desa/policy/wesp/wesp_current/2014wesp_country_classification.pdf
3. Chile Happiest Country in South America http://santiagotimes.cl/2018/03/17/chile-happiest-country-in-south-america-says-un-report/
4. Norway. CIA. The World Factbook, 2018.
5. This shows a discrepancy with the World Bank Data that reports $70.911 in Table 2.1. It is important to mention that discrepancy among different databases is confusing, but it is necessary to show multilevel data to increase awareness of the constraints researchers face investigating sustainable development with the new human centered focus.
6. OECD Better Life Index (http://www.oecdbetterlifeindex.org/topics/work-life-balance/)
7. https://www.heritage.org/index/country/unitedstates
8. https://www.heritage.org/index/country/chile
9. WB Overview of Chile (http://www.worldbank.org/en/country/chile/overview)
10. http://www.worldbank.org/en/country/chile/overview#3
11. Chile. 2017 Factbook of the Central Intelligence Agency.
12. Emol.com (http://www.emol.com/noticias/Economia/2018/02/26/896605/OCDE-presenta-estudio-economico-poniendo-enfasis-en-la-productividad.html)
13. https://www.heritage.org/index/country/singapore
14. World Bank's Singapore country profile (http://www.worldbank.org/en/country/singapore/overview)
15. World Bank's Singapore country profile (http://www.worldbank.org/en/country/singapore/overview)
16. https://www.heritage.org/index/country/singapore
17. https://www.heritage.org/index/country/singapore
18. https://www.heritage.org/index/country/hongkong
19. https://www.heritage.org/index/country/singapore

4

Global Pledge for Quality in Education

And a Critique on Misleading Quality

Don't let schooling interfere with your education.
—Mark Twain

In 2002 the World Bank (WB) invited me to present a quality for education model I had developed with the purpose to assess continuous process improvement to optimize the use of limited resources available to educate all students for a better life. The model highlights the critically important role of quality educators and education anchored in quality standards to foster economic growth and inclusive societies. In 2001 McGraw-Hill had published my book *Management and Quality in Education. A Model for Evaluation* and the quality ideas were already raising new expectations and aspirations to improve the quality of education.

My presentations inaugurated the WB's Global Online Conference Network launching subjects with the most significant impact on development.

Educonomy, pages 55–67

The presentations were transmitted for the first time live online to all the countries connected to the new WB Global network. My book is in Spanish, therefore my presentation was transmitted to all the organizations affiliated to the WB network in Latin America.

Since then, quality in education became an axiom in the sector that started to emulate and adopt the quality management movement that was showing extraordinary results in elite organizations of the productive sector in developed and some developing countries.

Many educators and institutions took quality seriously and sought training and support in quality management to deploy the model. A word of warning, while others grabbed *quality* as a buzzword and an appealing feature, those unable to reach required efforts necessary to achieve quality standards, coined the label *quality assurance* to sell empty promises that deceived many worldwide.

Quality can be promised but can never be assured. Quality is a road, not a destiny. Quality assurance is an oxymoron. Quality is continuous improvement. If there is no systematic evidence of continuous improvement in people, processes, services, products, then quality standards are unattainable. If workers are not engaged with their work—any work they do—then they cannot advance to continuous improvement; if organizations are unable to create a sustainable wellbeing culture, then quality standards are unreachable because quality starts with people for people. Quality is a responsibility of producers to meet the needs and expectations of customers who buy or users who receive goods or services, and the same quality standards apply to businesses and government agencies. Quality has no limits for improvement; but it has foes—in the acceptance of mediocrity. Everybody can attain and build quality, but to attain quality standards requires effort, engagement, and perseverance.

I learned the value, principles, and practices of quality from Edwards Deming, the father of quality and improved as the examiner of the Baldrige National Quality Award of the United States and as the adviser to homologous National Quality Award Programs in numerous countries in Latin America.

My careers in education and economics led me to *adopt* the quality principles and *adapt* them to education to find solutions urgently needed in education by close observation of methods that had worked in other sectors. And rightly so, in 2002 the U.S. Baldrige National Quality Award developed a category for education to stimulate and support educators and educational institutions at all levels to learn and deploy an optimization methodology leading to quality standards.[1]

The quality management model I designed for education is aligned with the assessment criteria, principles, and practices of the U.S. Baldrige National Quality in Education Award program. But it is based on my experience and it enhances the role and responsibility of people in quality achievements. For over 20 years I have been training educators and professionals in business and other sectors and publishing on the subject. I help educators discover their talents, what makes them unique as individuals, and help them excel as members of quality teams aimed to form generations of students who will improve society—not only get a good, passing grade. I train educators to optimize the use of their limited resources to produce formidable education for all students, how to organize and get systematic efforts that facilitate continuous assessment, and how to measure improvement and celebrate quality achievements. And yes, I have celebrated quality with so many teachers in many countries!

Quality Challenges in Education

In contrast with other industries in the productive sector, and highly aware that in the Information Age professional and institutional sustainability is anchored in attainment of continuous improvement and quality standards to survive, the quality transformation is much harder in education. To the largest extent, this is because education and educators lack awareness of the crucial role of the profession and educational institutions and their impact on the formation of talent and human capital nations required to succeed in the Knowledge Economy.

Since the first industrial revolution, education has developed as a supply-leading demand-following industry. The pressing demand for rapid growth of the education industry developed it as a major employment sector more that as one of the most important industries in the productive sector of the economy responsible to educate generations of people, discover their talent, and develop their human capital essential to increase economic growth and promote inclusive societies.

In contrast with other industries that help customers or clients, traditionally best teachers have been associated with strict pedagogues who failed high numbers of students. Until today, the concept of education is used as a synonym with pedagogy and pedagogues, embedded in methods of teaching, instead of andragogy—meaning leading and helping learners advance using the Socratic method of educated and respectful debate to develop the talent, skills, and critical reasoning the Knowledge Economy demands of all students to succeed.

In education, schools hire educators not based on the ability and the capacity of applicants to motivate students to learn, to become independent, to stimulate self-cultivation and value lifelong learning, but on certificates and accreditation that may have no relation to students' success.

Schools of education, teacher training programs, institutions, and educators to a large extent ignore the critical impact they have on sustainable development. The Educonomy discussed in Part III addresses these critical issues that require prompt and high attention.

Global Pledges for Quality in Education: Important Initiatives, Minimal Results

Today there is consensus among global and international organizations to advance initiatives to improve the quality of education to foster development and sustainability. Among them are the International Labor Organization (ILO), the UN, the OECD, the World Bank, and the European Union. But this has been a long term good intention with marginal improvement. Things must change, and change fast, to avoid surmounting waste of human minds needed to increase human wellbeing.

ILO

ILO has shown high awareness of the impact and effect of educational quality in the productivity of the labor force and increase in wages, salaries, and income. ILO is advancing initiatives supporting the training of quality teachers. Moreover, ILO warns that a lack of quality in education will drastically curtail attainment of the UN's 17 Sustainable Development Goals (SDGs) aimed to eliminate poverty from the face of earth.

Europe 2020

The initiative EUROPE 2020 emphasizes continuous improvement in education as an essential element of progress for all the countries in the Union.

The World Bank

The World Bank pledge for quality education is clear, stating that education is fundamental to development and growth, from increasing enrollment to promoting learning for all.[2] With the quality education objective in mind, the World Bank Group is significantly increasing the level of investments in education to help countries with a large variety of programs.

UN-UNESCO

The UN's UNESCO Director-General Audrey Azoulay has expressed high concerns for the need to provide access to education for children and youth worldwide and particularly in endemically deprived regions. She has emphasized that the most critical issue is not access or quantity of education, but it is the quality of education.[3]

Azoulay has stated the urgency of improving the quality of education for all based on comprehensive approaches and targeting resources that effectively reach children and youth, with special emphasis on girls. She stated that education quality is the most pressing need to unlock progress to achieve the UN's SDGs.

Efforts Are Missing Quality in Education Target: UN Education 2030 Agenda

But results so far do not look promising. A report released in February 2018 by UNESCO's Institute for Statistics (UIS) on children out of school worldwide revealed that despite decades of efforts to get every child in a classroom, progress has stopped. Data shows that 263 million children, adolescents and youth worldwide—one in every five—are out school and this figure has not changed in the last five years. These results were published when the delegates gathered in Paris for the fourth SDG-Education 2030 Steering Committee meeting. This committee is the body that provides strategic guidance on the advancement of the Education 2030 agenda. SDG4 includes a concrete commitment to ensure that every girl and boy will receive *quality* primary and secondary education by 2030.

Maria-Teresa Lepeley (MTL): The main obstacle I see for UNESCO and the UN to meet the SDG4 target is the use of inadequate formulas to measure quality. Most of all, the problem is confusing quality with test scores. I see this unidimensional formula as the main obstacle for continuous improvement and quality standards in education. The urgency is not to empower UN initiatives but to measure their success in empowering quality teachers worldwide. Additionally, it is important the UN assess teachers and schools responsible not only for students' grades or scores in standardized tests, but also for how schooling is improving education in terms of the lives of all students. Otherwise, the waste of human talent and human capital will continue with exponential losses and gaps in the quality of education in the Knowledge Economy.

Children and Youth Out of School

UNESCO reports that the rate of access to education varies by age group. At the primary level, the out-of-school rate has not changed in the last decade and remains at 9% of children (6 to 11 years) or 63 million worldwide who are out of school. At the lower secondary level (12 to 14 years) 61 million adolescents and at the upper secondary level 139 million youth (15 to 17 years) are not enrolled in school. The youth in the 15 to 17 age cohort are four times more likely to be out of school than children of primary age and twice as likely to be out of school as those of the lower secondary age.

Regionally in sub-Saharan Africa, one in every three children, adolescents, and youth are out of school, with girls more likely to be excluded than boys. For every 100 boys of primary age out of school, there are 123 girls out of school.

UNESCO reveals a deep gap between out-of-school rates in low and high income countries. With upper-secondary out-of-school rates of 59% in low-income countries compared to 6% in high-income countries. I consider this one of the most significant evidences that GDP growth is critically important for development, contrary to those who believe otherwise, and mostly come from high income developed countries. Furthermore, low income countries face a heavier burden of public finances necessary to cover expenses in education. In relative terms, lack of quality in education in low income countries is a surmountable challenge that international development organizations need to monitor closely.

A Learning Crisis Caused by Ignorant/Irresponsible Schooling

According to Silvia Montoya, director of UNESCO's Institute of Statistics (UIS), the problem of access to education is only part of the picture. She highlights a *learning crisis* where the most critical problem is that half of all children and adolescents worldwide are not learning (UNESCO, 2017).

UIS reports that one in six children and adolescents attending school are not reaching minimum proficiency levels of performance in reading or mathematics. Montoya states that education is failing to deliver for every child and this problem requires close monitoring to ensure that all children in school are learning what they need. To this end, UIS, which is the official data source for SDG4, is developing new indicators on equitable education about learning outcomes.

UIS's data[4] show the critical need to improve the quality of education while expanding access to ensure that no learner is left behind. The conclusion of a study also includes the importance of benchmarking and the concept of minimum proficiency levels. According to the researchers, these results predict a learning crisis with potential to jeopardize progress of global education goals and many other SDGs that depend on the quality of education and having literate and numerate populations.

Indeed the waste of human potential revealed here confirms once again that getting children into the classroom is not enough. It clearly shows that teachers and schools must assume their professional responsibility to ensure that every child is learning. According to UNESCO, this is at least minimal skills in reading and math.[5]

MTL: I emphasize that minimal standards have nothing to do with quality education or preparing all children for a better life. Minimal standards are equivalent to a supermarket selling food that is about to get rotten. Schools should learn their lesson. Memorizing basic material and developing skills in test taking is not educating human beings for a better life. Teachers who work in schools that serve vulnerable student populations need to receive extraordinary support from the system and the institution to fulfill their professional responsibility meeting students' needs.

UIS states that these results are rooted in three common problems:

- First, lack of access with children who are out of school having little or no chance to reach a minimum level of proficiency.
- Second, a failure to retain students in school and keep them on track.
- Third, the issue of education quality and what is happening within the classroom.[6]

MTL: Again I emphasize that this has nothing to do with quality of education, which means preparing all children for a better life, but much to do with memorizing and test taking in math and reading with low implications in students' lives.

UIS reports that the results are shocking:

- More than two-thirds of the children and youth not learning are actually in school, meaning that they are not hidden or isolated from their governments and communities, but they are sitting in classrooms with their own aspirations and potential.

- UNESCO confirms reaching these children but emphasizes that to stay in school and grasp only the basics is not enough.
- Policy makers must understand students' needs and address the shortcomings of schooling.
- UNESCO emphasizes that education requires a high commitment and resources but more than anything else new approaches to measuring and improving the quality of education.[7]

UIS states that this can only happen with data and that is why the organization is working closely with partners in countries worldwide to help nations explore options to move forward. UIS states that the discussions on benchmarks touch all major education issues.

MTL: I add that benchmarking is very important to attain continuous improvement and sustainable quality standards in education, but teachers must receive training in quality standards to empower students to attain for a better life, not only to memorize data and testing skills to get higher scores in math and reading; which is still the principal objective of UIS. To attain a better life is a most challenging proposition for everybody, but it is far more difficult for learners from low income households who confront surmounting constraints aside from education.

Table 4.1 shows the number and percentages of students attending school who are not learning to meet minimal standards, according to UIS, segmented by country income levels. The numbers show that the most pressing problem of not learning and lack of quality in education are in lower–middle income countries, representing the highest proportion of

TABLE 4.1 Population of Students Not Learning in School by Country Level of Income

Primary and Lower Secondary School Age	School Age Population (in millions)	% of School Age Population	% of Children Not Learning
High income countries	117	11%	2%
Upper middle income countries	307	29%	16%
Lower middle income countries	493	46%	60%
Low income countries	154	14%	22%
World	1,072	100	100

Source: Adapted from UNESCO Fact Sheet No. 46. September 2017. p. 15.

TABLE 4.2 Percentage of Schooled Children Not Learning by Gender and by Region

Region	% School Age Children Not Learning NL Total	% NL Boys	% NL Girls
North America & Europe	14%	17%	12%
Oceania	22%	24%	19%
Easter & South Easter Asia	31%	32%	28%
Latin America & the Caribbean	36%	38%	34%
Western Asia & Northern Africa	57%	58%	56%
Central & Southern Asia	81%	84%	77%
South Saharan Africa	88%	86%	90%

Source: Adapted from UNESCO Fact Sheet No. 46. September 2017. p. 3.

students attending schools (46%) and also the highest percentage of students who are not learning (60%).

Table 4.2 presents the proportion of children attending school but not learning or reaching minimal scores in standardized testing in reading and math. The results in Table 4.2 show that in 6 of the 7 regions girls perform better than boys, except for girls in the sub-Saharan region. Here it is important to find out why boys in general show lower performance in test taking.

Tables 4.1 and 4.2 confirm that for UNESCO and its statistic unit, the main objectives are anchored in basic memorization and test taking skills as proxy for student learning. But as I said above, minimal standards do not relate to continuous improvement and optimal standards associated with fundamental quality standards and learning for a better life, beyond test taking.

Here are the queries posted by UNESCO's UIS unit and below are the questions I propose that need to be asked to advance to quality standards. Differences are significant, and so are the efforts that governments of countries worldwide, and international development organizations in particular, should do to advance from minimal standards to quality parameters without leaving students behind.

UIS: What are the minimum levels of learning we expect children to achieve?

MTL: If this were a quality concern the question should be:
What are the most effective ways to recognize and enhance the talent in each child?

UIS: Should there be one benchmark for developing countries and another for 22 UIS Fact Sheet No. 46 | September 2017 developed countries?

MTL: The developed–developing dilemma was solved long ago, so it is mystifying that an organization such as UNVESCO continues to wrongly use the same standards to measure progress in developed and developing nations, but in so doing is also widening a gap that is detrimental for all.

UIS: Or should they be defined at the country level?

MTL: Quality is an individual and institutional responsibility embedded in people. Until UNESCO and all other development organizations understand this, real quality standards based on continuous improvement will be unreachable for its members.

UIS: Do children and their households have the right or entitlement to a minimum level of learning?

MTL: Nobody is entitled to any minimum levels of learning. This is a most dangerous and harmful assumption of an international organization funded excessively to improve the life of people. If UNESCO was truly concerned with quality of education, the query should have been: What is the level of responsibility UNESCO has to assume to improve the lives of children in schools around to world and to encourage families of out-of-school children to help them experience schooling?

Expenses in Education (Forget About Returns to Investment)

UIS confirms the difficulty that most countries and international development organizations confront to accurately calculate how much countries spend on education and where funding comes from or how it is spent. To a large extent, this happens when countries lack reliable statistics and systems for collecting and analyzing data on education financing. Therefore, calculations of rates of return to investment in education, when they exist, are elusive and may even be hazardous in countries where national stats have to collect data from a large number of different sources often using different classifications (UNESCO, 2016).

Additionally, countries funds for education that to a considerable amount are provided by households and non-governmental organizations (NGOs) are excluded. Or when these funding sources are collected they may be in aggregate form difficult to analyze.

UNESCO highlights the importance of collecting reliable data of financial flows to help governments understand how funds are disbursed, which groups are disadvantaged in accessing the funding, and what must be done to improve cost efficiency and effectiveness. Lack of reliable financial data impedes cost assessment and management at national and international levels.

Furthermore, UNESCO states that calculating accurate unit costs for education is not possible in many countries and the significant gaps in international data availability has high potential to prevent effective monitoring of progress towards the Education 2030 framework and SDG4. Given that SDG4 is to provide quality education to all students and promote lifelong learning opportunities for all, this highlights a significant obstacle for quality improvement.

In any case, Table 4.2 shows data available in UNESCO to present a picture of the expenses in education the selected countries used to analyze the complementarity of the income and wellbeing formula. Table 4.3 shows the expenses in education of the two countries in Europe, Norway and the Netherlands; two countries in the Americas, the United States (high income, developed) and Chile (high income developing country); and two countries in Asia. Data for Hong Kong is not available in UNESCO. The purpose of Table 4.3 is to inform the magnitude amount of investments these countries spend in the schooling of their people. UNESCO's confirmation of the economic shortcomings of many countries to report expenses and funding sources makes this problem a major national issue.

TABLE 4.3 Expenditures in Education as Percentage of Countries' GDP and Percentage of National Government Expenditure by Educational Levels

Country	% GDP in Education	Education Expenditure as % of Total Government Expenditures	% Expenditure in Primary Ed as Total Education Expense	% Expenditure in Secondary Ed as Total Education Expense	% Expenditure in Higher Ed as Total Education Expense
Norway (2014)	7.6%	17.0%	10.0%	21.6%	28.6%
Netherlands (2014)	7.0%	12.0%	7.0%	22.5%	30.6%
United States (2014)	4.9%	13.6%	6.5%	31.0%	27.5%
Chile (2015)	4.9%	20.0%	13.0%	25.6%	25.7%
Singapore (2013)	2.9%	20.0%	n/a	22.0%	35.3%
Hong Kong	n/a	n/a	n/a	m/a	n/a

Source: Adpated from UNESCO (http://data.uis.unesco.org/#)

The most critical problem about quality in education is economics. While the issue of access and quantity of schooling for all is important and it is a responsibility of public education, the measurement of output using only standardized test scores is extremely limited to show the benefits learners gain from schooling in relation to investments.

UIS reports that it is exploring, with partners, the possibility of developing a global composite of indicators to reflect issues related to access, quality, and equity of education. UIS's forthcoming discussion will include: How can governments improve students' learning when they do not have effective instruments to evaluate outcome and quality?

Meanwhile, UNESCO and its unit of statistical analysis express that the results reinforce calls for far greater global investment in education at all levels to ensure progress towards SDG4, including more resources for data gathering and analysis to monitor the pace and equity of that progress. These issues will be on the agenda of the fourth SDG-Education 2030 Steering Committee, the main global consultation and coordination mechanism for education in the 2030 Agenda for Sustainable Development. The committee, that meets once or twice a year to provide strategic advice on policies, financing, monitoring, and reporting on advocacy, is composed of 38 members representing a majority of the member states, together with eight UN agencies, the Global Partnership for Education, the OECD, regional organizations, teacher organizations, civil society networks, in addition to representatives from the private sector, foundations, and youth and student organizations.[8]

UNESCO states that countries can save millions of dollars investing in effective learning assessments but emphasizes that these savings would pale compared with the individual and collective benefits if each of the 617 million children and adolescents are able to meet and beat minimum proficiency levels and assume their right to a quality education.

I close this discussion stating that quality in education is not a right, it is a responsibility. A personal and shared responsibility that every teacher and every school and institution offering educational services must assume to attain continuous improvement and sustainable quality standards to eradicate pervasive approaches that have led to these devastating results and waste. The following chapters show the road to progress and quality in education.

Notes

1. Baldrige National Quality and Excellence Program in education. https://www.nist.gov/baldrige/self-assessing/baldrige-sector/education

2. World Bank education (http://www.worldbank.org/en/topic/education)
3. World Bank education (http://www.worldbank.org/en/topic/education)
4. UNESCO (2017). http://uis.unesco.org/sites/default/files/documents/fs46-more-than-half-children-not-learning-en-2017.pdf
5. UNESCO (2017). http://uis.unesco.org/sites/default/files/documents/fs46-more-than-half-children-not-learning-en-2017.pdf
6. UNESCO (2017). http://uis.unesco.org/sites/default/files/documents/fs46-more-than-half-children-not-learning-en-2017.pdf
7. UNESCO (2017). http://uis.unesco.org/sites/default/files/documents/fs46-more-than-half-children-not-learning-en-2017.pdf
8. http://data.uis.unesco.org/#

PART III

The Educonomy and Its Three Pillars

5

The Educonomy

There is one good, knowledge; and one evil, ignorance.
—Socrates

In 1987 when I wrote the research thesis *Higher Education and Economic Development: The Case of Chile* (Lepeley, 1987), this was the first research on economics of education in the Department of Economics at the University of Miami. Then, George Psacharopoulos with the World Bank, was among my main sources of information in this emerging field about the impact of education on growth and development and the special effects in developing countries (Psacharopoulos and Sanyal, 1981; Psacharopoulos and Woodhall, 1986).

Three decades later, Psacharopoulos is once again as highly concerned as I am about education's pending promises of improvement that international development organization programs are constantly postponing and unable to achieve. Readers will confirm in the following section the

Educonomy, pages 71–114

stubbornness and recurrent failure to improve the quality in education that has become pervasive and insidious. The reader will find many coincidences between Psacharopoulus' (2014) findings, in the study *Benefits and Cost of Education Targets for the Post–2015 Consensus* published by the Copenhagen Consensus Center for Education Assessments Papers, and the concerns I have reiterated in the previous chapters that created my motivation to develop the Educonomy model.

First, it is helpful to review the details of the career of an education economist who has made major contributions to this important but still emerging field.

During his career, Psacharopoulus, has had extensive impact on the way education is viewed in relation to economics and its development across the board and particularly in developing nations. This information is critical because nations in general, but developing nations in particular, invest a substantial proportion of their national budgets in educating people (and so do international development organizations). Yet, the returns of investment in education remain low and hardly monitored effectively to repair and improve results. Waste is surmounting and people are increasingly tired and desperate for solutions.

Psacharopoulos was born in Greece, obtained a BA in his home country and an MA and PhD in Economics from the University of Chicago in 1964 and 1968. Early on, he took an interest in the economics of education, particularly in the returns of education and in comparative studies across nations (1992). His conception of how investment in education can be approached has influenced research studies and policy extensively in developing nations (Psacharopoulos & Sanyal, 1981; Psacharopoulos & Woodhall, 1986). Psacharopoulos has used human capital theory as a focus on macro planning of education as an integral part of his work (Psacharopoulos & Tzannatos, 1992). He views human capital development through education as a means to more productive societies. He has emphasized that economics is an integral utility in the process of educational planning, guiding planners in determining resource allocation to optimal use for efficient and effective school systems.[1]

Unfulfilled Educational Promise Obstructing Sustainable Development. Urgent Need for Solutions!

In his study *Benefits and Costs of Education: Targets for the 2015 Development Agenda. Post–2015 Consensus*, Psacharopoulos (2015) presents a comprehensive assessment of the benefits and costs analysis of education with ample discussion of the advantages and shortcomings of this methodology.

Psacharopoulos predicts that an overall conclusion of the study is that the vast majority of the post–2015 education global targets would not be achieved by 2030, as I have done all along. His recommendation is the need to prioritize based on cost-benefits analysis findings.

He attributes poor outcome to a long history of international organizations setting numerical targets for education which have been unachievable. He highlights the following examples:

- In 1961 UNESCO convened a high level conference of African States focused on the development of education in Africa setting a goal that by 1980 primary enrollment should be 100%, relative to 40% in 1960. In 1980, the net primary enrollment ratio in sub-Saharan Africa stood at 56%.
- In 1990 UNESCO, UNICEF, the World Bank, and UNDP joined forces in another high level conference to launch the "Education for All" (EFA) campaign with the goal of universal primary education by the year 2000. In 1999 the net enrollment ratio in Africa was 57%.
- Given that earlier targets had not been achieved in 2000 the Dakar World Education Forum set a new target for 2015. This target was reaffirmed at the 2000 United Nations Millennium Summit where world leaders set a goal of achieving universal primary education by 2015 (UNDP, 2013): "Ensure that, by 2015, children everywhere, boys and girls alike, will be able to complete a full course of primary schooling" (UNDP, 2013, p. 20). The primary enrollment ratio was set as the monitoring indicator. The 2013 figures confirmed that about 60 million children were out of school and over 100 million youth aged 15–24 lacked basic reading and writing skills (UNDP, 2013).
- In 2011, the World Bank issued its education strategy for 2020 pledging learning for all meaning that "all students should acquire the knowledge and skills they need to live happy, productive lives" (World Bank, 2011, p. 7). Although the target year of this noble goal is 6 years away, Psacharopoulos wonders how this target can be achieved given the huge gaps in educational achievement documented in the recent PISA report (Psacharopoulus, 2015; OECD Education at a Glance Reports, 2013, 2016).

But Psacharopoulos (2015) claims that the never-fulfilled education target is not only a phenomenon in developing countries but also in Europe:

- In 2000 the European Council set a goal that "the proportion of early school leavers should be no higher than 10% in 2010" (European Commission, 2000, p. 1). Early school leavers include 18 to 24 year olds with only lower secondary level education and without further education and training. In 2008, only 6 out of the 27 EU countries had reached that goal (European Commission, 2009). According to Eurostat 2013 data, 14% of those aged 18 to 24 are early leavers from education and training with only lower secondary education.

Psacharopoulos and other scholars emphasize the detrimental effects that no lessons have been learned from past grandiose but unrealistic education target goals in the post-2015 Millennium Development Goals (MDGs) discourse (Psacharopoulos, 2014; Clemens, Kenney, & Moss, 2007).[2]

The reasons most often cited for failing to meet targets are: insufficient foreign aid (ignoring that plenty of financial support does not explain the many reasons why parents prefer not to send their children to school); cultural factors (in some countries parents do not allow girls to attend school beyond puberty, poverty rates impact school enrollment when child labor is necessary to supplement family income, and lack of information on lifetime benefits of education); and political climate (high incidence of orphans and single-parents and expectation that the quality of schooling is so low that parents have low expectations that education can help their children).

Psacharopoulos (2015) assessed that the magnitude of the international call for defining the post-2015 millennium goals and targets contrasts deeply with the dominant characteristic of the proposals that are very general in nature. Despite the well-intended directions for educational systems, there are extremely few specifics to lead to concrete improvements.

Additionally, numerous unattained goals have been postponed from the 2015 agenda to the 2030 agenda 17 Sustainable Development Goals SDGs (UN, 2015), including:

- establish sufficient education system accessible to all at all levels,
- lifelong learning,
- continued pursuit of lifelong learning,
- equal right to education, and
- socioeconomic equality.

Adding to these new 2030 goals:

- reduce adult illiteracy by 50% and expand lifelong learning;

- all children and youth should complete primary and lower secondary education;
- all countries have strong education systems in place which support learning;
- improve school readiness reducing by 50% the proportion of young children, marginalized and vulnerable groups, not attending early childhood care and education programs;
- all children and youth ought to receive and complete *a quality primary and lower secondary education* with expected learning outcomes;
- ensure all children receive *a good-quality education* and have good learning outcomes; and
- provide equal opportunity to learn the basics, whatever special circumstances.

All the goals or targets are expressed in very general terms that defy rigorous economic analysis that include "strong" or "sufficient" educational systems.

The keywords "all" or "every child" are used repeatedly, meaning zero target, such as:

- Ensure every child, regardless of circumstance, completes primary education able to read, write, and count well enough to meet minimum learning standards 4.
- Ensure every child, regardless of circumstance, has access to lower secondary education in terms of indicators for monitoring achievement and enrollment of 100% of school age children attending school by 2030.

According to Psacharopoulos (2015), pulling all together the post–2015 MDG goals could be grouped in the major clusters aligned with economics of education literature: preschool, primary, secondary, tertiary, education quality, vocational education, and education finance.

I extensively agree with Psacharopoulos about the shortcoming of SDGs related to the attainment of educational goals. My main concerns on education are twofold: first, UN SDGs highlight the critical importance of quality education for all only in Goal 4, therefore, neglecting (if not rejecting) that quality education is essential and a determinant to develop necessary competencies to meet all the other 16 SDGs. Secondly, and most critical, the UN's misunderstanding and consequently misleading conception about quality in education. For the UN, quality in education is still a process-oriented approach that misses essential alignment with the human centered systematic methodology of continuous improvement that is central to sustainable quality standards in education (Lepeley 2001, 2017a, 2017b, 2018), as discussed in my book *Human Centered Quality Management in Education: A Model for Deployment, Assessment, and Sustainability*, 2019).

I recognize the challenges that the UN has faced to identify the development goals and missing targets recurrently. This is an extraordinarily complex global agenda that requires cooperation, alignment, and integration of all sectors—private and public, productive and government—at the national and global levels that still ignore the basics of 21st century quality in education principles and practices.

Raj Kumar, founding president and editor-in-chief of Devex, a media platform for the global development community said that the 17 SDGs add up to much more than each individual goal and targets. He states that critiques about the number of goals and targets missed the point about the differences between 2015 SDGs versus the earlier MDGs whose 2015 targets also went unmet. He claims that today's global goals (GG) are no longer about donors and recipients, because the GGs are owned by all countries so they are goals about leaders accountable to their citizens, among other things, about the imperative of leaving no one behind and focusing on the most vulnerable people—people with disabilities and indigenous communities. He has emphasized that Unilever CEO Paul Polman, who was a member of the panel that drafted the goals, recalled how challenging it was to find an organizing principle to tie together so many disparate ideas from a diverse array of world leaders. But they landed on the concept of partnership that differentiates the UN's new SDGs from the old MDGs era. He assessed this was probably the most powerful message from the SDGs in the 2017 World Economic Forum Conference in Davos, given that at a time of great uncertainty, when world leaders and corporate CEOs were trying to find common grounds, the idea that the biggest global challenges are identified with targets and metrics that can only be solved in partnership by all people working together, offers a confident roadmap (Kumar, 2017).

Economics of Education: Cost-Benefit Analysis and Rates of Return

In the empirical literature, most cost-benefit studies in education are based on rates of return (RoR). The reason RoR are so popular among economists and researchers is because they compare easily across countries, exchanges, and discount rates. There are two types of RoR to education.

Private RoR compares the costs and benefits of education incurred by and realized by the individual student who undertakes the investment. Social RoR compares costs and benefits of investments at the macroeconomic or societal dimension.

Psacharopoulos (2015) clarifies potential confusion on the "social" RoR to investment in education. In traditional mainstream economics of education "social" rate refers to the private rate adjusted for full cost of schooling, rather than just what the individual pays for education. However, in the economics literature the social RoR should also include externalities. That is, benefits beyond those captured by the individual investor. For example, lives saved because of improved sanitation conditions followed by more educated women who do not participate in the formal labor market—since they do not receive a salary these externalities go uncounted for. Given the limited empirical evidence on the external effects of education, social RoR estimates are commonly based on directly observable monetary costs and benefits of education many of which have intrinsic but not monetary value which makes them difficult to evaluate and are usually ignored if there are not monetary proxies.

Psacharopoulos (2015) highlights that traditional social RoR to education are called "narrow-social," while returns that include externalities are called "wide-social." The distinction between narrow- and wide-social returns is more than theoretical. Adding externalities to the narrow-social returns can lead to different policy conclusions.

Benefits and Costs of Economic Analysis Applied to Education

As an educator who became an economist to solve problems in education, I am highly aware of the benefit of economics analysis to study problems that lead to solutions in education. Among them, to understand the important effects of education on development, which in the Knowledge Economy, has critical implications on sustainability at all levels, that is, organizational, national, and global (Lepeley, 2001, 2017a, 2017b, 2018; Lepeley, Kimakovitz, & Bardy, 2016).

But I recognize that there are problems that obstruct fluid communication and interaction between economics and education, and between economists and educator. There are barriers that need to be solved because they present important developmental challenges. One of the most notorious is a different use of analytical approaches. The common use of math and money that economics and economists rely on to explain social phenomena frighten educators and distance them from economic analysis.

In contrast with other social sciences, economists rely on math and money as instruments to a significantly higher degree than other social sciences in the calculation of regressions and optimization formulas that add validity and reliability to economic analysis. But different approaches introduce substantial biases between economics analysis and education applications that obstruct a pressing need for integration. Lack of improvement in the education programs discussed above, to a large extent, is evidence of deep gaps between these two social sciences. In spite of the abundance of economic studies with potential solutions for education, economics is not reaching affected partners in education.

In my research and economic related presentations to educators, I try to use as much descriptive statistics as possible to facilitate communication and understanding of economic analysis. This is the pattern I follow in this book to reach economists and educators to bridge integration of economics and education. This supports the need to create the Educonomy to consolidate improvement.

When I train educators in quality management—which is in reality a deployment of economic optimization formulas of private, organizational, and social RoRs—I mainly use descriptive methodology to introduce economic concepts. Participants in my programs trust me because they consider me an educator and one of their peers, but most educators are reluctant to learn and become engaged in economic analysis and to interact with economists. Even though I train them in economics they are not aware until the end of the programs. When I reveal that I have trained them in economic optimization they first stare at me with incredulity and later they feel proud they have learned some economic optimization. As an economist and educator I have comparative advantages to reach both sides of the isle. We need more educators to study economics, and more economists to get involved in education. Cross fertilization is key to advance development and sustainability, and the validity and reliability of both sciences: economics and education. And, the costs of postponing integration is too great.

The Need for the Educonomy

My proposal to integrate economics and education are embedded in the Educonomy. From now on, I will discuss the concept and its components which are highly aligned with the imperatives of the Knowledge Economy and pressing demands of the human centered Balanced Sustainable

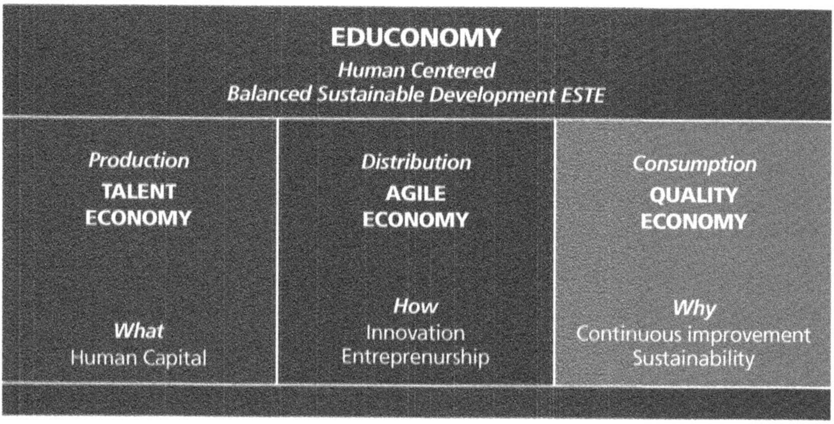

Figure 5.1 The Educonomy.

Development ESTE (economic, social, technology, environment) model within the context of the global VUCA (volatile, uncertain, complex, ambiguous) environment where economics and education play critical roles.

To be functional and effective, the Educonomy is built on three pillars: The talent economy, the agile economy, and the quality economy. Each of these pillars or components are discussed in detail in the following chapters to strengthen the core functions of the Educonomy. In this section I highlight the economic theories behind Educonomy that press the need for a paradigm shift in education from a supply-driven industry of the industrial past into a demand-led sector required in the Knowledge Economy to meet demands of 21st century customers of education.

Need for Paradigm Shift: From Supply-Driven to Demand-Leading Education

Education, including educators, institutions, and systems, all have an extremely high correlation with economic growth and development. But the links are not well understood and this leads to inefficiencies and waste of valuable resources. And overall, to a significant waste of the talent of generations of people who go through formal schooling for an important proportion of their lives with the exclusive purpose to get a better life and more opportunities.

But there is a missing link between economic accounting and education outcome that was identified half a century ago by Edward Denison, one of the designers of the GDP formula, which he coined the *measure of our ignorance* (Denison, 1985). This is a significant proportion of the GDP that cannot be explained only by accounting the traditional factors of production: capital, labor, and land/resources that pertain largely and primarily to the imperatives of the industrial past.

But in Knowledge Economy, it is imperative to diminish the size of the measure of our ignorance with respect to GDP to identify, understand, and solve constraints that impact and often obstruct sustainability.

At the end of this chapter, I discuss the World Bank 2018 initiative *Learning to Realize the Education's Promise.* This initiative is very similar to the program I presented at the World Bank about my Quality Management for Education Model in 2002. This is not unusual, lagging behind is the norm not the exception in education still focused on imperatives of the industrial age when machines were the engine of progress and humans the factors under command and control to meet demands of factories. The traditional inflexible structure of education obstructs change. Change takes decades. The status quo is strong. But in the Knowledge Economy the future of many generations is at stake. Agility is more urgent than ever before to maximize human talent and avoid waste of human capital. Today, quality standards in education for all are the consensus, no longer just another option. Change has to pervade education to meet sustainable development demands.

Today, growth and development are sustainable only if embedded in the principles of human wellbeing as I discussed in the previous chapter. And progress is a reality when human beings assume the responsibility that individual and collective wellbeing are highly correlated and needed to advance in parallel.

Human Is the Engine

After 30 years working in education with quality standards, I have observed that programs and policies—institutional, local, national, or international—focused mainly on processes and ignoring the needs and the wellbeing of people at work, are impaired and fail.

The argument of human beings as the engine is simple: people are the decision makers and executors who lead or limit and expand or restrain economic, social, technical, and environmental activities for better or for worse. Consequently, to blame markets or capitalism or income inequality for problems and global failures is to ignore the fundamentals of human nature and how the world works. In the era of knowledge and information, this misunderstanding is a surmounting obstacle for progress.

In Educonomy—Talent, Agility, and Quality Share the Driver Seat

The missing links that move the Knowledge Economy, and society, technology and the environment are embedded in the Educonomy. Yet, although a significant number of people and organizations, agencies, and governments worldwide are claiming urgency to improve education quality to foster development, many fail to recognize how education impacts the economy.

This book is the result of many inquiries, a great deal of risk taking, and a mountain of innovation and new views of education and economics. This is an integration of these two social sciences in urgent need of innovation because in terms of wellbeing, both have changed little since the first Industrial Revolution and both are critically important to foster future human centered sustainable development. Although both are transformative, none will be able to achieve success in isolation. And neither is sufficiently aware that a high degree of complement is essential and agility is crucial to diminish the costs of perpetuating the status quo.

I am opening a Pandora's box in the same fashion I opened innovation in quality management in education 2 decades ago.

Economics and Education as Optimizers

Economics is to resource optimization as education is to talent and human capital optimization.

The purpose of human centered economics as a *social science* is to optimize the use of limited resources and maximize the wellbeing of people in a sustainable way.

The purpose of education as a *social science,* is to optimize and help all students identify their talents and their capacity to attain personal wellbeing in life in order to optimize their contribution to society. Humanly speaking, a person unable to fulfill personal needs cannot help improve society.

Don't let schooling interfere with your education.

—Mark Twain

Although education and schooling are commonly used as synonyms they are different concepts, and Mark Twain made this clear. Education is the ongoing process of acquiring information and transforming it into knowledge to enhance human values, beliefs, attitudes, and to develop habits and skills that improve wellbeing and help individuals make more significant contributions to improve society. Internal drivers of education are curiosity, creativity, perseverance, and engagement in learning. External drivers of education include parents, family, schooling, media, and increasingly, the Internet. Schooling is one among many external aids of formal education that learners of all ages choose to advance their knowledge to attain wellbeing.

Schools are *distributors* of educational services *produced* by educators. Schools are major *suppliers* of educational services in all nations. Schools and educational institutions at all levels and educational systems, all shape the *supply of education.*

Students/learners are users and consumers of educational services. Students represent the customers and clients of educational institutions. Students and learners integrate the demand for education. Learners pay for the educational services received either directly or indirectly through taxes and with national funds owned by all the citizens.

Understanding Education Supply and Demand

There are caveats to the integration of economics and education. Common economic concepts like consumers, customers, or clients do not exist in education, and educators are reluctant to adopt and adapt these concepts to the education lexicon. This is one of the obstacles in the transformation from the traditional supply-driven educational industry to the needed Knowledge Economy demand-led sector. The economic lexicon is not easily transcribed to education. To simplify the complex educational focus and necessary transformation of supply to demand functions I use a personal experience most people have had in school.

Do you remember a teacher who inspired you? Who may have changed your life for the better? Do you recall what that teacher did to help you? Or why? Looks simple! Yet this is not the rule but the exception in education.

That special teacher was a demand-led educator. That teacher met job requirements to help you discover your talent and understood your needs. That person lifted *you and your* ability up which gave you incentive to work harder and more enthusiastically to attain your goals. And you improved, and probably changed your life for the better. I was fortunate to have some of those wonderful teachers and they changed my life for the better. I remember them all, some are alive others are not. But they are all inspirations for this book.

In theory, this is what is expected of every educator: to help students improve their lives—regardless of the discipline or subjects they teach in every class. Teachers should create a sense of purpose, discipline, and direction in each learner; to complement and strengthen the education that some parents give to their children at home or to compensate for some parents who do not have the ability to do so because their basic needs are unmet.

Engaged Teachers and Quality Education

Engaged and inspiring teachers at all levels are critical to enhance the lives of learners at all ages. And particularly to help children whose parents do not have the preparation, capacity, social or economic condition, or skills to provide fundamental support to instill in their children the value, commitment, and responsibility for continuous self-improvement to face life challenges. All children attend school to receive a quality education from quality teachers but particularly these children need inspiring teachers to overcome precarious family conditions and avoid vicious cycles of poverty and hopelessness. Teachers who fail to achieve these basic responsibilities are inept to educate students and should not be in a classroom. The human costs are too high in terms of waste in life potential.

In contrast with all other industry that produce goods and services, the responsibility of education is to prepare human beings to get a better life and attain their own wellbeing as a precondition to contribute to society's wellbeing.

Teachers Can Teach What They Know

Life is not easy for anybody. It is a most complex endeavor and it is impossible to teach students when teachers do not have the institutional and professional wellbeing required to promote and deploy quality principles. Students spend many years of their lives in schools with significant human investments in time, effort, and opportunity costs. Therefore, all students should receive quality standards and education that optimize their options to face the perils and challenges of life as problem solvers instead of problem creators. Are all schools and all educators meeting this critical responsibility as a demand-led industry?

Traditionally, education has been structured as a *supply-driven* industry. Although this is hardly acknowledged, it gives education a significant degree of monopoly power on programs, practices, rules, norms, and controls of schools in a system that is banned in most industries.

The providers of education, originally religious institutions and since the 19th century, largely systems affiliated with the government, have taken education as a bastion for progress, dictating directions and centralizing objectives, in many cases led by political interests of the administration at hand instead of the wellbeing of students these systems serve.

But in the Knowledge Economy the imperatives of the Fourth Industrial Revolution that are changing the world, including technology, connectivity, social networks, and artificial intelligence are causing major disruptions in traditional education systems and changing the economic effects of education in development and sustainability.

Changes Affecting Education and the Economics of Education

Deep changes are reflected in education, evolving from the traditional teacher lecturing students in a brick and mortar classroom to online platforms and fast growing educational settings; from community schools to global educational options. Today, higher education learners worldwide have many alternatives, from attending a local college to take courses online in open universities or MOOCS[3] and enrolling in courses that until not long ago, were open to privileged high performing students or affordable only by the very wealthy, like MIT Opencourseware.[4]

At lower educational levels, Montessori education adjusts closely to the needs of learners and to learner centered quality standards. Although Montessori education was originally designed for small children, its methodology provides close alignment with educational demands at all levels. Moreover, Montessori methods can integrate education and workplace demands of the 21st century as do the best schools and educational systems in the world.

The Montessori Method was developed by the Italian physician and educator Dr. Maria Montessori (1870–1952). It is a century old learner-centered educational approach based on scientific observations of children from birth to adulthood. The andragogy approach views the child as an individual, eager for knowledge and capable of initiating learning in a supportive, thoughtfully prepared learning environment aimed to develop physically, socially, emotionally, and cognitively. Characteristics of the Montessori education which are central to the demand-led educational sector include:

- students of mixed age in same classrooms;
- student choice of activity from a prescribed range of options;
- uninterrupted blocks of work time;
- a discovery/constructivist model: students learn concepts empirically working with materials rather than by theoretical instruction;

- instructors and learners use educational materials developed purposefully and mainly made out of natural and aesthetic materials;
- work is in a thoughtfully prepared environment where materials are organized by subject area, within reach of the child, and appropriate to children's size;
- freedom of movement within the classroom and with classmates and teachers; and
- trained Montessori teachers follow the child and are highly experienced in observing personal characteristics, tendencies, innate talents, and abilities.

I discuss characteristics of the Montessori method because it highly aligns with successful schools, colleges, and universities that seek quality standards in education (Lepeley, 2001, 2019).

When and Why Education Drifted Away From the Learner Focus?

When did education drift apart from the focus on learners? What went wrong with education?

Did you ever have a teacher who curtailed your talent or dissuaded, not to mention mocked, your ideas or ideals? Can you recall why? Or how?

Most likely you can recall a memory like this. It is not unusual. This is common when education functions as a supply-driven demand-follow industry. It is the common outcome when parents and students ignore quality standards of education and are unable to request them.

Demand for Education and Direct Consumers: *Students and Parents*

Students—and in some educational levels parents—constitute the *direct demand for education.* They are indeed the direct consumers of education and educational services.

Demand for Education and Indirect Consumers: *The Workforce*

The workforce shapes the indirect demand for education. The axiom is that organizations that hire graduates are affected by the quality of the education they receive.

The quality standards I discuss in the book are human centered and anchored in the wellbeing of learners/students as consumers, customers, clients, and users of education. This also includes the wellbeing of educators as producers of education, who are unable to foster wellbeing of students unless they have the same wellbeing standards at work and in life. My model quality management model goes beyond the limits of traditional institutions and deviates from the traditional supply-driven connotation that characterizes education. Instead, I emphasize the demand side as a necessary condition to advance the human centered balanced sustainable development ESTE model (HC BSD ESTE) that serves as the base for the Educonomy. The alignment of education and the economy is no longer an option but it is an imperative. And the most effective way to complement them is the Educonomy.

In the 21st century, the paradigm shift in education from a supply-driven industry to a demand-leading sector is unstoppable and irreversible. The broad base impact of technology has increased exponentially, the number of learning channels and the freedom to learn in nontraditional places creates surmounting sources of competition for formal education and institutions.

Wikipedia, the online encyclopedia, with permanent self-actualization is a treasure that few could have imagined a decade ago. Homeschooling, where parents assume responsibility for the education of their children, with extensive online support from regulatory agencies is growing fast to avoid mediocre public schools imposed on students by place of residence. The U.S. Institute of Education and Sciences reports that the proportion of school age K–12 children receiving homeschooling doubled from 1.7 in 1999 to 3.4 in 2012,[5] or close to 2 million students.

Pressing Needs to Integrate Economics and Education as Parts of a Continuum

Special attention needs to be placed on Schools of Education and Schools of Economics in universities worldwide as central axes of the Educonomy transformation. Both need to realize that the old supply leading prerogative in education is in extinction. To survive the challenges and disturbances of the global VUCA (volatile, uncertain, complex, ambiguous) environment in developed and developing countries worldwide the demand-leading imperative is pressing education for change in its paradigm.

Increasingly, the focus of attention is no longer the discipline, but how disciplines in general, produced and delivered by educators, can help learners attain better life prospects than if they would have stayed at home—how each educator, as a producer of education, is *indirectly* impacting the economy through the graduates, positively or negatively. This is a dimension of education that economists and educators need to be aware of. Furthermore, how economics and education converge to advance human wellbeing and inclusive societies considering that problems in education and economics that pertain to sustainable development are increasingly complex and solutions are always multidisciplinary. The Educonomy provides venues and alternatives necessary to advance.

Education, Quality, and Wellbeing

Examples of effective schooling in European countries consistently get the highest global rankings in social development, transparency, economic competitiveness, and happiness. Norway, Finland, Switzerland, Sweden, and the Netherlands are among the best. Norway and the Netherlands were analyzed extensively in previous chapters to demonstrate characteristics of the HC BSD ESTE model. These countries have agile educational systems that respond fast to changes in the world economy and help learners adapt faster to new conditions in job markets.

When making comparisons about educational systems it is important to keep in mind the special characteristics of countries in terms of population size, income per capita, and education level. Otherwise, it is easy to be trumped in wrong appraisals. The countries aforementioned are relatively small and have low populations (5 million in Norway and Finland, 10 million in Switzerland and Sweden, and 17 million the Netherlands). They have the highest income per capita in the world and the highest percentage of educated people. These are not coincidences but are the result of long term educational policies and development strategies. Good national conditions that citizens value allow governments to charge higher tax rates in exchange for higher responsibility to administer the welfare state that characterize European countries. The special conditions of European countries jeopardize comparisons with countries with significantly larger populations, different national and per capita income, and levels of education of the population. The perils are higher comparing high performance educational systems in Europe with low performing educational systems in developing countries that adopt models but fail to adapt them to local conditions and circumstances frequently causing more harm than help to improve quality standards to help students and the workforce. This is a common mistake that leads to misleading remedies at all educational levels. When the audacity to adopt foreign models is not aligned with high capacity to adapt them to local circumstances, failure and waste are commonly the results.

Economics of Education: Utility Theory and Wellbeing

Across the book I have emphasized that a major challenge to foster human centered sustainable development is quality in education for all. This is quality embedded in optimization of human capital and resources to secure highest RoRs to investments in education. In a nutshell, at the microeconomic level, the purpose of economic theory is to put the limited resources available to the best use aiming to optimize human wellbeing. To secure this economic principle economic analyses, start with *utility* assessment.

In classical economic studies, *utility theory* is based on the principle that people have tastes and preferences for goods and services available in the market and are free to choose among different alternatives. A person maximized utility selecting the best options that satisfy personal needs and expectations. The summation of personal *utility units* compound human *preferences.* Utility functions are central to all economic analysis because they give origin to demand curves. Figure 5.2 shows a sample of *indifference curves* of three people whose options to choose and substitute between good X and Y provides the same level of utility. *Indifference curves* express a person's level of satisfaction with different combinations of goods or services.

Indifference curves are the most basic function used to determine aggregate *demand and supply* functions in microeconomic analysis. In the trade and transactional *demand–supply* functions, *price P* is the common denominator that balances supply and demand for goods and services in the marketplace. *P* guides producers to produce the amount of products or services necessary

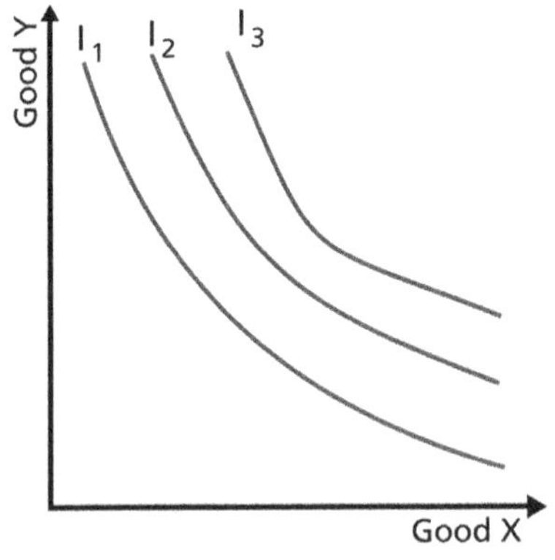

Figure 5.2 Indifference curves show the same level of satisfaction in exchanges of goods Y & X. *Source:* Wikipedia (https://commons.wikimedia.org/w/index.php?curid=4737756)

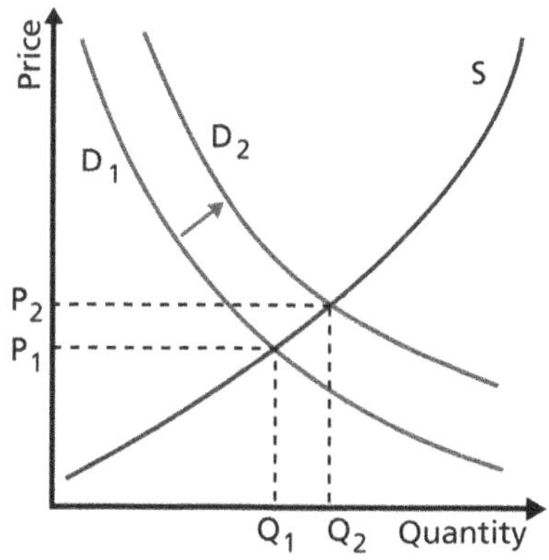

Figure 5.3 Demand and supply curves show balance between production and demand of goods at intersection points P_1–Q_1 and P_2–Q_2. *Source:* Wikipedia (https://commons.wikimedia.org/w/index.php?curid=7159492)

to satisfy the needs of consumers and how much they are willing to pay for goods or services to optimize wellbeing.

At macro-economic level *P* in markets and nations where people are free to choose, and where companies are free to invest to produce the quantity of goods and services customers will demand.

Supply and Demand Distortions in Education: *P* the Missing Link for Objective Assessment

In the supply driven educational sector the supply and demand (S&D) functions that determine optimal quantity and quality of services differs from free markets shown in Figure 5.3. S&D in education lack transparency and are not calibrated by a price system that represents people's choice, level of utility, quality, or quantity of education. Centralized educational systems command prices, amount supplied, and demand volume. There is no, or low, competition to produce education that optimizes students' wellbeing. These are obstacles that hinder thc freedom to choose and the quality standards the direct and indirect consumers of education seek. But this hurts students in low income cohorts the most, who have less access to information than better informed and better connected consumers.

Educational systems anchored in centrally planned platforms, financed by government agencies in developed and developing nations that administer funds collected from taxes people pay, commonly lack agility necessary to change. This structure is protected by the status quo, obstructing efforts for continuous improvement, deterring comparisons with the best in the system necessary to induce constructive competition and curtail pursuit of quality standards.

Quality and Freedom to Choose

Students and families can opt for and support education quality when they have options to freely choose and enroll in institutions that produce and deliver educational service aligned with students' needs that meets demands of the workforce.

Freedom to choose education is introduced through government subsidized programs including charter schools that are privately administered and publicly financed by the government through educational vouchers for students.

The voucher system allows students and families to choose institutions according to quality standards they seek. Freedom to choose penalizes low performing schools but provides them comparative standards and incentives to improve and compete to attract students. Options to compete increase confidence to remain in the system and improvement justifies funding from central national agencies.

In traditional public educational systems in the United States and in many other countries, including most developing countries, students and their families have limited options to choose and must attend schools assigned to them associated with an address and place of student's residence.

Given the restriction to choose, students who attend public schools get lucky when they can enroll in schools that are emblematic for high standards, amount of resources, and quality among the best in the nation.[6] But the demand for these schools is so high in nations around the world that they have long waiting lists and use a lottery system to accept new students. Naturally this approach, which seems to be fair at first sight, deceives a large proportion of applicants.

Quality Challenges in Education: Information and Transparency

Personal and institutional responsibility, information transparency, and commitment are essential factors to attain quality standards in education. Lack of transparency and misinformation hinder efforts to advance and assess continuous improvement. Quality standards are the result of comprehensive assessment and reporting of data to monitor process improvement.

From the educational dimension, highly centralized operations can be an obstacle for collection and distribution of information and transparency to help students and parents select schools—or for organizations in the labor force to identify schools that train graduates that meet their demands and facilitate closer links with institutions.

Although technology has opened broad access to information and the Internet facilitates decision making, there are hazards and communication risks that expose errors that require increasing awareness and cross-checking. Perfect information does not exist and misinformation is always a risk. For everybody to make education decisions, it can be costly in terms of time, money, and future life prospects.

An argument that foes of "freedom to choose quality schools" post is that parents with more education have advantages and are better informed to make decisions about schools for their children, and this perpetuates a vicious cycle of exclusion of the less informed cohorts that perpetuates inequality. This is true to some extent. But not because parents with less education ignore that their children will benefit from better education and more opportunities in life. But primarily because governments and educational systems do not make special efforts to reach out to parents in low income cohorts to inform them about the impact of quality and educational alternatives.

The access and use of iPhones and Internet connections are increasing exponentially and popularizing information among low income groups, helping these groups evaluate school characteristics and educational options and institutions in terms of quality standards.

How School Quality Impacts Housing Demand

In countries where parents are forced to enroll their children in public schools assigned by an address of residence, unable to choose schools based on quality standards, the price of housing fluctuates according to corresponding school quality. Neighborhoods with emblematic public schools significantly increase demand and price of housing. This trend increases income inequality when other public schools in the area fail to meet comparable high standards.

Quality and *Constructive Competition* in Education

A critical element to attain sustainable quality standards in all sectors is competition. Education is no exception. Competition is a fundamental concept in economics and essential to avoid monopoly or oligopoly power in any industry. When educational institutions are not allowed to compete, they have less incentive to improve and tend to perpetuate bad practices and failing rates.

My sustainable quality management model shows specific differences in dimension of competition. The model promotes constructive competition as a critical element to foster improvement—this means to learn from the best and assume responsibility to be exemplary, sharing quality practices with other educational institutions and organizations in the labor market and the community. In contrast, *destructive competition* is unacceptable because it ignores fundamental ethical standards and overlooks social responsibilities, using greed and mistrust formulas with potential to hinder individual, organizational, or community wellbeing.

Constructive competition is an important element of quality embedded on ethical standards of fairness and engagement with continuous improvements that are shared and exchanged to benefit all. Quality standards become sustainable when they are broadly shared and aligned across educational institutions and organizations in other sectors of the community as a common pursuit of excellence. The *quality connectivity imperative* is the focus of National Quality Award programs linking all sectors with shared quality standards and assessment criteria.

National Quality Awards and U.S. Baldrige in Education

Here are the links to NQAs in the United States and Europe, two of the examples previously discussed that are aligned with similar programs in over 70 countries around the world, including countries in Asia where Japan was the world quality pioneer, and a number of nations in Latin America. I was a member of the board of examiners of the United States Baldrige National Quality Award (NQA)[7] which was created in 1987. Since 2002, Baldrige is the only NQA that includes recognition for quality standards in educational institutions at all levels that successfully deploy the Baldrige criteria.[8] The Baldrige training program is now called the Performance Excellence Program[9] to avoid confusion and perils of misuse and abuse of the quality concept, that I already discussed. The European Quality Award (EFQM) has existed since 1991, administered by the European Foundation of Quality Management.[10]

For over three decades, NQA programs around the world provided significant contributions to guide organizations seeking quality standards in most industries and across productive and service sectors to increase organizational performance and national productivity. NQAs have increased transparency of quality standards leading to high performance, productivity, and competitiveness and the development of better working environments and wellbeing in the workforce (Ochoa et al., 2018; Essens & Lepeley, 2018).

Supply and Demand in Education: Costs of Misalignment With the Workforce

Economic analysis and the utility theory of human preferences are aligned with wellbeing when educational institutions provide quality standards. My sustainable quality management model and NQAs in nations around the world promote close alignment between education and the workforce to promote performance and productivity. Countries are increasingly pursuing education = workforce alignment to face unavoidable disruptions in the global VUCA environment on one hand and on the other to revert stagnant conditions most of the last decade.

In the Introduction, I discussed a study conducted by Gallup about the low level of engagement with work reported around the world. Those results converge highly with stagnant levels of performance and productivity reported in the last decade. It is illusory to think that someone who does not feel engaged with work can produce at high capacity. Many organizational models are failing to revert low performance because they are targeting capital or physical resource objectives that consider people just as human resources, not as central for organizations to exist and become sustainable.

In contrast, quality management is human centered as a condition to attain sustainability and this approach counteracts industrial management and economic models. Moreover, quality focuses on the wellbeing of people as an essential condition to improve performance and productivity in a sustainable way. Previous discussion about the importance of multidisciplinary approaches and need for convergence between economics, psychology, and neuroscience are essential to understand the forces that drive or hinder performance in the production. These are forces that education should adopt and adapt to optimize inputs to produce and distribute quality educational services to strengthen the Educonomy.

Lack of knowledge of economic optimizations discussed above and methods to monitor quality standards and measure systematic improvement in education are a large part of the problem. These shortcomings undermine the responsibility of schools as producers of educational services and dent a crucial supply quality axiom: to help learners, *not* only to learn a subject, *but* to improve a human life.

Research Findings Supporting the Education Quality Imperative

Findings of research studies confirm that students' engagement with school and learning is highly correlated with teachers' engagement with work (Busteed, 2014a, 2014b; Gallup, 2015). Therefore, optimal alignment of individual wellbeing of teachers and learners is essential to attain sustainable collective wellbeing. Educators are responsible to produce and deliver educational services—but humanly speaking—they can fulfill their tasks and responsibilities for continuous improvement only if their needs and wellbeing are first satisfied by the institution where they work.

Sustainable quality is based on management principles and practices congruent with Aristotelean eudaimonic philosophy of self-cultivation and responsibility for continuous improvement of the self to better help the organization and society next. This order is critical to attain inclusiveness and sustainability (Lepeley, 2001, 2017a, 2018; Lepeley, von Kimakovitz, & Bardy, 2016).

Personal and organizational alignment on talent development, self-actualization, and continuous improvement is the common denominator that underlines the Educonomy and is an essential component to advance economic growth in sync with sustainable development in the Knowledge Economy (Powell & Snellman, 2004).

Powell and Snellman (2004) from Stanford University define the Knowledge Economy as the result of the transition from an economy based on natural resources and physical inputs to one based on intellectual assets. They identify the benefits embedded in significant growth in the stock of knowledge and the expansion of new industries—notoriously information and computer technology and biotechnology. And they mention potential shortcoming when the Knowledge Economy focuses heavily on knowledge production but pays less attention to the dissemination of knowledge as a crucial key in increased productivity. They emphasize that the gains of the Knowledge Economy are enhanced when new technologies complement broadly with organizational practices. They claim that knowledge dissemination is needed to advance the analysis of the *skills mismatch debate* and how all workers, from executives to low skilled, can acquire technical skills to perform in the new settings in the 21st century. Because the *skills mismatch debate* reveals a serious lack of standard metrics to appropriately measure knowledge aligned with skills, pressing researchers to rely on obsolete occupational labels instead of emerging data. Powell and Snellman call attention to thousands of polytechnic schools worldwide that have changed to become universities, emphasizing that such *upgrading* is part of the pressing for a *quality assurance mockup* that needs to consolidate in realistic quality of education, connecting students with the workforce through education to optimize participation in the Knowledge Economy. These authors claim that accurate measurements and analysis ad hoc with the demands of the Knowledge Economy are not still solving critical challenges in the social science research to connect an abundance of quantitative indicators with a scarcity of qualitative studies in organizational practices and educational programs.

Capital Resources Are Restrictive and Limited: Talent and Human Capital Are Limitless, With Quality Education

The purpose of the Educonomy is to fill in this gap that is obstructing growth and balanced sustainable development. It is aimed to identify and substitute obsolete approaches in education, organizations, and development strategies with the human centered drivers of the Knowledge Economy. The analysis is timely and solutions are urgent to avoid further harm.

From the economic dimension, a special consideration to strengthen the Educonomy is surmounting evidence that while physical capital and RoRs are low and restrictive in the present environment, talent is abundant and human capital growth has no limit. Nonetheless at the individual, organizational, and national level, the growth of human capital depends largely on personal efforts and on the quality of education educators and organizations produce and students receive.

Advent of the Educonomy

I developed the Educonomy construct synchronizing and integrating economic and educational theories and practices that until now are implicit but need alignment to advance in the Knowledge Economy based on the concerns spelled by Powell and Snellman (2004). The Educonomy relies on economic principles that optimize educational resources necessary to optimize human wellbeing, minimizing waste and costs. Economic as much as human variables shape the Educonomy development formula.

The Educonomy is built on three pillars to achieve objectives: (a) talent, (b) agility, and (c) quality standards all connecting the economy with education. The Educonomy is the basic drive of the ESTE HC BSD, integrating economic, social, technology, and environment progress centered on the wellbeing of all people and avoiding harmful effects and consequences for present and future generations.

The Three Pillars of the Educonomy

- The talent economy
- The agile economy
- The quality economy

The talent economy addresses production functions in the Educonomy and the *what* questions and answers for developing talent in rapidly changing economies. What kind of talent is necessary to increase the stock of human capital at the individual, organizational, and national level to foster economic growth and inclusive and sustainable development in the short, medium, and long term. The talent economy is discussed in Chapter 6.

The agile economy addresses distribution challenges in the Educonomy, focusing on the *how* questions and answers regarding the work and efforts at individual, organizational, and national levels needed to adopt and adapt to change. Agility is essential to adapt to change optimizing benefits and minimizing costs of growth and sustainability in VUCA (volatile, uncertain, complex, ambiguous) environments. The agility economy is discussed in Chapter 7.

The quality economy focuses on consumption challenges of the Educonomy addressing questions and answers about *why* quality standards are the common denominator of the production, distribution, and consumption chain leading to sustainability synchronizing wellbeing at individual, organizational, and national development levels. The quality economy is discussed in detail in Chapter 8.

The sustainable development corollary is that the Educonomy operates on these three fundamental and inseparable pillars to advance the Knowledge Economy, which until now lacks coherence and integration to solve challenges the social sciences face to connect an abundance of quantitative indicators with a scarcity of qualitative measurements of wellbeing at the individual, organizational, and developmental level.

Figure 5.4 summarizes the three pillars described above that supports the 21st century Educonomy as the centerpiece of the ESTE HC BSD.

The Educonomy concept was coined by Brandon Busteed, executive director of the Education Division[11] at the Gallup Organization.[12] The

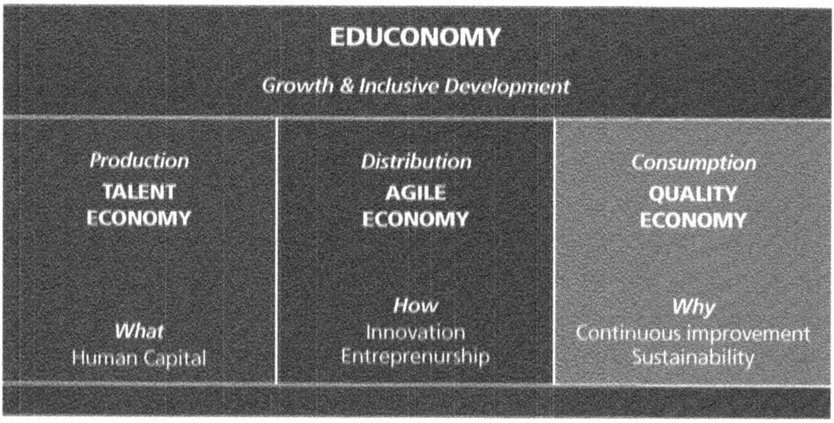

Figure 5.4 The four components of human centered ESTE balanced sustainable development.

concept was not an innovation of the educational sector. It was the result of increasing concerns of business and organizations in the productive sector observing that while productivity increases are closely related to education in terms of the knowledge, attitudes, and skills of school and college graduates, education is not responding fast enough to the rapidly changing demands of the labor force.

The number of claims that the output of education—graduates at all levels—lack emotional or Soft Skills, cognitive skills, and abilities necessary to meet the fast changing demands of a workforce entrenched in the global VUCA environment (Lepeley & Albornoz, 2013; Lepeley et al., 2016; Majluf, 2016; Massaro et al., 2016; Tarr & Weeks, 2016).

The Educonomy Is Anchored in Wellbeing

Gallup's education initiative that provided the bases for its Educonomy initiative are associated with a specific wellbeing model that evolved from global studies of the workforce based in the book *Wellbeing: The Five Essential Elements* by Tom Rath and Jim Harper (2010).

Wellbeing in the Workforce

Gallup has pioneered the study of wellbeing at all levels and introduced the concept of *strengths-based development* based on employees' engagement as a main drive of performance and productivity embarked in a wellbeing framework of the workforce.[13] In 2013, more than 20 million people in 150 countries participated in a landmark study that led to the construction of a wellbeing model for the *great life*. The Five Essential Elements of Gallup's wellbeing are displayed in Figure 5.5.

Their groundbreaking research revealed information necessary to advise how organizations can boost employees' integral wellbeing, but it also sent needed and long overdue signals to education about student wellbeing. And most importantly, how educators and institutions can develop talent and prepare students to maximize opportunities in the workforce, aligning life satisfaction with careers, good health, financial security, and community involvement.

The findings allowed Rath and Harper to confirm that much of what it is commonly assumed to improve wellbeing in the workforce was misguided or wrong. Common assumptions that life improves by making more money, losing weight, strengthening relationships, or segmenting life, is the incorrect approach. The five elements they identify to compound human wellbeing—career wellbeing, social wellbeing, financial wellbeing, physical wellbeing, and community wellbeing—are closely interconnected and combine

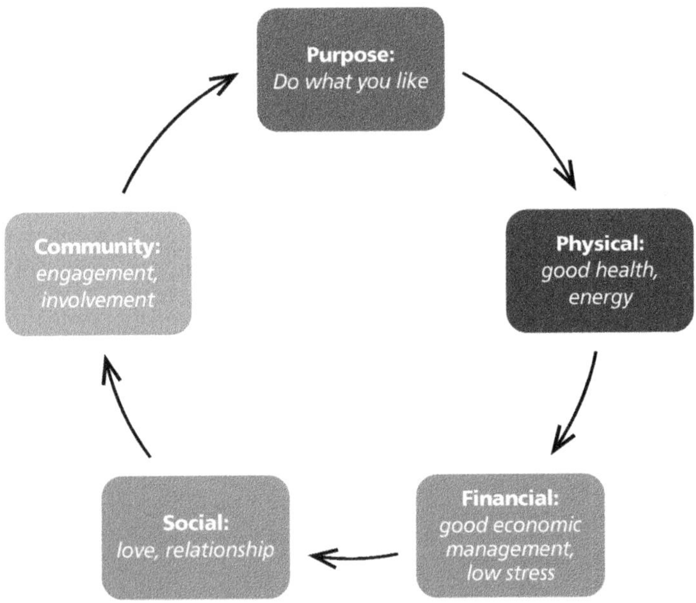

Figure 5.5 Gallup's What Does a "Great Life" Look Like: The Wellbeing Cycle. *Source:* Rath & Harper. 2010. Wellbeing. Gallup Press.

to shape *life wellbeing* over a lifetime. Segmented approaches have greater potential to fail.

Wellbeing in Education

The United States, as most countries today, conduct extensive numbers of studies to assess the state of education. In terms of financing, continuous evaluation is required because nations are making increased investments in education that demand higher levels of accountability and updated information to assess RoRs on investment in order to allocate funds efficiently and be aligned with the most pressing needs of people—and also to update obsolete financing schedules that are no longer valid. In terms of student learning and educational performance, a broadly used method of student assessment is based on standardized testing. There are growing concerns that this testing methodology, designed away from students, fails to measure a student's progress beyond cognitive ability. Moreover, standardized tests are commonly mistaken as a measurement of quality education which is highly misleading because it omits to measure students' wellbeing. Therefore, there is increasing need to differentiate between cognitive skills and quality standards. Standardized tests measure levels of learning in a specific subject. Quality standards in education measure students' wellbeing. Standardized tests are applied to groups; quality standards are personalized and directly related to needs and expectations of students (Kaufman, 2013). The main shortcoming of standardized tests is that they do not cover personal dimensions of student wellbeing.

Standardized tests are discussed in detail in Chapter 8, "The Quality Economy." I emphasize here that standardized tests do not represent quality standards aligned with comprehensive assessment of student wellbeing embedded in my sustainable quality in education model. Testing in general represents one aspect among many dimensions required to assess how education is serving students' needs to increase wellbeing. For most students, standardized test scores are not good predictors of life or work achievements. But as the importance of education increases to advance development, and educational systems get bigger and investments grow exponentially, there is pressing need for education to show results. Standardized tests expedite assessment of student segments and facilitate comparisons across schools, nations, and educational systems around the world. The problem is that although these standards facilitate comparisons they do not help to advance students wellbeing across educational systems.

PISA is one of the best known global standardized test. The Programme for International Student Assessment (PISA)[14] started in 2000 as a triennial international survey of 15-year-old students aimed to measure scholastic performance in mathematics, science, and reading. The program is directed by the Organization for Economic Cooperation and Development (OECD) and surveys students in member and nonmember nations with the purpose to evaluate educational systems. The results provide comparable data that allow countries to compare themselves with others and ideally improve educational policies and outcomes.

In 2015, over half a million students, representing 28 million 15-year-olds in 72 countries and economies, took the international 2-hour PISA test. For the first time, in addition to assessment of students in science, mathematics, and reading, OECD introduced new items to test collaborative problem solving and financial literacy.[15]

To strengthen this new venue, PISA has developed a student wellbeing framework to assess student's beyond cognition in three disciplines contingent with more realistic student aspects of a student's life. Figure 5.6 shows PISA's contributors to student's wellbeing in school.

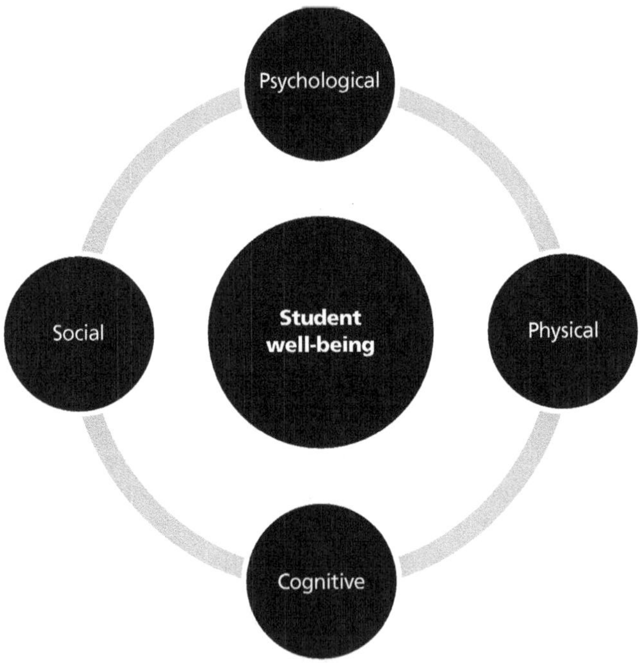

FIgure 5.6 PISA's contributors to student's wellbeing. *Source:* PISA 2015 (http://www.oecd.org/education/pisa-2015-results-volume-iii-9789264273856-en.htm)

Category specifications:

- Psychological refers to *students' life satisfaction, sense of purpose, self-awareness, and absence of emotional problems.*
- Physical refers to *adapting a healthy lifestyle and students' overall health.*
- Cognitive refers to *students' proficiency in applying what they know to solve problems.*
- Social refers to *students' relationships with family, peers, and teachers, and students' feelings about their social life.*

PISA's student's wellbeing closely resemble the Gallup's *Wellbeing in the Workforce* presented above. This shows that leading global education policy makers are finally synchronizing strategies with those developed and used effectively in the productive and business sector for decades to develop talent and advance agility and quality standards in education. This was an overdue demand as I demonstrate in the following chapters that I started 2 decades ago with quality management standards integrating education and the productive sector.

Student Wellbeing in Education

Gallup has also conducted comprehensive studies in education to assess students' needs in relation to the status of education and identification of problem areas in the United States. These results provide a solid frame of reference to validate the quality education standards I will use to underline solutions linking Educonomy with human growth, development, and human centered sustainability.

I agree with Gallup about the critical and long overdue need to intensify and clarify the direction of the links between education and the workforce. This dimension is essential to effectively balance the supply of education (students qualified for work) with the constantly changing demands of the workforce (talent and human capital necessary to increase performance and productivity).

In 2014, Gallup's executive director of education, Brandon Busteed, who coined the concept of Educonomy, addressed leaders in education, business, and government, and called attention to the urgency to turn this made-up word into a reality. Busteed presented the Educonomy concept at the United States's Education Commission of the States' National Forum on Education Policy agenda. His presentation explored links between education and long-term success in life and work.[16] In his presentation, Busteed conveyed to education leaders the importance to focus on and measure outcomes that matter most to people and students like *finding a good job to attain a good life*. He timely emphasized the need to advance the *Educonomy* as an essential field of study and inquiry to successfully align educational systems with the workforce and job creators.[17]

Although his study reflects the United States' results, I use them here with global implication because (a) they show the importance to correlate supply and demand for education in order to optimize the use of resources and talent to increase human capital and social wellbeing; and (b) the problem areas identified apply extensively in developed and developing countries, based on evidence of similar problem areas I have observed in the last 30 years in my practice as professor and quality management specialist from the educational and economic perspectives.

This Gallup study, linking education and long-term success, is based on a sample and surveys of 1 million American parents, students from 5th through 12th grade, business leaders, educators at all levels, superintendents, college presidents, principals, college graduates, and young Americans aged 18–34. The findings are shown in the next section.

Demand for Higher Education Is High

- 95% state that it is important or somewhat important to get a certificate or degree beyond high school.
- 44% in the last year thought about going back to school to get a certificate or degree.

But Gallup finds quality is in question (or what I call education's mission or responsibility):

- 46% perceive U.S. higher education is the same or worse than in other countries,
- 58% perceive U.S. higher education is the same or worse than in the past,
- 29% perceive that traditional U.S. colleges and universities offer high-quality education, and
- 19% perceive community colleges offer high-quality education.

Americans associate education quality with getting a good job:

- 88% higher education students mention it as priority,
- 67% of all Americans mentioned it, and

- 38% of parents with children in 5th to 12th grades mentioned going to school beyond high school as very important to getting a good job.

Students' perceptions of teachers' care are low:

- 23% of high school graduates and 16% of college graduates perceived that teachers care about their problems and feelings,
- 18% of high school graduates and 11% of college graduates perceived that teachers knew their students' hopes and dreams.

Student engagement in decline:

- Student engagement in school drops precipitously between 5th and 12th grade:
  - 76% of elementary school students feel engaged with school, and
  - 44% of high school students are engaged.
- The longer students stay in school, the less engaged they become.
  - These Findings demonstrates that if education were fulfilling its mission, the trend should go in the opposite direction.
- Teacher engagement is the most important driver of student engagement (Hastings & Agrawal, 2015).
  - Student engagement does not increase unless teacher engagement is high.

Teachers' engagement low:

- 69% of K through 12th grade teachers are not engaged in their work, and
- teachers show the lowest level of engagement and the highest burnout among all the professions surveyed.

Teaching conditions are stressful:

- K through 12th grade teachers are the least likely among 12 professional groups to agree that "At work, my opinions count"; and
- 46% K through 12th teachers report high degrees of stress.

Job preparedness questionable:

- 43% of students in grades 5th through 12th grade say they plan to start their own business, but

  - only 7% of the students work in an internship or job in an organization where they apply their entrepreneurial energy.
- Twice as many young Americans who worked on long-term projects that took several classes to complete and used what they learned to develop solutions to real problems in their community in the last school year valued work quality much higher than students lacking this experience.
- Schools and colleges do not offer jobs, employers do.
  - When schools and businesses do not integrate, students miss opportunities to develop talents demanded in the workforce.
  - Misalignment hurts students and the workforce, decreases ROI in education, hinders potential for growth, and generates surmounting waste of talent and resources.

Schools measure wrong predictors of success:

- 11% of business leaders think college graduates are well-prepared for success at work,
- 14% of Americans feel college graduates are well-prepared to suc ceed in the workplace, and
- 96% of chief academic officers of colleges and universities are somewhat or very confident their institutions are preparing college students for success in the workplace.

Most important: to get a job, not a degree:

- College graduates working in internships or jobs able to apply what they learned in the classroom, work on projects that take a semester or more to complete, and are actively involved in extracurricular activities or organizations during their college studies, double their chances to be engaged with work later in life.
- Only 6% of college graduates strongly agree with these statements.
- The majority of Americans agree that the main reason to attend college is to get a good job; not a degree.

But, in high contrast with the information in Table 5.1, research findings show that student's hope is a stronger predictor of college success than these parameters.

TABLE 5.1 Gallup: How Education Measures Success and Misleads on Quality Today

Inputs	Outputs
High school GPA	GPA
Rank in class	Rank in class
Standardized tests (SAT, ACT)	Degree attainment
	CLA

Source: Gallup

Deep Disconnect Between Education and the Workforce

The Gallup–Purdue Index of Great Jobs and Great Lives emphasize the need to shift from what's wrong to what's strong in terms of best predictors of college success, looking at: responsibility, discipline, empathy, ideas, perseverance, achievement, continuous learning, maximizer, analytic, and futuristic. I agree with all these principles which I have emphasized throughout and I add that (a) identification of areas of improvement is essential to advance; (b) considering that unless there are concrete plans about the *how* to do it, *what* to do, and *why* it is important to continuously improve, then outcomes will be blurry.

Gallup highlights that since the 1970s, when the U.S. government began measuring the number of business creations and closings, the year 2014 was the first time the number of business closings (100,000) surpassed the number of business creations (70,000). Busteed emphasized that business creation is fundamental for economic growth. Expanding workforce has significant positive impact on economic expansion and social inclusiveness.

For education to meet the employability needs of students, it is essential to secure strong and functional integration between educators, employers, and entrepreneurs, who are more flexible to create jobs at a faster pace than large corporations. It is necessary to pay attention and update traditional education that overvalues course grades and test scores and underestimate entrepreneurial talent of students as innovators and potential job creators. Microsoft's Gates and Facebook's Zuckerberg are among a growing number of examples of self-made entrepreneurs, innovators, and job creators that provide evidence of the dimension of education and workforce mismatches.

Mismatches between education providers and labor force demands hurt school and college graduates. In order to correct these shortcomings, increasing numbers of employers are changing hiring practices from traditional and exclusive reliance on grades and test scores to social skills and personal interviews, or they use other methods that are better predictors of performance and productivity. Grades do matter to include in a CV and to get an interview, but so do personal relationships and a well-rounded educational experience.

Weak integration between education and labor force demands provides evidence that educational institutions are perpetuating the supply-driven approach over demand-led by students, parents, and the labor force. Failing to meet these demands hinders students' opportunities to find jobs at a time when college student loan debt has reached a trillion dollars and graduates need work and income to repay and increase wellbeing to start a productive life.

Gallup's proposal to increase integration between education and the workforce recommends employers across sectors and industries to offer paid and unpaid internship to high school and college students. And also to offer *externships* to teachers and faculty who have not worked outside schools and academia. Familiarizing teachers with activities and challenges in the productive sector is essential to prepare students for reality beyond theoretical constructs. This option would help educational institutions support teachers and comply with the responsibility to increase educators' engagement to stimulate students' engagement. A proposal of this nature has potential to become an important, national initiative to help employers fulfill their social responsibility in sync with effort to increase students' needs to find jobs, workers' performance, and national productivity.

Busteed closed his presentation emphasizing that educators at every level and sector must look for ways to align curricula with long-term projects that connect students' learning in classroom with real problems in the workforce to strengthen the Educonomy (Busteed, 2014b).

Constraints Affecting Supply-Driven Education: Teachers' Shortage

Education is a high stress profession. All educators who work and earn a living in front of a class and feel responsible for the wellbeing of their students in a classroom or online, know this well. Consistently, studies show that almost half of K–12 teachers report high levels of stress and a high percentage do not feel engaged with their work. These are detrimental statistics of the profession responsible for educating and forming the character and the minds of children, learners, and citizens worldwide.

These are clear signs that the traditional supply-driven education industry is not working. If education would be a demand-driven industry, where parents, students, and the labor force would have a voice and a choice, all teachers and professors would be the best, the brightest, the most ethically driven and caring professionals. Instead, data shows that the future of the teaching profession may go in the opposite direction.

Between 2007 and 2017 the number of students interested in pursuing studies in education has decreased significantly in the United States and this trend is expected to continue. In 1975, 22% of college students majored in education, a higher share than any other major. By 2015, fewer than 10% of Americans are pursuing studies in education. The shift from the education major is notable among women (David, 2017). The share of female college students majoring in education shrunk from 32% to 11% as more female students pursue coursework in sciences, business, fine arts, communications, and computer science (Passy, 2018). Forecasts show that this trend will continue.

According to the U.S. Department of Education, public schools nationwide do not have enough teachers. Shortages are occurring because of increasing demands for enrollment in public schools. In 2017, 50.7 million students attended public elementary and secondary schools. It is forecasted that by 2025 the number will be 51.4 million.

To maintain the current class size, ratios would mean hiring thousands of more teachers, aside from efforts across school districts nationwide to reduce class sizes. An already reduced number of qualified teachers exacerbate the problem with attrition. In the last decade, 8% of American teachers left the profession, almost double the rate of Finland and Singapore, where teacher shortages are less acute and students are higher achievers. Richard Ingersoll, professor of education and sociology at the University of Pennsylvania indicates this pre-retirement turnover is driven by dissatisfaction. While low salaries play a role, Ingersoll emphasizes that teachers are more frustrated with their lack of active participation in schools' decision-making and curriculum. Attrition is worse in urban districts where teachers are micromanaged in accountability.

In 2014, a report of the Consortium for Policy Research in Education showed that educators with training in teaching methods and pedagogy are less likely to quit teaching (Ingersoll, Merrill, & May, 2014). And teaching longer has benefits because a teacher's degree alone is not necessarily correlated with improved student performance, while more teaching experience is.

The Demand-Side of Education: Students, Parents, and the Workforce

There is a fast growing number of research studies on the demand side of education conducted by business and consulting organizations that share increasing concern with the kind and scope of education students receive in schools and how it fails to increase performance and productivity in the workforce.

The social sector division of McKinsey & Company published a study on factors that make students' thrive in education. The main inquiry of the study was to identify what kind of education is needed to make students thrive amid relentless change brought about by technology and globalization. The inquiry was focused on evidence that improvement of educational outcomes has proved to be elusive and the quality of education continues to be a major challenge at the national level.

The study analyzes education from four dimensions: (a) impact of student's mindsets on learning outcomes, (b) teaching practices, (c) school day length, and (d) childhood education. The data was collected from the 2015 PISA administered by the OECD.

Results show that for 15-year old students', attitudes and beliefs are the most important determinant of educational outcome. Although students' attitudes vary, the most critical to thrive is the ability to calibrate motivation of daily life by doing more than expected and working on tasks with continuous improvement as targets. Student attitudes and beliefs influence active learning outcomes to a significantly higher degree than academic performance (PISA's score) or home environment and socioeconomic factors combined.

Other attitudes and beliefs that better predict student outcomes include having low test anxiety and believing that their school work will be useful to advance future career plans. Students who believe they can succeed if they work harder outperform students with a fixed mindset and beliefs that their capacity is limited.

McKinsey researchers found that students' attitudes and values alone cannot overcome all economic and social barriers, or to what extent parental or school interventions can shift students' attitudes. But they emphasize that this research confirms that student's attitudes and values matter significantly on students who live in challenging and most precarious circumstances, this a critically important finding for educational systems and societies seeking income parity and inclusiveness.

Education Demand for Soft Skills

Results on the impact of student's attitudes and beliefs coincide with studies I have conducted on Soft Skills[18] with colleagues from the United States, Europe, and Latin America, about the need for schools at all levels—and particularly business schools—offer courses to develop student's soft skills that increase self-confidence and caring for other people and facilitate teamwork and mutual understanding. Our studies demonstrate that teaching and training students in soft skills at lower educational levels is necessary to build and strengthen students' perseverance and motivation needed in the upper school levels to meet the increasing and changing demands in the workforce (Bardy & Massaro 2013; Lepeley & Albornoz, 2013; Lepeley et al., 2016; Ochoa et al., 2018; Majluf, 2016; Tarr & Weeks, 2016). We also found that schools of education and teachers training programs need to train teachers and educators at all levels in Soft Skills to prepare them *how* to teach, *what* are soft skills, and *why* are they so important.

A job outlook related to a soft skill course[19] that MIT offers online in edx.org reports that

- soft skills are today's power skills in the workforce.
- U.S. employers face major gaps in employee preparedness in soft skills, which account for one-third of skills requested in all U.S. job postings. (Source: EAB, Tackling the 'Soft' Skills Gap, 2016).
- Writing, communication, and organizational skills are scarce, and in demand across occupations and technical fields. (Source: Burning Glass Technologies, The Human Factor, 2015).
- The soft skills most employers look for in employees are: oral communication skills, teamwork, decision-making, and critical thinking. (Source: EAB, Soft Skills That Matter to Most Employers, 2016).

Education Demand and Teaching Styles

The McKinsey study confirms that high-performing and fast-improving school systems are powered by quality instruction. Additionally, students' learning outcomes showed to be higher when there is a balanced combination of teacher-directed instruction in most classes and inquiry-based teaching in some classes. Currently 1/2 of U.S. students are receiving insufficient teacher-directed instruction. In spite of a strong positive effect of inquiry-based pedagogy, students' capacity to deal with inquiry-based methods depends highly on knowledge gained through teacher-directed instruction. But inquiry-based teaching is more challenging to teach and teachers who attempt it without sufficient training and support struggle and students decrease educational outcome.

The study highlights the need for quality standards in schools of education and teacher training programs, emphasizing that lesson planning and school-based instructional leadership and decision-making are required to increase principals' and teachers' confidence. While the results show that teacher-directed instruction has higher impact on PISA scores, researchers emphasize that inquiry-based practices are more effective promoting students' "joy of science" and instilling belief that doing well in school will help them have a brighter future. This confirms the need to blend and balance teacher-directed instruction with inquiry-based teaching.

Education Demand and Optimal School Day Length

Educational systems at the federal, state, and district levels in the United States are continuously assessing optimal length of school days which are often challenged by diverse advocacy groups. According to the study, student outcomes improve by 4% for each additional 1/2 hour of instruction up to 6.5 hours per day. But, extending the work school day from 6 to 6.5 hours would significantly increase education expenses, affect student commutes, after-school activities, and school start times. Moreover, the study shows that students in Finland and Germany achieve superior results than the United States with shorter school days. This confirms that length of a school day has lower correlation with time than with teachers' quality. In the United States improving quality per school hour is a critical factor impacting students' wellbeing.

Education Demand and Early Childhood Education

Education studies conducted in numerous countries show that quality of early childhood education (ECE) improves social and academic outcomes and produces gains sustainable for many years. Moreover, the lack of quality standards in early childhood programs has high potential to impair a child's development potential. The results of this study shows that ECE has a positive impact that according to neuroscience studies applies to all regions in the world.

Research shows that the United States faces serious quality problems in ECE. Children in low socioeconomic groups benefit less from ECE in spite of evidence that this cohort has the most critical need for the best ECE to get out from the poverty cycle. All suggest that there are significant problems with ECE quality in the United States for low-income families and toddlers. In 2018, the U.S. Department of Education is sponsoring comprehensive assessment and development of ECE programs that include preschool development and early learning development grants[20]

Global Consensus on Urgency to Improve Quality in Education

At the present time, the urgency to improve quality in education goes far beyond demands and appeals of the productive sector. But in nations worldwide, quality is playing a key role and is one of the most critical challenges imposed on the international development organizations.

Previously, I have discussed how international organizations are focusing on quality improvement in education and identified the shortcomings to meet required targets.

The United Nations' 2030 SDGs program's focus of attention in the 4th Goal is: *Ensure inclusiveness and equitable quality education and promote lifelong learning opportunities for all.*[21] UNESCO, the education division of the UN, is placing urgency on quality improvement in education, above and beyond the need to expand access, as one of the most pressing needs to unlock progress and achieve the UN's 2030 SDGs agenda. I have discussed the European Union's Smart Growth 2020[22] importance to focus on continuous improvement in education and how the International Labor Organization (ILO) is emphasizing improvement in the quality of education to meet the demands of an evolving global labor force.[23]

In 2018, the World Bank published the report "Learning to Realize Education's Promise" (World Bank, 2018). It claims to be the first report devoted entirely to education and its critical impact on human wellbeing in times of rapid economic and social change.

The Report states that the best way to equip children and youth for the future is to place their learning at the center. To achieve this objective the World Bank study explores four themes: (a) education's promise, (b) need to shine a light on learning, (c) how to make schools work for learners, and (d) how to make systems work for learning.

A summary of the World Bank report emphasizes three messages in education, three dimensions of the learning crisis, and three policy actions to address the crisis as shown in Table 5.2.

TABLE 5.2 Summary of the 2018 World Bank Report Learning to Realize Education's Promise

Main Messages of the Study	Dimensions of Learning Crisis	Policy Actions to Address Crisis
Schooling is not the same as learning	First dimension of crisis: poor learning outcomes	Need to make student's learning assessment a serious educational goal
Schooling without learning, more than wasted opportunity, is great injustice.	Second dimension of the learning crisis and causes: • Children arrive unprepared to learn. • Teachers lack skills or motivation to teach effectively. • Inputs fail to reach classrooms or to affect learning. • Poor management and governance undermine schooling quality.	Need to act on evidence in order to make schools work for learners
There is nothing inevitable about low learning in low- and middle-income countries.	Third dimension of the crisis: deeper systemic causes.	Need to align actors to make the system work for learning

Source: World Bank (2018)

Quality Management in Education: Back to Basics, Looking at the Future

Sixteen years after my World Bank presentations on *Management and Quality in Education: A Model for Evaluation* (Lepeley, 2001) to inaugurate the Online Global Network Conference on *Innovation in Education of the 21st Century*, the World Bank is launching this report emphasizing the student centered quality education imperative that I presented at the WB conference in 2002. Again this is not unusual in education. Actually, it is the norm in the sector, and with few exceptions worldwide. Change is slow and can take decades. In spite of the immense costs that delays of this nature generate in terms of talent and human capital of generations wasted, this new World Bank initiative could have not been more timely to enhance the crusade I make to develop the Educonomy. This strengthens significantly the points I make in this book: In the global VUCA environment, when many unavoidable disruptions affect all people, quality in education is not an option it is an imperative.

Education can no longer lag far behind but must assume responsibility to lead, to advance the human centered wellbeing for sustainable growth and inclusive societies. Otherwise, the lack of quality in education for all will perpetuate itself as the main cause of income inequality and poverty in developed and developing countries.

Once Again, the Problem Is Not Income Inequality, It's Lack of Quality in Education

Much attention has been focused on the controversy of income inequality. The trend was ignited by capital focused analysts convinced that capital is the master and people are servants. This is a regressive posture that contradicts fundamental principles of human centered sustainable development. To claim that money and capital are the cause of all maladies in the 21st century is to confuse cause with effects that perpetuate inequalities of the 19th century.

David Brooks (2005), a trustworthy *New York Times* journalist and author, wrote an op ed column titled *The Pillars of Cultural Capital* about the unfairness of economic and social stratification in the Information Age. He calculated that highly educated parents pass their advantages to their children, while the children of less educated parents fall behind and as a result life prospects are broadly unequal. A child growing up in a family earning over $US 90,000 a year has a 50% chance of getting a college degree by age 24. A child of a family earning between US$ 35,000 and $61,000 has a 10% chance. And a child of a family earning under US$ 35,000 has a 0.17% chance.

Brooks confirms that the cause of the problem is not income inequality, it is a lack of quality in education for all.

The three pillars of the Educonomy are presented in the next chapters.

Notes

1. George Psacharopoulos World Bank (https://blogs.worldbank.org/team/george-psacharopoulos)
2. *Financial Times* (https://www.ft.com/content/51d1c0aa-5085-11e5-8642-453585f2cfcd)
3. MOOC (massive open online course) "is an online course aimed at unlimited participation and open access via the web. In addition to traditional course materials such as filmed lectures, readings, and problem sets, MOOCs may provide interactive user forums to support community interactions among students, professors, and teaching assistants (TAs)." MOOCs is a form of dis-

tance education introduced in 2006 that has expanded worldwide. (https://en.wikipedia.org/wiki/Massive_open_online_course)
4. MIT Opencourseware (https://ocw.mit.edu/index.htm)
5. IES U.S. Government (https://ocw.mit.edu/index.htm[1])
6. School Without Walls, Washington, DC (https://en.wikipedia.org/wiki/School_Without_Walls_(Washington,_D.C.)
7. https://www.nist.gov/baldrige/publications
8. https://www.nist.gov/baldrige/publications/baldrige-excellence-framework/education
9. https://www.nist.gov/baldrige/how-baldrige-works
10. http://www.efqm.org/what-we-do/recognition/efqm-award-history
11. http://news.gallup.com/authors/Busteed.aspx?a=161327&p=1&utm_source=link_wwwv9&utm_campaign=item_229397&utm_medium=copy[2]
12. Gallup (http://www.gallup.com/home.aspx)
13. Gallup Clifton Strengths. (https://www.gallupstrengthscenter.com/?utm_source=google&utm_medium=cpc&utm_campaign=Strengths_ECommerce_Brand_Search_US&utm_content=strengthsfinder&gclid=EAIaIQobChMI9tTU0YGK2wIVklmGCh1w4wxFEAAYASAAEgLnE_D_BwE)
14. OECD PISA (http://www.oecd.org/pisa/aboutpisa/)
15. OECD PISA (http://www.oecd.org/pisa/aboutpisa/)
16. PISA (https://www.oecd.org/pisa/Well-being-Infographics.pdf)
17. PISA (https://www.oecd.org/pisa/Well-being-Infographics.pdf)
18. Soft skills are a balanced combination of emotional intelligence; ethical values; respect for self and others; effective communication; critical thinking; decision-making; risk taking; learning from failure; constructive leadership; interpersonal, social skills; and team work in high demand across all industries and jobs. Soft skills are deployed through: continuous improvement, quality standards in all a person does, active listening, effective written and verbal communications.
19. https://www.edx.org/professional-certificate/ritx-soft-skills
20. U.S. Department of Education. ECE. (https://www2.ed.gov/about/inits/ed/earlylearning/index.html?src=rn)
21. UN SDG 4 (https://sustainabledevelopment.un.org/sdg4 and Chapter 2)
22. EU Smart Growth 2020 (http://ec.europa.eu/regional_policy/en/information/publications/guides/2011/regional-policy-for-smart-growth-in-europe-2020 and chapter 2)
23. ILO education (http://www.ilo.org/global/industries-and-sectors/education/lang—en/index.htm)

6

The Talent Economy

Members of organizations, who many assume are best at learning, are in fact not very good at it. I am talking about well-educated, high-powered, high-commitment professionals.

—Chris Argyris (1957)

Demand for Talent in the 21st Century

In his 2014 *Harvard Business Review* article, "The Rise (and Likely Fall) of the Talent Economy," Roger Martin, director of the Martin Prosperity Institute and former dean of the Rotman School of Management at the University of Toronto, claims that talent is the main asset in the global economy. He uses the United States to demonstrate how talent has driven the transformation of the productive sector and economic growth in the last half century. He warns though that when talent is circumscribed to a small group of corporate executives the harms to society may surpass the benefits of talent.

But Martin restricts talent to the elite of corporate executives and financiers who have led corporations and risen to be among the richest—indeed

Educonomy, pages 115–140

to a few executives who have optimized their own benefits by taking advantage of the spurring demand for talent driven by the dynamics of change, economic transformation, and cyclical crisis. Martin argues, correctly, that high demand for talent made this executive elite earn high incomes that have contributed to exacerbate the income inequality gap between the talented few versus the bulk of routine workers.

To solve the income inequality gap, Martin proposed increases in government regulation and taxes, and the cooperation of top executives earning big incomes to help others rise to the talent top.

But Martin overlooks the enormous progress that talent-driven corporations have brought to people and society, not only in the United States but worldwide with significant increase in the wellbeing of people based on job creation for millions of workers. I contend Martin's proposal for solutions because neither high government regulations nor tax increases have worked to decrease income inequality. And given the speed of change and overall the sluggish bureaucratic government capacity to react, his proposal would be even more detrimental in the future.

Talent Diversity Leads to Organizational Sustainability

I cite Martin's study because it is a clear example that contrasts with my arguments about the shortcomings of income inequality analysis. Martin (2014) ignores that the main problem for society is not income inequality (this is the effect), it is lack of quality in education (this is the cause of income inequality).

It is time to acknowledge that talent is not a privilege of a few, because all human beings have talent. The problem is to continue ignoring that, despite many years of education and enrollment in the system, many graduates are unable to recognize or develop their talents to improve individual performance necessary to secure a good job in the workforce.

Martin (2014) is right to call for the cooperation of top executives to decrease income disparities. There are volumes of literature addressing these challenges from the scope of human centered management (HCM) and corporate social responsibility (CSR; Lepeley et al., 2016; Lepeley, 2017a; Bardy, 2018; Ochoa et al., 2018), an increasing number of corporations assuming their role in CSR, and a large number of business schools worldwide ready to meet the corporate demand offering courses in CSR. Most focus on CSR as a necessary condition for sustainability. The trend is supported by social initiatives in the World Economic Forum's *The Fourth Industrial Revolution*,[1] global business consultant companies like McKinsey,[2] and Gallup.[3] But this is just the beginning of new shades of talent and there is a long way to go.

Martin cited a study conducted by the creative mind of Richard Florida, a fellow at the same institute, about *The Rise of the Talent Economy* (Martin, 2014). This study analyzed talent and the composition of the United States workforce based on the Department of Labor job classifications and the content descriptions focusing on creative-intensive and routine-intensive jobs. The difference between routine- and creative-intensive jobs is that the latter require higher independent judgment and decision-making. The findings show that in the last half century the proportion of routine-intensive jobs has decreased significantly and the demand for creative-intensive jobs is fast increasing.

In 1963 only 16% of the top 50 companies in the United States included an emerging breed of jobs identified as creative intensive, performed by employees like scientists, engineers, marketers, and salespeople who were leading the companies and driving competitive advantages and success in the marketplace. Among those corporations were IBM, Eastman Kodak, Procter & Gamble, and others. All had a common denominator of success: human talent.

In 2013 over 50% of the top 50 U.S. companies were talent-based, among them Microsoft, Apple, and Google. In the last decades, the U.S. economy, as many other economies in developed and developing countries, are shifting from exploitation of natural resources to optimizing the potential of human creativity and talent. As economies advance from the resource-based first industrial revolution to the fourth industrial revolution of the knowledge age, deep changes in production functions are pressing organizations in all sectors to rely on human talent. Consequently, human talent today generates higher returns to investment than natural or capital resources. Moreover, in the global VUCA environment and a highly integrated world economy, the same forces are impacting production and organizations across developed and developing countries. Increasing demand for talent is a global phenomenon.

Evolution of Demand for Talent

The global increase in demand for talent is not surprising, what is new are the effects of shifts in production strategies adapting to emerging technologies that are transforming the workforce, economies, and societies worldwide.

Studies focused on talent anchored in traditional descriptions such as the U.S. Department of Labor are limited and are becoming obsolete given the fast changes in the economy that affect all jobs, including the routine intensive. Change makes workers increasingly aware, if not forced, to constantly develop personal talents and update skills to attain or maintain good jobs and avoid to be displaced by artificial intelligence and robotics.

To face emerging challenges, industries and organizations in productive sectors are increasing decentralization to become agile to adopt change and adapt to disruptions minimizing its costs. To become agile, organizations need to become less hierarchical and increasingly flatter to expedite decision-making. To be successful in this changing environment, not only the executive cohorts but all employees need to use their talent and creativity to help organizations advance to continuous improvement and to display quality standards of high performance, productivity, and competitiveness to become sustainable (Lepeley, 2017a).

Increasingly, organizations realize the important responsibility they have to develop and promote a culture that fosters wellbeing and supports all people, from owners to employees, who work *in* and *for*[4] the organization aimed to increase the level of engagement with work and the better use of their talents to optimize their contribution (Ochoa et al., 2018). There is growing awareness that the success of upper organizational echelons depends on the pool and individual talent of people who work in lower quarters who must share the same quality standards (Lepeley, 2017a).

In 3 decades as a researcher, and training and facilitating deployment of human centered quality management standards in organizations in developed and developing countries (in the productive and public sector), I have not seen a case where the talent of executives is sufficient to reach and sustain quality standards, high performance, and productivity across organizations. Invariably, these standards are achieved when the organizational culture helps all the people to work harmoniously, share their talents, and when supervisors stimulate employees to do their best and recognize their achievements. If these elements are lacking, segmented efforts do not achieve successful and consistent results. The age of hierarchical organizations is long gone and it is harmful for an organizational culture of wellbeing and sustainability.

When I was an examiner of National Quality Awards (NQA) and led teams of examiners in evaluation visits to organizations applying for the award, and selected among a large number of applicants based on written reports deploying the NQA criteria, I used a simple strategy to evaluate advances in the quality direction. When visiting organization facilities with our hosts, I looked for an employees' restroom as far away as possible from the executive headquarters. I separated from the group of executives and headed in that direction. The executives customarily suggested taking me to a restroom in the executive quarters. I never accepted because my purpose was to check in situ the condition of the employees' restrooms. When they were as clean and neat as the executive restrooms, it was one of the best indicators I could collect visually and objectively to confirm concerns for people's wellbeing and quality standards embedded in the heart of the organization. The main principle is that quality management means quality for all.

The same quality standards resonate for human talent. Employees who feel that their talent is not fruitfully used by the organization show lower levels of engagement with work. Although they may work *in* the organization, they have not reached a level of wellbeing necessary to drive commitment to work also *for* the organization (Ochoa et al., 2018). Organizations that fail to recognize and make optimal use of workers' talent, across all levels of responsibility are wasting a most valuable asset to succeed in an era of fast change. Organizations that consider workers' training and development as an expense instead of an investment in human capital jeopardize sustainability (Lepeley, 2017a).

How Well Is Education Preparing Students for the Talent Economy?

Commonly, talent is associated with superstars in the business sector, or outstanding achievements in sports, movies, and corporations. But in the talent economy as a pillar of the Educonomy this notion is misleading.

The principle here is that every human being has talent. But in most cases it goes undetected. In spite of the large proportion of life that people spend enrolled in educational institutions, few recognize that the principal mission and responsibility of educators and educational institutions at all levels, is not to deliver information on specific disciplines and make sure the student remembers, but it is to help students discover their talents and how they can optimize wellbeing, applying their talent to a specific discipline.

But this principle is new. The development of student's creativity and innovation in education until now is a pursuit of a small number of free thinking education pioneers, but it is not a relevant feature of traditional education. Talent development is essential to attain quality standards in education.

Beyond grades in courses, ranks in classes, scores in standardized tests, or educational attainment that are the traditional ways to show progress in the educational system, as educator I am perplexed by the low level of awareness that students at all levels have about their talents. As an economist, I am concerned how much talent is spared by ignorance and omissions that could significantly improve the students' passion for learning, performance, productivity, and human wellbeing.

To test for talent awareness in my MBA classes and quality management professional training, I ask participants if they know their talents. I commonly see surprised faces and excited smiles. Then I ask them to make a list of their main five talents in 2 minutes. Close to 10% of the class are able to list five talents. Most are not. People in general have difficulty identifying their talents, including the professionals. This is a significant failure of education. Students need to be aware of their talents, not as a show-off exhibitionist feature, but as a responsible and valuable personal asset of self-cultivation that can help others. Education should assume responsibility to help students discover and nurture their talents to do better in school and in turn to improve society. It is not easy or natural in most cultures to identify the altruistic side of personal talents. At the end of this chapter there is a List of Talents, natural or acquired. Awareness can stimulate personal improvement and stimulate collective wellbeing.

Talent Misconceptions in the 21st Century

Talent is associated with genius and virtuosos. And sure, they have talent. But none of them would have reached the level of prestige unless someone else—parents, teachers, coaches, supervisors—had not found that these persons had special talents that could be nurtured and harvested to get the highest possible returns to nature, genetics, and neuro capacity.

Unlike money and capital, that some people have and others lack, every human being has some kind of talent. The problem is that education is not tapping in on one of the most valuable inputs: human talent.

Education wastes surmounting amounts of time and effort of teachers and students trying to correct student's areas of weakness. In spite of exponential evidence that human limitations, flaws, and weaknesses are genetically induced, it is almost impossible to turn into strengths.

The Montessori educational method previously discussed discovered this and it has been applying student personalized methodology successfully for over a century. Personalized education is the key for improving and attaining quality standards in education. It is also the leading strategy in the most prestigious educational systems in the world.

A most crucial question for education, educators, and systems is: If we know what works in education—and what does not—what justifies continuous waste and misuse of resources?

The purpose of the Educonomy is to optimize RoRs to investments in education at the personal and social level, to ensure the benefits surpass the cost of the limited resources every nation, district, and community assigns to education all focus on human wellbeing.

Human Talent and Quality Education

I closed the previous chapter on the Educonomy emphasizing that the problem is not income inequality; but lack of quality in education. I warned about the threats and high costs of confusing the effect (income inequality) with the cause (lack of quality for all in education) to find solutions. To avoid or postpone working on solutions demonstrates growing negligence of educational systems to comply with their mission and main responsibility: discover and nurture the talent of learners of all ages that go through the system. This is one of the key aspects of the Educonomy to attain sustainability.

Taking advantage of the RoR to money and capital investment is limited, but in the Knowledge Economy, human talent has no limit. Failing to consolidate continuous improvement and quality standards of education for all, meaning assuming responsibility to discover and nurture the talent of all learners, is ignoring a most feasible solution, if not the only one, to increase the economic growth and decrease income inequality and poverty.

I bring attention to the discussion about the shortcomings of the gross domestic product (GDP) accountability formula (C+L+R)[5] to measure social variables previously discussed. The economist Edward Denison (1985), one of the developers of the GDP formula, coined the term "the measure of our ignorance" to describe a considerable segment of GDP increases that cannot be explained with pure monetary accounting. But I have emphasized that aside from its social assessment limitations, GDP accounting is critically important to explain *how*, *what*, and *why* economies grow. GDP is the most effective instrument that exists, used by countries around the world, to measure changes in national production and income distribution that have economic implications in wellbeing. GDP is a methodology of monetary accounting that was not designed or intended to measure social progress or problems. Denison announced this clearly from the beginning. What is surprising is that in half a century no effective solutions have been developed but instead, proposals to substitute GDP spur here and there.

In Chapter 2, I also discussed that to face the social accountability shortcoming of GDP, new methods to measure development, beyond economic growth, are necessary. For instance Bhutan, a small country enclaved in the

Himalayas Mountains with a long and rich Buddhist spiritual tradition, developed and has used the gross national happiness (GNH) since the 1960s. But in spite of GNH's strategy and Bhutan's rhetoric to distance themselves from GDP, the results of the 2015 GNH national survey show evidence that GDP, and specifically, income, is the second most important element for Bhutanese people to attain happiness. This is concrete evidence that the GDP methodology is unavoidable to objectively *assess* development and to advance human capital evaluating RoRs to investments in education including its externalities. In my 2017 article, *Bhutan's Gross National Happiness: An Approach to Human Centred Sustainable Development* (Lepeley, 2017b), I analyze the case of Bhutan and the complementarity between GDP and GNH.

GDP and GNH Are Complement, Not Substitutes

GDP and GNH are complements, not substitutes (Lepeley, 2017b). Ignoring this positive relation hinders economic growth and obstructs investments in human capital. Although the implications are substantially higher for developing countries, developed countries, where most of the proposers of GDP abolition come from, are also affected. Among them, *The World Happiness Report*,[6] published yearly since 2012 and sponsored by United Nations, follows a similar trend albeit the analysis explicitly includes GDP parameters.

Who would deny that money cannot buy happiness, wisdom, or talent?! But, from the dimension of economic theory, denial of the value and need for economic growth is a profanity from the core principles of human centered economics and sustainable development. Clarifying that human centered economists consider money and capital as instruments to meet human needs necessary to attain wellbeing; not as masters that command the lives of human beings and economic systems.

A typical example of denial of the importance of GDP is the Easterlin paradox that came about in the 1970s and perpetuated in spite of its flaws (Dierner et al., 2013; Stevenson & Wolfers, 2008; Veenhoven & Vergunst, 2014). The paradox was coined after a study conducted by the University of Southern California professor of economics Richard Easterlin (1974), suggesting that GDP growth and income per capita had no relation with the level of happiness in developed nations. Easterlin interpreted that high increases in income in the United States between 1946 and 1970 had not resulted in similar levels of personal happiness. These claims fostered an ongoing debate and critics have grown exponentially over time and for different reasons. An abundant number of studies contradicts the paradox, some argue that when GDP grows, the perception of happiness always increases; others show statistical correlations that happiness increases with a lag and more slowly than income. Moreover social variables, such as freedom, trust, perceptions of lack of corruption in government and business, and more leisure time for vacations and entertainment also influence the sense of happiness that Easterlin's study failed to capture. If we ask a high income family in a high income developed nation if more money makes them happier, most likely their answer would be "No." If we ask the same question to a low income family in a low or medium income developing nation, their answer will be definitely "Yes."

The argument I consider most important to reject the Easterlin paradox is based on the fundamental principle of utility theory which I have discussed in previous chapters. In short, the more a person consumes of a specific good, the less important that specific item becomes in the long run. In economics this is called *diminish returns* to *marginal utility*. I do not go in depth defining these concepts here, but those interested in economics can find extensive information on utility theory and related subjects in the following links[7–12] and a comprehensive analysis of marginal utility in Wikipedia.

Talent Demand in the Workforce

In traditional work environments where employees are still considered human resources—comparable to all others as inputs of production functions—the typical HR office plans processes for highly predictable environments, repetitive ways of getting work done, and along organizational lines and boxes that define how people are managed. But change is deeply impacting organizations forcing them to become more agile. Old organizational strategies no longer fit planning in the long run but new approaches are necessary to sensing and seizing opportunities to adapt as fast as possible to constantly changing environments. In the global VUCA environment, organizations must discover and are pressed to use and deploy the talent and creativity of all their people to remain productive and competitive.

Talent management in organizations and the workforce refers to the capacity to anticipate future requirements of human capital to plan, produce, and meet forthcoming demands. As a field of study, talent management became popular with the pioneer McKinsey's 1997 research and publication of the book *The War for Talent* (Michaels, Handfield-Jones, & Axelrod, 2001).

The war for talent term was coined by Steven Hankin of McKinsey & Company and the book with the same name was authored by Ed Michaels, Helen Handfield-Jones, and Beth Axelrod. It refers to the increasingly competitive landscape for recruiting and retaining talented employees. The book does not describe a set of superior management processes but mainly emphasizes the importance of talent for the success of organizations.

Confirming my previous argument about the difficult to identify talent, the concept was never explicitly defined in this book. Except for a note in the "Preface" that says "talent eludes description: You simply know it when you see it" (Michaels et al., 2001, p. xii). But the authors define managerial talent as a combination of a sharp strategic mind, leadership ability, emotional maturity, communications skills, ability to attract and inspire other talented people, entrepreneurial instincts, functional skills, and the ability to deliver results" (Michaels et al., 2001, p. xiii). In spite of the fact that talent defies clear definition, the underlying assumption is that in the Knowledge Economy the *knowledge worker,* coined by Peter Drucker (1959), is crucial for competitiveness and organizational sustainability.

The war for talent was intensified by demographic shifts primarily in the United States and Europe characterized by an increasing demand for workers along with a decreasing supply because post-baby boom generations have decreased faster than they are able to be replaced. But in the last decade the same trend pervades all developed and most high income developing countries.

In McKinsey's 2018 book *Talent Wins: The New Playbook for Putting People First,* associates Ram Charan, Dominic Barton, and Dennis Carey (2018) argue that although executives and organizations in all sectors and worldwide highly recognize the competitive advantage of human capital, still many are unaware that the practices they use are stuck in the 20th century and most ignore they are wasting surmounting amounts of talent. The book provides new formulas for acquiring, managing, and deploying talent in agile, digital, analytical, technology driven strategic environments that have provided new approaches to develop and optimize talent in companies such as ADP, Amgen, BlackRock, Blackstone, Haier, ING, Marsh, Tata Communications, Telenor, Volvo, and also in entrepreneurial startups of Silicon Valley.

This book claims to align the rigor needed to manage financial capital to human capital. It elevates talent to the level of finances as a necessary condition to create sustainable talent-driven organizations. The book is anchored in the following seven part plan:

- Integrating talent and capital
- Making talent drive strategy
- Designing and redesigning the work of the organization
- Scaling up individual talent

- Creating an organization strategy to foster talent
- Reinventing the role of HR
- Living the talent agenda

Unleash Talent and Agility

When executives in talent-driven companies launch new initiatives they make sure they have the right talent before going deeper into strategic and financial planning. McKinsey emphasizes that agile and team-based organizations are the best way to ensure that organizations are able to match right talent with right strategic initiatives.

In the human centered management model I developed in the book, *Human Centered Management: 5 Pillars of Organizational Quality and Global Sustainability*, and it is displayed in Figure 6.1. I coincide with McKinsey about the critical importance of agility to optimize development of talent management. But in addition to work teams, which in this case are responsible for

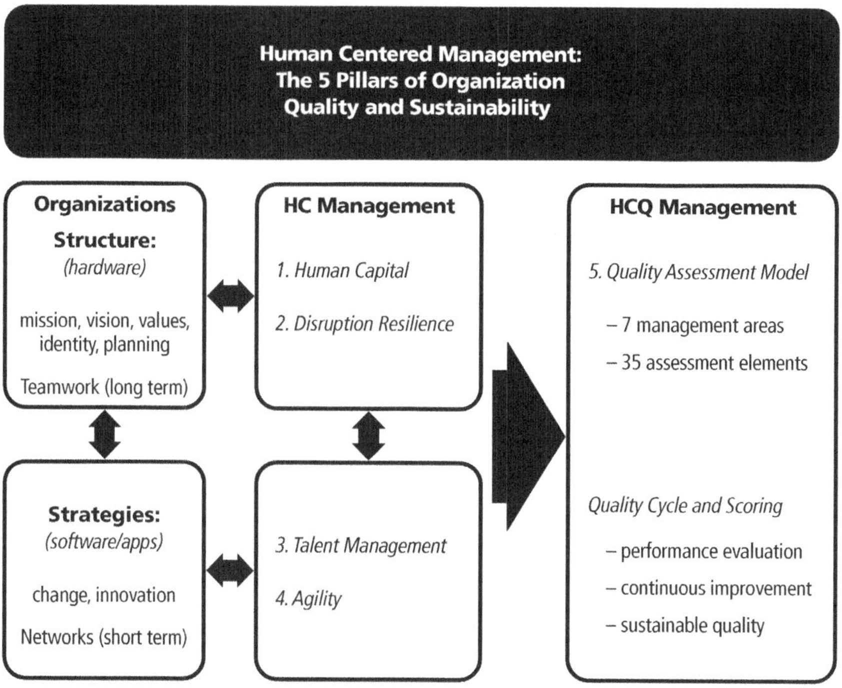

Figure 6.1 Human centered management. The 5 pillars of organizational quality and sustainability. *Source:* Lepeley (2017a).

organizational structure, I propose that the organizational strategies are led by short term change and innovation networks with capacity to reach higher level of agility needed to deliver expected results.

How Facebook's Zuckerberg Manages Talent

McKinsey (Barton et al., 2018) describes how Facebook, an organization that consistently aligns top talent with critical strategic initiatives, counteract rigidities. When CEO Mark Zuckerberg decided that the company had to make a dramatic shift from a desktop business model to a mobile one, Zuckerberg told his product teams: "Come in with mobile. If you come in with a desktop product I'm going to kick you out" (Barton, Carey, & Charan, 2018, para. 25). McKinsey argues that a clear vision does not guaranteed much and actually the CEO graveyard is full of visionaries who fell back to earth when their teams couldn't deliver. But Zuckerberg delivered with the help of top executives COO Sheryl Sandberg and CHRO Lori Goler. Facebook launched a full-scale attack on mobile. Every product team got a mobile developer. Desktop products were discarded. Teams delivered mobile offerings. Not all were hits, but enough made the cut for Facebook to over deliver to its members, who were growing increasingly dependent on smartphones. By the end of 2016, mobile accounted for 84% of the company's revenue (Barton et al., 2018).

Why was Facebook's culture able to foster success? Lori Goler, who joined the company in 2008, described a culture of autonomy and initiative, where different kinds of leadership were found at every level. People are able to find their way to projects that interest them to get engaged. Some teams stay together for years, others disband after just a few weeks. Star programmers can get rich without ever having to join management. Management ranks get filled by people who enjoy overseeing and developing talent. Facebook's structure is agile enough to ensure continual connection between talent and strategy. The organization can move talent quickly to support a clear, steadily communicated vision, but new products emerging from those teams can modify the vision, creating strategic shifts. The company is constantly organizing and reorganizing itself to optimize talent deployment and adapt to unpredictable market and technology shifts (Barton et al., 2018).

Launching Talent and Holding Fears

Haier CEO Zhang Ruimin says that today's CEOs must learn how "to lose control, step by step" (Barton et al., 2018, para. 28). This is indeed a frightening idea for anyone accustomed to traditional, hierarchical, and top-down leadership. But the second half of the quote is: "step by step." Leading talent organizations is something that needs to be learned and managed incrementally. The steps required are: alignment at the top, continual talent search and development, commitment to link talent and strategy, and agile and flexible strategies—all are important (Barriere et al., 2018). But, it is also important to build on solid structural grounds to trigger a multiplier effect that can exponentially increase the value talent delivers to the organization. In talent-first organizations, grasping new ideas leads to better new ideas, and watching creative thinking is amplified across divisions to all levels of seniority and expertise, and allows to reap the benefits of explosive value that arises from expected and unexpected parts of the company (Barton et al., 2018).

In the Talent Economy: Talent Management Is a Business Discipline

Unilever is a company with 161,000 employees in more than 150 countries that operates globally in consumer goods with products like Lipton tea and Magnum ice cream to laundry detergent and skin care. Under the leadership of Paul Polman,[13] its chief executive since 2009, the Anglo-Dutch group has sought to drive growth through innovation and reshaping its portfolio while reducing operational complexity and focusing on sustainability as the key theme. Leena Nair, Unilever chief human resources officer (CHRO), joined the company in 1992 as a management trainee. Prior to taking her current role, she was the group's global head of diversity and inclusion. She has said: "A most important competitive advantage a company has are the ideas, the ingenuity, and the passion of its people." In January 2018, Nair had an interview with McKinsey publishing's Rik Kirkland that took place on the sidelines of the annual meeting of the World Economic Forum in Davos, Switzerland to discuss how HR leaders can play a key role driving value creation by leveraging data analytics focusing on value-creating roles and developing close partnerships with finance teams. Here are the most relevant points she made about talent-driven organizations:

- The company is discussing how to deploy investment into certain countries, markets, and categories but in parallel assessing if there's organizational readiness, because when companies make investments but people are not ready, meaning that there is not enough talent, investments do not thrive. Making strategic investments in financial capital and human capital at the same time is critical.

- Increasingly, the company needs to be far less hierarchy-conscious and more agile about value creation. It often happens that value is being created in roles that may be two or three steps below a CEO. So the company is creating multifunctional and empowered teams looking for particular categories in particular countries. It may happen that the person handling P&L (profit and loss) might not be a senior in terms of hierarchy, but has an important role creating value as a key organizational strategist.
- The company is the #1 employer of choice in 44 of the 52 markets where it recruits according to external measurement Nielsen Universal. In markets where the company is more attractive, the company can attract the right kind of people which means costs of recruitment fall and recruitment yield is higher.
- Unilever's Sustainable Living Plan has been one of Paul Polman's signature initiatives translating into meaningful work and purposeful work. Because the fast pace of change is so intense that people do tend to feel overwhelmed and threatened and one of the most effective organizational assets is a culture anchored in a sense of meaning and purpose as the key feature of the talent strategy to help people discover their own purpose and deploy them into roles where they can live their own purpose. The results of employee surveys show 92% of people are proud to work for Unilever and they want to work for Unilever. Employee-engagement scores are higher than competitors and benchmark companies and retention numbers are far lower than the market in almost every country the company operates.
- This is the impact of what a meaningful purpose does to employees' engagement, motivation, and attrition. *Companies with purpose last, brands with purpose grow, and people with purpose thrive in uncertain times.*[14]

Talent Management and Agile Practices

Talent management in an age of digital disruption deserves special talent. By rethinking its approach to talent management and introducing agile working practices, Guardian Life Insurance Company of America, one of the largest U.S. mutual life insurers founded in 1860, aims to stay ahead of disruptive competitors because history and scale offer only limited protection against technology-driven disruptions. McKinsey's Rik Kirkland interviewed its chief executive officer Deanna Mulligan about how a large company is responding to adopting artificial intelligence-based technologies, but also innovating its approach to talent management.[15]

New Sources of Talent

Traditionally, Guardian Life Insurance did not have comparable benchmarked to assess the talent pool, but company expansion is pressing to recruit people with different backgrounds who have been through disruptions to lead this company go through emerging disruptions. By and large, new recruits are not people from insurance companies.

Guardian Life is looking at completely different sectors and discussing leadership teams in the gig economy from Uber drivers all the way up to CEOs. How to use of talent that wants to be independent. How to bring in people who normally the company would hire as officers but instead hire them to do specific jobs, because some experienced people prefer to work this way. The company is retooling because not only millennials want to work as employees but also agile and flexible people who are not permanent employees. The company wants to provide space and technology a diversity of workers need.

Making Talent a Top Priority

The company is assessing: how to optimize the link between talent and strategy, and how to free people up from feeling a human "resource" to focus on development of human talent. To achieve this objective, an executive-leadership team meets weekly for a talent-priority discussion, putting more responsibility on the business people to work in closer alignment with HR to transform traditional functions into talent management. The company is aiming to push forward people to drive the business, searching for people across all levels in the organization, assessing what they do and how they serve customers, as opposed to where they are in the hierarchy. People in the entire company are being trained in agility. Although the IT group has been agile for quite a while, agility is now spreading everywhere and to everyone in the company. To unlock the value of talent, the company's structure and strategies need to be more flexible.

Optimizing Talent in the Age of Automation

The company is piloting several applications of AI (artificial intelligence) in office processes, customer service, and underwriting, using data analytics and advanced technologies like facial recognition to conduct underwriting analysis and really working with people to explain IT. The company forecasts that between 5% and 10% of the jobs will be replaced by robots, so people have to learn to work with artificial intelligence and robotics to understand the benefits and costs of automation. There are "robot play dates," where people in the office work with small robots or take a class on robotics. For example, people who are answering phones and serving customers learn to program little robots and understand how robots can assist them serving customers. The company makes efforts to make people feel comfortable with change, comfortable with AI, and comfortable with robotics because organizations will need people who understand how to partner with AI to serve customers better.

Talent Opportunities for Some and Societal Challenges for Many

Guardian is a mission-driven large company with abundant time and resources, so the company can retrain its people in new skills to help them meet future disruptions and changing demands. But Mulligan posts a number of critical questions about the disturbances and developments that people in charge of the economy and society should be concerned about, but overall educators and educational institutions at all levels should be concerned about it.

- What happens with organizations that do not have abundant resources for retraining its employees?
- What happens to employees who work in organizations that are preparing them for the future?
- What happens to people who are unemployed or not yet employed?
- What is the responsibility of larger companies?
- What is the role of large companies as leaders in society to think how to retrain and re-skill the population?

Mulligan emphasizes that all the Fortune 500 CEOs are deeply concerned about these issues and what to do to help solve these problems.

To finish this chapter where I have covered the most critical areas required to develop, assess, and manage human talent, I revise the economic underpinnings of talent embedded in human capital theories. Talent is worthless if it does not contribute to increase the stock of human capital every human being has.

Investing in People and Talent

Investing in people, educating students in school, and training and retraining people in the labor force to help them keep their jobs and learn new skills, demands high investments. But these investments are unavoidable if societies want to move ahead, and a national priority in the short-term horizon for both developed and developing countries.

The talent economy is responsible for the analysis of changes and disturbances that affect the labor and effective articulation of labor demands with educational systems. The responsibility of the talent economy is to ensure that education can bridge the gaps that today exist with emerging demands of the labor force. The talent economy will put education at the forefront of innovation and progress to fulfill its responsibility to optimize the RoRs to investments in education for individuals, systems, and nations.

It Takes Talent to Develop Talent

It requires talent to recognize and develop talent. One of the roles of the talent economy is to ensure that the best and brightest are responsible to design, produce, and deliver education. To continue ignoring this principle is to neglect the importance of education and its critical impact on sustainable development and inclusive societies. It is to overlook that in the Knowledge Economy the RoRs to investments in human capital have surpassed RoRs to investment in physical capital and it is to be blind to ethical and unbiased allocation of investments in education.

Investing in people has always been important but it is more important today given the prospects for higher returns when investments are allocated to optimal use. In the 1980s when I worked on my economic thesis on the impact of higher education on economic growth, which was a brand new field then, two Nobel Prizes in Economics that I will discuss next, were major influences in my work. Both developed and pioneered studies in human capital and provided the basis for theoretical analysis of what is today central to the Educonomy.

Theodore Schultz and Gary Becker were the founders of the principles behind human centered economic theories I present in these books; without them my road would have been much harder and cumbersome.

Both were professors of economics at the University of Chicago. Theodore Schultz won the Nobel Award in 1979 and Gary Becker in 1992. To close this chapter, I transcribe their experiences embedded in their Nobel speeches to demonstrate their talent in the development of human capital.

Theodore Schultz

Theodore Schultz (1902—1998) earned a doctorate in agricultural economics. He was chair of economics at the University of Chicago from 1946 to 1961. He received the Nobel award for his work in human capital theory and economic development. His theories convey that the speed of economic recovery is founded in a healthy and well educated population. While education makes people more productive, healthcare helps people work and produce in a sustainable way increasing the return of investments in education. He pioneered studies on poverty and exposed the challenges and mismatch of foreign aid to help low income people attain a better life by failing to educate them properly and to use their talent to improve the effectiveness of development programs. He was a promoter of vocational education to stimulate industrialization and reconstruction after WWII in Europe, the United States, and extensively in developing countries.

He is the author of the pioneer book *Investing in People: The Economics of Population Quality* (Schultz, 1982 and a large number of related articles that include: "Capital Formation by Education" (Schultz, 1960), "Investment in Human Capital" (1961), the books *The Economic Value of Education* (Schultz, 1963), *Investment in Human Capital: The Role of Education and of Research* (Schultz, 1971), and the edited books, *Investment in Human Beings* (Schultz, 1962), *Investment in Education: Equity-Efficiency Quandary* (Schultz, 1972), *Economics of the Family: Marriage, Children, and Human Capital* (Schultz, 1974).

THEODORE W. SCHULTZ—BANQUET SPEECH[16]

Theodore W. Schultz's speech at the Nobel Banquet, December 10, 1979

Your Majesties, Your Royal Highnesses, Ladies and Gentlemen,

Your Royal Academy of Sciences expressed a deep concern about the economic problems and the welfare of poor people throughout the world in awarding the Nobel Prize in Economics this year. It is a noble concern worthy of the best talent not only in economics but also in other branches of knowledge.

Permit me, however, to be less serious about economists for a moment.

I have been asked: What do economists do? My reply is: When economists face disagreements, they appeal to a long-established, basic Law of Talk, which is, "The more intelligent people are, the more certain they are to disagree on matters of social principle and policy, and the more acute will be the disagreement." Herein lies the proof that economists are intelligent!

Economists, however, do not do what needs to be done to make friends, they neglect history to the consternation of historians. They give too little attention to the cultural and social values to please the humanities. Their mathematics does not impress the mathematicians. Scientists do not take kindly to the application of costs and benefits to science. Governments are ever wary of being friendly with academic economists. The only real friends economists have are impersonal adverse events: inflation, unemployment, and hard times.

But this is not the whole truth. Scientists made it possible to increase the resources of society. Humanists, historians and social scientists clarify human values. Economists analyze the interplay between human preferences and scarce resources.

Folklore notwithstanding, economists do count their words as poets do, but for a different reason. It is not *beauty* that economists seek; their aim is to *save time*. I know that you also value your time highly.

Gary Becker

Gary Becker (1930—2014) was professor of economics and sociology at the University of Chicago. He was considered one of the most important social scientists of his time. He received the Nobel Prize in Economic Science in 1992 and the U.S. Presidential Medal of Freedom in 2007. A survey of economic professors named Becker as their favorite living economist over the age of 60, followed by Kenneth Arrow and Robert Solow.[17] Becker further developed Schultz's theories on the importance of human capital consolidating this important field in economics. He defined that different types of human behavior affect rational and utility maximization, including individual utility and altruistic behaviors. Becker earned a BA at Princeton University in 1951, and a PhD at the University of Chicago in 1955. He was influenced by Milton Friedman whom he called "by far the greatest living teacher I have ever had" (Klein & Daza, 2013).

He taught at Columbia University from 1957 to 1968, then returned to the University of Chicago. In 1965 he was elected Fellow of the American Statistical Association and of the American Academy of Arts and Sciences in 1972. He was a member and president of the Mont Pelerin Society. He received the National Medal of Science in 2000.

He is the author of the book *Human Capital: A Theoretical and Empirical Analysis, With Special Reference to Education* (Becker, 1964) where he argued for the need to expand human capital. His research influenced many about the importance of individuals to make choices of investing in human capital based on rational benefits and cost that include return on investment as much as cultural benefits. He explored the different rates of return for different people and the resulting macroeconomic implications. He distinguished between general and specific education and their influence on jobs and promotions.

Becker was a prolific researcher and writer. These are some of his publications: "A Theory of the Allocation of Time" (Becker, 1965); *The Economics of Discrimination* (Becker, 1971); "A Theory of Social Interactions" (Becker, 1974); *The Allocation of Time and Goods Over the Life Cycle* (Becker & Ghez, 1975); *The Economic Approach to Human Behavior* (Becker, 1976); "Human Capital, Effort, and the Sexual Division of Labor" (Becker, 1985); *A Treatise on the Family* (Becker, 1991); *Nobel Prize Lecture: The Economic Way of Looking at Life* (Becker, 1992); and *Social Economics Market Behavior in a Social Environment* (Becker, 2000).

GARY S. BECKER—BANQUET SPEECH[18]

Gary S. Becker's speech at the Nobel Banquet, December 10, 1992

Your Majesties, Your Royal Highnesses, Ladies and Gentlemen,

I would like to express my gratitude to the Royal Swedish Academy of Sciences for the superb honor conferred on me. It is not necessary to have special reasons to be happy to be here, but I do feel especially pleased. This Prize gives recognition in the most influential way possible to all economists who endured many obstacles, criticisms, and even ridicule to study and analyze broader aspects of behavior than is traditional in economics.

During the first half of this century, economics became more of a systematic science, but it also became increasingly isolated from the study of society, law, and government. I was fortunate to have had outstanding teachers, several who later won this Prize. They supported my desire to use economic theory to try to understand discrimination against minorities and other questions that were much broader than those that had become the core of economics. I am grateful for their insights and encouragement.

I am not revealing any professional secrets when I state that not very long ago this type of research was not popular among most economists and other social scientists. But attitudes are changing, and there are now thriving schools of scholars in many fields using what is called the economic approach to analyze nonmarket and social behavior.

Economics is a very young science in comparison with the physical and biological sciences. Still, much is now known about economic and social life, although perhaps even more remains to be learned. For the economic and social world is mysterious, and it sometimes changes quickly and in surprising fashion. Every time we peel away some of the mystery, deeper challenges rise to the surface.

Economics surely does not provide a romantic vision of life. But the widespread poverty, misery, and crises in many parts of the world, much of it unnecessary, are strong reminders that understanding economic and social laws can make an enormous contribution to the welfare of people.

The Latest on the World Bank and Investing in People

In a conference in Uruguay on March 21, 2018 the president of the World Bank Group, Jim Yong Kim, stated that investing in people is not an option, it's a must. He remarked that people have become the most important factor in the wealth of nations. Knowledge, skills, and know-how—collectively known as human capital—are today an enormous share of global wealth, bigger than natural resources, factories, or industry.[19] Kim emphasized that the world is at a crossroads of advances in technology that will require countries to invest more and more wisely in education and health if they want to remain competitive in the economy of the future. He stated that Latin America is no exception where 60% of the region's wealth lies in its human capital, according to a World Bank analysis.

Many Organizations Confront Talent Challenges, Education Confronts the Most

I started this chapter on the talent economy with this quote from Chris Argyris: "Members of organizations, who many assume are best at learning, are in fact, not very good at it. I am talking about well-educated, high-powered, high-commitment professionals." Argyris was professor emeritus at Harvard University, a business theorist and co–founder of the field of organizational development, well known for his seminal work in learning organizations, but in this case his quote applies equally and paradoxically to many professionals who work in education. For to the largest extent we are trained to teach but not to learn. But times have changed and the talent economy is something educators have to learn to navigate better than any other profession.

All the material I have used in this chapter to sustain the principles and practices of what I am calling and defining as the talent economy come from economics and organizations in the business sector. McKinsey, a global business consulting company that pioneered talent and talent management has been a principal source and guide. McKinsey concerns are legitimate because the company needs to be at the forefront of business innovation to help clients become productive and sustainable. But this seems odd and ludicrous when we think that education is the par excellence profession and the sector responsible to develop the talent of students who have to perform and succeed in the labor force, in society, and in economies worldwide.

Multiple searches for studies on talent management in education returned zero results. Neither the Academy of Management archives with all its journals, nor Google Scholar fed results. In the United States, *Education Week* magazine articles relate talent with gaps and gifted children education. The U.S. Department of Education's Center for Great Teachers and Leaders at American Institutes for Research relates talent management with recruitment, hiring, and retention but not as a subject teachers need to master to develop the talent in students. Even in Wikipedia the concept talent management does not exist. This calls for something I will have to do after I finish writing these series of books.

What is clear, is that talent management in education is an overdue endeavor in a sector whose main responsibility with society is to develop the talent of students. The creation of the talent economy as a fundamental part of the Educonomy is most evident than ever as a most critical element of advance balance sustainable development ESTE.

This discussion has provided the necessary evidence pressing for the creation of the Educonomy and its three inseparable pillars: the talent economy, the agile economy, and the quality economy.

Appendix
Partial List of Human Talents

Ability to deal with failure
Ability to focus
Ability to handle change
Ability to make friends
Ability to spot new trends
Academics
Accounting
Adaptability
Advertising
Affiliate systems

Analyzing the past
Art
Articulate
Asking questions
Athleticism
Awareness
Bookkeeping
Brainstorming
Communication skills
Computer literacy
Computers/IT
Conflict resolution
Creativity
Critical thinking
Decision making
Detail orientation
Dexterity
Drawing
Economic vision and optimization
Empathy
Emotional intelligence
Encouraging
Enthusiasm
Fairness
Financial management
Financial planning
Forecasting
Foreign language
Futuristic
Global vision
Graphics
Health/fitness
High energy
Hiring/recruiting
Identify strengths and areas of improvement
Imaginative
Initiative
Innovation
Inspiring
Integrity/honesty
Intuition
Leadership
Learner

Legal
Listening
Logistics
Maintenance/routine tasks
Making connections
Management of actions
Management of foreign languages
Management of ideas
Management of money
Management of people
Management of tasks
Marketing
Mathematics
Mystical
Musical
Negotiating
Networking (across virtual connections)
Networking (person to person)
Persuasion
Photography
Planning
Positiveness
Problem-solving
Programming
Project management
Public speaking
Raise money
Reading
Relaxation
Reliability
Relieve stress
Research
Risk management
Sales
Self management
Self-assurance
Self-discipline
Sense of humor
Sign language
Singing
Social intelligence
Social networking
Software

Storytelling
Strategic planning
Systems management
Taxes
Teaching/training
Time management
Trouble-shooter
Typing
Visualization
Volunteering
Wisdom
Woodworking
Writing

Source: Author and https://www.michaelhartzell.com/blog/bid/17550/howto-6-list-of-strengths-talents-you-may-have

Notes

1. World Economic Forum: https://www.weforum.org/center-for-the-fourth-industrial-revolution/home
2. McKinsey: https://www.mckinsey.com/global-themes/leadership/making-the-most-of-corporate-social-responsibility
3. Gallup: http://news.gallup.com/opinion/gallup/170417/different-think-corporate-social-responsibility.aspx
4. I emphasize the concept to work *in* and *for* organizations because there is a notable difference. While working *in* an organization implies that individuals perform job duties to earn a salary, to work *for* the organization implies engagement with job and commitment with the organizational mission leading to continuous improvement, quality standards, and long-term sustainability.
5. Where: C = capital, L = labor, R = resources
6. http://worldhappiness.report/ed/2017/
7. Demand curve and utility (https://courses.lumenlearning.com/boundless-economics/chapter/the-demand-curve-and-utility/)
8. Theory of Consumer Choice (https://courses.lumenlearning.com/boundless-economics/chapter/theory-of-consumer-choice/)
9. Market equilibrium (https://courses.lumenlearning.com/boundless-economics/chapter/market-equilibrium/)
10. Price elasticity of demand (https://courses.lumenlearning.com/boundless-economics/chapter/price-elasticity-of-demand/)
11. Price elasticity of supply (https://courses.lumenlearning.com/boundless-economics/chapter/price-elasticity-of-demand/)
12. Public goods (https://courses.lumenlearning.com/boundless-economics/chapter/public-goods/)
13. Paul Polman, Unilever (https://www.unilever.com/about/who-we-are/our-leadership/paul-polman.html)

14. McKinsey interview with Unilever CEHRO Leena Nair, March 2018. WEF. (https://www.mckinsey.com/business-functions/organization/our-insights/talent-management-as-a-business-discipline-a-conversation-with-unilever-chro-leena-nair)
15. McKinsey interview with Guardian's CEO Deanna Mulligan, March 2018. (https://www.mckinsey.com/business-functions/organization/our-insights/the-ceo-of-guardian-life-on-talent-in-an-age-of-digital-disruption?cid=winningtalent-eml-alt-mip-mck-oth-1803&hlkid=0ce7c2f0705a411b8b7aadafa245c6f6&hctky=2823006&hdpid=98519504-4067-4df6-99f8-0773efdf06d1)
16. Theodore Schultz, 1979 Nobel Award Lecture. https://www.nobelprize.org/nobel_prizes/economic-sciences/laureates/1979/schultz-speech.html
17. Gary Becker (https://en.wikipedia.org/wiki/Gary_Becker)
18. Gary Becker Nobel Award Speech (https://www.nobelprize.org/nobel_prizes/economic-sciences/laureates/1992/becker-speech.html)
19. http://live.worldbank.org/human-factor-investing-in-people-today?cid=ECR_E_NewsletterWeekly_EN_EXT&deliveryName=DM2385

7

The Agile Economy

Do not go where the path may lead;
go instead where there is no path and leave a trail.
—R. W. Emerson

What Is Agility?

Zalando is the prototype of a firm in the agile economy. It was founded in 2008, and today, it is publicly listed as a Berlin-based company leading Europe's online fashion with a platform amalgamating the sector. Eric Bowman, its vice president in engineering, explained in a recent interview with McKinsey's associates that Zalando's strategy is to digitize fashion and move the company from a digital store to an online platform. Between 2015 to 2017, Zalando increased its digital infrastructure from 800 to 1,700 employees and the digital effort represents 14% of its staff. Bowman argues that purpose, autonomy, and mastery are essential to build agile organizations. He defines agility as being able to respond quickly to changing business contexts, to work well in parallel, and minimize the number of decisions

Educonomy, pages 141–181

and choke points. He compares agility with arranging a bunch of thorny roses in a pot. Agility is about cutting off the thorns to speed the floral arrangement without getting hurt. In the business environment there are many ways for teams to get trapped: on technology, organizational structure, culture, old mind-sets. To advance at the required speed, agility is about removing the thorns! (Cadieux & Heyn, 2018)

The Agile Economy

Agility expands from the micro to strengthen the macro level. Accenture is a tech support global company that provides services in strategy, consulting, digital, technology, and operations to organizations—including a large number of Fortune Global 500 companies—in 120 countries and in more than 40 industries aiming to improve work and lives. In 2016, Accenture produced a comprehensive report titled *The Platform Economy: Innovation From the Outside–In.*[1,2] This report illustrates the dimensions and outreach of change regarding how businesses are transforming industrial organizations in a new digital world. Companies worldwide are unleashing the power of technology developing platform-based business models and strategies that, according to Accenture, are driving the deepest global macroeconomic changes since the industrial revolution.

In the digital economy platform, ecosystems are becoming the foundation for value creation. In the new environment, tech companies and digital-born organizations (DBOs) like Amazon, Google, and Alibaba are prototypes. But the number is growing exponentially. Therefore, understanding the power of digital technologies is crucial knowledge for organizations to take advantage of benefits and competitive advantages of agility to minimize the costs of change and disruptions.

The success of new DBOs rests on two key elements: (a) technology platforms built to support a business, and (b) platform-based business models that are deeply changing how business and organizations operate. Eighty-one percent of the executives in the Accenture report indicate that platform-based business models will be crucial to their growth strategy within the next 3 years. To date, platform companies represent $2.6 trillion in market capitalization worldwide in value-creating power of platform ecosystems or digital assets.[3] Many companies are combining resource-based with platform-based businesses, like Apple and Amazon. Nevertheless, whether a company owns a business platform or is plugged into an external one, the important thing is adopting a platform strategy and adapting it to the business know-how to exploit its benefits. This fast progressing macroeconomic shift is disrupting business models from large incumbents to small startups in all sectors and industries worldwide.

Bloomberg's November 2017 article, *America's "Retail Apocalypse" Is Really Just Beginning* (Townsend, Surane, Orr, & Cannon, 2017), shows that the retail store decline is becoming so ingrained in the United States that it has gained its own Wikipedia entry.[4] Although some people contend the pessimist argument saying that retailers opened more than 3,000 stores in the first quarter of 2017, chain stores reported that 6,800 would close. It must be considered that the news of retail closures occurs during a booming economy with sky-high consumer confidence, unemployment historically low, and an increasing rate of overall economic growth. All these are common drivers for a retail boom, yet more store chains are filing for bankruptcy and more are distressed than during the last financial crisis. For Bloomberg, the reason is not only Amazon taking market share but long-standing chains overloaded with debt.

Until now, struggling retailers have largely been able to avoid bankruptcy by refinancing to buy time, but the market has shifted, pushing investors to reconsider lending to them. Toys "R" Us, a national toy chain, served as a sign of what lies ahead.

The ripple effects of the retailing sector can have a direct hit on the industry that is the largest employer of low skilled and low income Americans. U.S. government statistics show that salespeople and cashiers in the industry total 8 million jobs. Between 2008 and 2009, 1.2 million jobs of store workers disappeared. The drop coincides with rapid acceleration in store closings but also while many of the largest retailers, such as Wal-Mart and Target in the United States are considering that stores occupy too much space with huge amounts of inventory that requires high capital investments.

Before the e-commerce boom, retail builders and investors were pouring huge quantities of money into commercial real estate when the suburbs across the country were booming. The result was the birth of the big-box era of massive stores in all categories from office suppliers like Staples to pet retailers such as Petco. But today, the boom is going bust. At the end of 2017, 6,752 locations were scheduled to close according to the International Council of Shopping Centers (excluding grocery stores and restaurants). That is double the 2016 total and close to surpassing the all-time high of 6,900 in 2008, during the depths of the financial crisis. Apparel chains have taken the biggest hit, with 2,500 locations closing. Department stores are downsizing and 550 have closed, leaving empty 43 million square feet.

In terms of impact in the workforce, the traditional path to middle income in retailing is associated with becoming a supervisor. There are

1.2 million of these jobs with an average annual salary more than twice a cashier at $44,000. In response to the loss of store-based retail jobs, the industry is adding positions at distribution centers to bolster online operations. But there are a few constraints. Many displaced retail employees live far from shipping facilities. Besides, hiring new employees in shipping activity would be skewed toward men while retail store employees are 60% women. Ripple effects are negatively affecting women workers.

The detrimental shrinking of brick-building retail business models contrasts deeply—and dangerously—with unparalleled growth of the digital economy, that accounted for 15% in 2005 and it is estimated to reach 25% of the entire world economy by 2020. And, platform business models represent a fast increasing proportion of this overall total.[5]

Nevertheless, not only the tech and digital-born organizations are using platform strategies. A fast growing number of business leaders are adopting the platform-based model and engaging in ecosystems of digital platforms, either owned outright or in partnerships. While a growing number of traditional department stores in the United States are decreasing retail inventory in physical buildings and stores, and uploading their merchandise to online platforms, the list goes on and on from car manufactures to digital health, smart cities, buildings, homes, retail pharmacy, customer analytics, and from financial services to education. Massive open online courses (MOOCs) that offer free online courses available for anyone to enroll in is deeply disrupting higher education worldwide.

Accenture predicts that the most powerful platform ecosystems of the digital economy will emerge from global resources-asset conglomerates that deploy digital transformation in their organizations aligned with increased capacity to take advantage of the disruptive power of platform ecosystems. These organizations can advance by aligning foundational physical resources—by leveraging assets with knowledge of the industry and cross-over effect with other industries. Accenture identifies three types of organizational structures: (a) resource-asset heavy (GE and GM), (b) mixed (Apple and Amazon), and (c) light (Google and AirBnB).

There is no doubt that the technology-driven macroeconomic shift will disrupt competitive strategies and business models of all organizations in all sectors (private and public) and industries, from asset heavy to asset light, from large to small size and startups too. Therefore, all organizations need to have a platform strategy or find a space in ecosystems driven by other companies. Or at least must take a defensive position to become sustainable and protect profitable margins for survival in core operations to defend from emerging forms of platform-driven competition.

Economic Transition From the Industrial Revolution to the Digital Revolution

To survive and thrive in the digital age, organizations need to understand the underpinnings of the transformation to safely redefine capacity and constantly assess performance improvement of structures and strategies, teams and networks, the talent pool, and human capital using world recognized quality standards based on continuous improvement (Lepeley, 2017a). The characteristic of successful organizations emphasize human centered management and mastering structures, and strategic use of digital technologies to build and strengthen platform business models. Lagging organizations that ignore or neglect the macroeconomic transformation could face entropy and pre-announced failure.

Table 7.1 shows the elements of business models and structures that mark the transition from the industrial/resource focused age to the digital/people centered technology-facilitating age.

Economic transition is imposing surmounting costs to industrial age heavy asset-resource based organizations and industries. In order to adjust, adopt, and adapt, industrial structures and strategies to the digital age agility is essential.

The human centered environment requires not only a new economic vision but a different management structure aligned with emerging economic prospects. To flourish in this environment a human centered

TABLE 7.1 Economic Transition From the Industrial to the Digital Revolution

Industrial Age Economy	Digital Age Economy
Resource-based growth	People-centered development
GDP growth	GDP + human wellbeing
Capital accumulation	Talent and human capital growth
Focus on quantity	Focus in quality
Emphasis on performance	Focus on quality standards
Performance outcome	Continuous improvement evidence
Supply driven	Demand leading
Physical assets	Digital assets
Heavy organizational structures	Mixed & light organizational structures
Value chains	Ecosystems
Products	Platforms
Organic driven growth	Asymmetric growth driven by networks
Diminishing capital returns	Increasing human capital returns

TABLE 7.2 Management Transition From the Industrial to the Digital Revolution

Industrial Age Management	Digital Age Management
Bosses	Leaders
Resource—process oriented	People centered
Use control	Trust focused
Short-term objectives	Long-term goals
Limited vision	Global vision
Attention on production quantity	Focus on quality standards of production
Attention on problems	Focus on solutions
Promote status quo	Promote change
Obstruct change	Incentive innovation
Risk averse	Risk taker
Avoid failure	Value failure as part of learning
Dodge comparisons	Value benchmarking
Endorse destructive competition	Support constructive competition
Control decision making	Delegate decision-making to experts
Strengthen hierarchical structures and strategies	Strengthen flat structures and strategies
Attention on rules and regulations	Emphasis on individual responsibility for results
Attention on what is wrong	Emphasis on what is right

management approach is a crucial element for economic progress. Here the asset/resource focused boss of the industrial age is substituted by human centered leaders with clear understanding of human nature, neuroscientific developments, and implications of education and training to optimize the talent pool and increase human capital in the organizations.

Organizations are increasingly decentralized in autonomous environments where personal responsibility replaces hierarchical structures. Table 7.2 shows the management evolution in leadership from resource-anchored bosses to human centered leaders ad hoc to the economic transition between the industrial and the digital age.

Impact of the Digital Age on Agility and the Labor Force

As important as it is to assess the effects of change in the economy and management, it is also important to observe the effects of the economic transition in the labor force. The following is a snapshot of the United States labor force that in 2016 included 150 million workers (DeSilver, 2016b).

- *Most people in the United States work in the service sector.* According to the Bureau of Labor Statistics, 102.6 million people or 71% of all nonfarm payroll employees work in private service-providing industries. The biggest employers are education and health services (22.7 million workers), followed by professional and business services (20.3 million), and retail trade (16 million). Manufacturing employed 12.3 million, 22 million were government workers with nearly two-thirds of them working at the local level.
- *15 million of U.S. workers are self-employed.* About 10% of the active workforce are self-employed and an additional 30 million people are working for them. Combined, the self-employed entrepreneurial labor force accounted for 44 million jobs or 30% of the national workforce. A quarter of the self-employed people hired employees, the median number of employees was three with an average of 8.6 workers.
- *Millennials, the digital generation, are the largest generation in the labor force.* More than 33% of U.S. workers are Millennials (adults ages 18 to 34). In 2015, Millennials surpassed the Generation X (ages 35 to 50) and became the single largest generational group in the workforce. Gen Xers' place as the dominant generation in the labor force lasted for only 3 years as the sandwiched generation between the Baby Boomers and the Millennials. The Prudential Company takes a futuristic look at the Millennial generation in the report *The 80-year-old Millennial.*[6] The findings are based on a 2017 survey of 1,000 U.S. Millennials between the ages of 21 and 38, 50% males and 50% females; 56% White, 22% Hispanic, 13% Black, 9% other; income US$ 4,000+; 32% urban, 45% suburban, 23 rural. The main question was: "What will life be like for Millennials in 2068?" Here is a summary of their views:
  - *Great changes are coming.* The most educated U.S. generation with the highest potential to pursue opportunities and dreams report high anxiety and vulnerability about the future in general and specifically about the future they and their children may face.
  - *Pessimistic about things Boomers and GX take for granted.* Show an uncertainty about economic growth and opportunity, being financially better off than previous generations, employer–employee contracts and retirement, social stability, and access to quality education and higher education. Eighty percent believe they will not be able to retire comfortably in the future.

  - *Anticipate many changes in their work and career.* Sixty-six percent think that full-time employment will largely disappear and freelancers will make 75% of the labor force. Sixty-eight percent believe that the main purpose of work will remain to earn enough money to keep a desirable standard of living. Surprisingly, this is not consistent with the Millennials stereotype view of putting purpose over profit.
  - *Some positive outlooks about potential changes.* Hispanic Millennials show highest positive agreement about future of work, health, and technology. Millennial men have a more positive outlook of technology in general and influencing their lives from relationships to transportation.
- *U.S. women earn 83 cents on the dollar compared with men, but the wage gap is narrowing substantially among younger workers.* Among workers ages 25 to 34, women's hourly earnings were 91% of those of men's median hourly wages for full and part-time workers. Among younger workers (16 to 24), the gender wage gap lessens further with women making 93% of men's salary. But Pew (Pew Research Center, 2013) states that there is no guarantee that this increase in earning parity of young women will be sustainable because earning of young women falls behind their same-age male counterparts when they age and have to deal more intensely with responsibilities of motherhood and family.
- *Education and wage gap between young workers with college degrees and less-educated counterparts has increased.* In every measure of economic wellbeing and career attainment, young college graduates outperform peers without a degree. With the cost of college soaring and student debt rising in recent years, there is a high debate about the value of a college education. College graduates ages 25 to 34 working full time earned annually about US$ 20,000 more than employed young adults holding a high school diploma. The pay gap disparity was smaller in previous generations. College-educated adults are more likely to be employed full time than less-educated counterparts and significantly less likely to be unemployed. Unemployment among adults with a bachelor's degree or higher was 2.5% versus 5% among adults with only a high school diploma.
- *Working teens has decreased significantly compared with earlier decades.* In the 1970s, 1980s, and 1990s, most teens could expect to be working for at least part of their summer vacation. But the number of teens working summer jobs has decreased since the

early 1990s. After bottoming out in 2010 and 2011 at 29.6%, the teen summer employment rate edged higher but was still about 32%. The decline of summer jobs reflects an overall decline in youth employment in recent decades, a trend also observed in other developed countries.

- *The NEET population.* Another face of youth employment, or the unemployment challenge, are the NEETs or young people *neither employed nor educated nor trained.* Seventeen percent of people in the United States ages 16 to 29, or near 10 million, are in this category in 2016. In 2013, the first year for which NEETs data was available, there were 11 million, or 18.5% of the 16–29 population. The U.S. NEET population includes more female than male (57% to 43%) and two-thirds have a high school education or less.
- *More gray in U.S. labor force. More older U.S. citizens are working.* Nineteen percent of ages 65 and older, or 9 million people, are employed full or part time. The ratio, has been steadily increasing since 2000, doubled from 3% to 6% of the workforce between 2000 and 2016.

Impact of Economic Transition on Women and Families[7]

The economic transition from the industrial age when women had low participation in the labor force compares drastically with the rapidly increasing participation of women in the digital age. These changes have special implications not only for women but on men and families that require increased agility to adjust to women's family imperatives as a pillar for inclusive societies. The following challenges require special consideration to advance the agile economy in the workplace.

Work–Family Balance

Harmonizing work and family responsibilities is a most complex challenge for working women (Kuschel & Lepeley, 2016, 2017; Lepeley, 2018). Balancing work and family affects heavily on women's careers. A Pew survey (2015) showed that in the United States 28% of working mothers or fathers considered it harder to advance in their job or career, but women are significantly more likely than men to express this view. Thirty-eight percent said that being a working parent makes it harder to be a good parent, with women significantly more likely than men to fall in this category. An examination of the literature on conflict between work and family roles suggests that work–family conflict exists when (a) time devoted to the requirements of one role makes it difficult to fulfill requirements of another, (b) strain from participation in one role makes it difficult to fulfill requirements of another, and (c) specific behaviors required by one role make it difficult to fulfill the requirements of another (Greenshaw & Beutell, 1985).

Career Interruption

For women, family-related career interruptions have much higher effect than for men. Fifty-three percent of working mothers with children under age 18 took a significant amount of time off from work and 51% reduced work hours to care for a child or another family member. The majority of mothers say they were glad with the decision although many realized it hurt their careers. Beyond the personal benefit for mothers, children benefit from a mother's care in most cases and across ages.

Working Parents Face Double Challenges at Work and at Home

Sixty-three percent of working adult men and women with children under 18, or those who have worked when children were growing up, said that being a working parent did not make a significant difference in career advancement, while 37% said that being a working parent negatively affected their ability to advance at work. Twenty-seven percent consider that being a working parent made it harder to advance and 7% said it made things easier. But here there was a significant gender gap. Forty percent of mothers currently working and raising children, or who worked when their children were young, said that being a working mother has made it harder to advance in their job compared with 15% of working fathers. Fifty-one percent of the mothers with children under 18 say that being a working mother makes it harder to advance careers compared with 16% of men with children under age 18.

Children's Age Makes a Difference for Mothers

Women with older children are less likely than women with younger children to say that being a working mother is harder to get ahead at work. Thirty-three percent of these women said that being a working parent made it harder for them to advance at work compared with 13% men with grown-up children. Among working mothers with children under 18, 55% say being a working mother makes it harder to be a good parent. By comparison, 39% of women whose children are 18 or older say the same.

Millennials and Parenthood

Young working mothers are the most likely to say that being a working mother makes it harder to get ahead in a career. Fifty-eight percent of millennial mothers who have worked said that being a working mother makes it harder to get ahead at work compared with 19% of fathers. Forty-five percent of mothers and 31% of fathers say that juggling work and family makes it harder to be a good parent. Mothers in the midst of childrearing have a more negative assessment than those whose children are grown.

Parenthook Expectations and Work

Young adults without children have strong expectations that having children hinders career advancement. Sixty-two percent of Millennials say that having children will make it harder to advance in their job or career. Thirty-four percent expect that having children will not make a difference in their career advancement and only 1% say having children is likely to help them advance. An equal share of Millennial women (63%) and Millennial men (62%) anticipate that having children will make it harder to advance careers.

Career Interruptions

To balance work and family many people accommodate work schedules or career ambitions. A significant share of adults have changed the course of their work life in order to care for a child or other family member, and women are much more likely than men to have done this. Twenty-nine percent of adult workers have reduced work hours to care for a child or other family member, 34% of women and 23% of men mentioned cutting back on hours at work to care for family. Twenty-seven percent of adults with some experience in the labor force have taken a significant amount of time off from work at some point to care for a child or other family member—33% of women compared with 21% of men. Fifteen percent of working adults say they quit a job to care for a family member, among them 22% of women and 9% of men report this. Ten percent of adults with work experience have turned down a promotion to care for a child or other family member, 11% of women and 8% of men. Mothers are much more likely than fathers to say they reduced work hours or took a significant amount of time off from work or quit a job to care for a family member. Forty-two percent of mothers say they reduced their work hours compared with 28% of fathers. Thirty-nine percent of mothers took time off to care for a family member compared with 24% of fathers. Mothers are more than twice as likely as fathers to quit a job to care for a child or other family member.

Parenthood and Work Promotion

Mothers and fathers are equally likely to say they have turned down a promotion for family reasons. But family caregiving is not limited to parents. Twenty-five percent of childless adults say they have taken care of a family member. Twenty-seven percent of men and 23% of women in this category say they reduced their hours, taken time off, quit their job, or turned down a promotion to care for family members.

No Regrets About Career Interruptions

When respondents were asked if they were glad with career interruptions to accommodate their family, the answer was a definite yes. Among adults who have reduced their work hours to care for a child or other family member, 94% say they are glad they did and the same share say they took off a significant amount of time to care for a family member. Of the adults who turned down a promotion or quit a job to care for a family member, few express regret. Eighty-eight percent of those who have turned down a promotion and 87% of those who have quit a job say they were glad they did it. Men and women who had career interruptions are equally likely to say they don't regret it.

Women Perceive Greater Impact From Career Interruptions

Respondents with significant career interruptions were asked what impact, if any, it had on their career. Sixty-six percent of those who reduced work hours or took a significant amount of time off from work to care for a family member say it did not have much impact on their career. For those who did feel an impact that hurt their career, 28% said it hurt their career overall, and 4% said it helped their career. But there is a significant gender gap with women, much more likely than men, to say that taking these steps to care for family hurt their career. Thirty-five percent of women who reduced work hours to care for a child or family member say it hurt their career overall compared with 17% of men. Thirty-four percent of women who took a significant amount of time off from work to care for a family member said it hurt their career, compared with 18% for men. Among adults who quit a job or turned down a promotion to care for a family member about half say it didn't have an impact on their career, whereas, for the other half, the impact was more likely to be negative. Thirty-six percent of those who quit a job to care for a family member said it hurt their career and 10% it helped. Thirty-nine percent of those who turned down a promotion say this hurt their career and only 5% say it helped.

More Older U.S. People Are Working and Working More Than They Used To

People age 65 and older are working more than at any time since the turn of the century and spend more time on the job than did previous generations (DeSilver, 2016a). In May 2016, 19% of Americans ages 65 and older, or 9 million people, reported being employed full or part time. The steady increase in share of working older Americans contrasts with the adult population as a whole, whose employment–population ratio fell sharply during the Great Recession and has yet to recover to pre-slump levels. In May 2000, 64.4% of all adults had jobs, a figure that drifted down to 62.5% in May 2008 during the recession. The strong presence of 65-year-olds-and-older workers is found across the age brackets 65- to 69-year-olds, 70- to 74-year-olds, and 75 and older. All are working at higher rates and this is the only age group about which this can be said. Not only are more older Americans working, but more of them are working full time. Only 36% of 65-and-older workers were working part time. The share of older men and women working has grown over time, but working during what is commonly thought of as retirement years remains a largely male phenomenon. Although less than 45% of the total 65-and-older population is men, they represent 55% of older workers. Older Americans work in various sectors of the U.S. economy and the workforce, with a few notable exceptions. Older workers are less likely to work in computer and mathematics, food preparation, construction-related occupations, accommodation and food service sector (3.4% versus 7.1% of all workers), and are more likely to work in management, legal, and community/social service occupations compared to the overall workforce.

The Jobless Generation of the Economic Transformation[8]

Around the world, almost 300 million 15- to 24-year-olds are not working. *The Economist* analyzes the causes and effects of this epidemic of joblessness with a global vision.

Unemployment among this age group in Sevran, a suburb of Paris, is over 40%. A continent away, in Athlone, a Cape Town suburb, a young South African mother of two, lacks a high-school qualification and has been out of work for 3 years since her contract coffee shop cleaner expired. But the jobless rate among young Black South Africans is around 55%.

But youth inactivity or NEET is worse. The OECD, an intergovernmental think tank, counts 26 million NEET young people in developed countries. A World Bank database compiled from households shows over 260 million young people in developing economies are "inactive." *The Economist* calculates 290 million are neither working nor studying. This is close to a quarter of the planet's youth.

Excluding young women in countries where they rarely participate in the workforce, the rate would be lower because South Asian women are one-quarter of the world's inactive youth. In developed nations, young women are doing better than men in the labor force. In general, many of the *employed* young adults have informal or intermittent jobs, and one-third are on temporary contracts which do not allow them to gain skills. In developing countries, the World Bank reports that one-fifth of the young work as unpaid family laborers or in the informal economy. Altogether, nearly one-half of the world's young people work either outside the formal economy or contributing less productively than they are able to.

Two factors affect young people more than other groups. First, the financial crisis had a big effect because employers fire first younger and last hired employees, so recessions in general raise youth joblessness disproportionately. Second, emerging economies with the largest and fastest growing populations of young people have the worst labor market absorption. Almost one-half of the world's young people live in South Asia, the Middle East, and Africa and also have the highest share of young people out of work or in the informal sector. The population of 15- to 24-year-olds in Africa is expected to rise by more than one-third to 275 million by 2025.

Europe's Lost Generation of Young, Educated, and Unemployed (Petroff, 2017)

In the Eurozone, it is reported that since 2010 the rate of youth joblessness has fluctuated between 19% to 25% with Spain and Greece reaching over 40%.[9] Joblessness in Southern Europe has surged as economies in Mediterranean countries have shrunk and avoided economic reform. But these stats underscore the struggle that young Europeans face trying to find jobs that match their aspirations and education. As a consequence, many are still living at home while others leave their families and move to other countries in search of work. Young people are frustrated. Failure to employ the young not only lowers present economic growth but looms future development potential. The young jobless trend is viewed as contributor to the rising populism threatening to overturn and penalize the political establishment for ignoring their situation. In European countries with substantial welfare, youth unemployment imposes a heavy burden on taxpayers as well. It is estimated that in 2011 the economic loss from disengaged young people in Europe amounted to $153 billion equivalent to 1% of GDP.[10] These numbers exacerbate the importance of the discussion because they exclude the gains youth workers would have added to these economies if their idle human capital would have had productive employment.

In Japan, youth joblessness surged after its financial crisis in the early 1990s, and has remained high. A large number of youth live with parents and are withdrawn from the workforce.

In South Africa, the high jobless rate is pressed by one of the slowest-growing economies in the region with rigid labor markets that impact employment rate. North African and Middle Eastern countries have the highest rates of youth joblessness among emerging economies due to sluggish economic and social instability, low growth capacity, and underperforming labor markets exacerbated by a mismatch between education and the demands of the workforce. Despite some recent reforms in the region, restrictions to fire older workers in southern North Africa and the Middle East and a bloated and over-regulated public sector, high taxes on labor, and high minimum wages increase the problem.[11] In India, big factories and firms have to deal with over 200 state and federal laws and regulations governing work and pay.

Studies based on U.S. statistics show that people who begin their careers with problems to get their first paid job are more likely to have lower wages and greater potential of future joblessness than those who get early jobs. In Argentina and Brazil, young people who tried to join the labor force during a recession and had problems to securing a first job fared systematically worse as adult workers.[12]

Youth joblessness is lower in dynamic growing economies and significantly higher in stagnant economies where unemployment is a constant economic and social development problem. Countries that allow monopolistic forces or cartels of any kind obstruct competition, charge high taxes on labor, have high minimum wages and strong regulations to fire people, and have the highest rates of young unemployment.

Migrations' Effects on Labor Markets and Nations

Urbanization

A trend that is disrupting nations around the world is urbanization. Although people have been moving to cities for centuries, the scale and pace of today's urbanization movement has no precedent. Urbanization is driven by the interest of people to live in cities attracted by economic possibility to earn a higher income and a better life. But largely, to leave behind deteriorating rural living conditions and the detrimental effects of mini scale agriculture (Lepeley, 2017a).

The dimension of the urban migration problem has escalated in the last decades. Today the world is in the midst of one of the largest mass migration from the countryside to the city. While Europe and the United States started urbanization in the 18th and 19th centuries, in the 21st century, Latin America and China and India, both with a population of more than a billion people, are the regions that show the largest urban shifts (Dobbs, Manyika, & Woetzel, 2015).

In 2014, 54% of people across the globe were living in cities. This number is expected to double by 2050. *The world is turning into a global city.*[13] Migrations and human mobility play critical roles in economic development, sustainability, and inclusive societies. City management and governments around the world are struggling to solve migration problems that cause significant disruption in urban development planning with significant effects on education, organizations, economic systems, and social development.

International Migrations

The number of international migrants worldwide has increased steadily in the last 15 years. One of the causes of the phenomenon is driven by global connectivity that allows people to learn about better conditions in other countries pressing them to relocate or seek asylum and leave behind the native nation. The number of international migrants grew from 173 million in 2000 to 222 million in 2010 and 244 million in 2015. The United Nations 2015 Migration Report presents data on people migration.[14] The high level of human mobility is disrupting nations and systems worldwide. This list illustrates challenges and dimension of human mobility (Lepeley, 2017a).

Largest migrations:

- Europe hosts 76 million migrants, Asia 75 million, United States and Canada 54 million, Africa 21 million, Latin America and the Caribbean 9 million, and Oceania 8 million.

- In 2015, two-thirds of all international migrants are living in 20 countries.
  - The largest number of international migrants (47 million) resides in the United States.
  - Germany (12 million)
  - Russia (12 million)
  - Saudi Arabia (10 million).
- In 2014, the total number of refugees in the world was estimated at 19.5 million.
  - Turkey was the largest refugee-hosting country worldwide (1.6 million refugees), followed by Pakistan (1.5 million), Lebanon (1.2 million), and the Islamic Republic of Iran (1.0 million).
  - More than half of all refugees worldwide came from three countries: the Syrian Arab Republic (3.9 million), Afghanistan (2.6 million), and Somalia (1.1 million).
- Women comprise slightly less than half of all international migrants.
  - The share of female migrants fell from 49% in 2000 to 48% in 2015.
  - Female migrants outnumber male migrants in Europe and North America.
  - In Africa and Asia migrants are predominantly men.
- The median age of international migrants worldwide was 39 years in 2015, a slight increase from 38 years in 2000.
  - But the migrant cohort is becoming younger in some regions. Between 2000 and 2015 the median age of international migrants declined in Asia, Latin America and the Caribbean, and Oceania.
- Most migrants worldwide originate from middle-income countries (157 million in 2015).
  - Between 2000 and 2015, the number of migrants originating from middle-income countries increased more rapidly than from countries in lower income groups.
  - The majority of migrants from middle-income countries are living in high income countries.
- Birthplace of migrants.
  - In 2015, 43% of the 244 million international migrants worldwide were born in Asia.
  - 25% of migrants (62 million) were born in Europe.

- 15% of migrants (37 million) were born in Latin America and the Caribbean.
- 14% (34 million) were born in Africa.

- Largest emigrations in 2015:
  - India had the largest diaspora/emigration in the world (16 million)
  - Mexico (12 million)
  - Russian Federation (11 million)
  - China (10 million)
  - Bangladesh (7 million)
  - Pakistan (6 million)
  - Ukraine (6 million)
- Positive net migrations:
  - Between 2000 and 2015, positive net migration contributed to 42% of the population growth in North America and 32% in Oceania.
  - In Europe, the size of the population would have fallen between 2000 and 2015 in the absence of positive net migration.

The Educonomy: Urgency and Agility to Fix Mismatches Between Education and Labor Force

One of the most stubborn problems of young joblessness in particular, and unemployment in general, is the deepening gap between education and the workforce. Educational systems worldwide that blossomed in the industrial age until today survive under its shadow enforcing a supply driven industry anchored on exploiting quantity at the expense of demand-driven quality standards to meet needs and expectations of students and the labor force.

The supply-driven industrial educational model is in direct conflict with a rapidly changing global economy relying on agile productive sectors that is discarding heavy asset business models of the industrial past to adopt and adapt light and flexible organizational models based on networks and platforms supported by technology.

With few exceptions, educational systems at all levels—but particularly in the subsidized and highly centralized and regulated public sector which is in most need of quality standards to better serve students in low income brackets—are lagging behind change and progress in the productive sector and the workforce. Educational systems and institutions that keep obsolete structures and strategies of the industrial past are a burden with high potential to harm more than help students to facilitate their access to the labor force. A review of the contrasting characteristics of the post-industrial and digital economies discussed above illustrates the depth of the problem and stresses the need for change to advance development and integration of the Educonomy.

At this stage, it is clearer that the congruency of my backgrounds in education and economics and careers as educator and entrepreneur have exerted the greatest pressure to write this book. But this concern is now shared by a growing number of people in business, academia, and the general public becoming increasingly aware of the implications of the problem and surmounting human and financial costs that are demanding solutions. The claims no longer come from economists who understand the economic impact of wasting talent and human capital needed to strengthen the workforce to foster economic growth, but increasingly from scholars and practitioners in other professions. Because developmental problems aimed to attain sustainability and human wellbeing are increasingly complex and solutions are always multidisciplinary.

The Demand Side for Higher Education

Nicholas Beutell (2013) in his chapter "The Value of a College Degree in Relation to Career, Occupational, and Organizational Metamorphosis" in the book *Higher Education: Economic and Social Mobility* argues that for students, as direct consumers of higher education, the meaning and value of a college degree is changing. While for the workplace, as indirect consumer and the most critical dimension of the demand for higher education degrees, change has been far more dramatic. The author highlights that the effects of the economic recession a decade ago left many college graduates either underemployed or unemployed generating a complex array of change in social mobility. Overall, going to college and obtaining a higher education degree has a substantial value in the U.S. society. I will argue that, in the 21st century, education in general and higher education in particular, have a high value for families and societies worldwide. But in the United States, in contrast with other countries, students and families unable to afford the high costs of a college degree, commonly assume significant debt to have their sons and daughter pursue—and hopefully receive—a college degree. And high school graduates continue to enroll and pursue college degrees in spite of rising tuition costs, longer time to graduate (more than 4 years), and uncertainty about the *real* value of a college degree in changing times.

Beutell (2013) concludes that, overall, the value of a college degree in the United States is changing, but on average, college graduates have a significant differential over high school graduates. In response to the question—"Has college been a good investment for you?"—86% of the graduates sense that it is a good investment, not only in monetary terms but in other areas like overall life satisfaction, health, and civil participation. Nonetheless, recent graduates are facing deep changes in the workplace and much more uncertainty compared with the more predictable workplaces of the 20th century. Graduates will be increasingly pressed to design their own career paths in more convoluted organizations, assume high responsibility for career planning, continuous learning, networking, and saving for retirement. This new degree of freedom and independence affects careers that have to navigate across organizations to draw validation and press for social capital outside the present employer. An environment that is far distant from the traditional one-employer-for-life pattern.

Beutell (2013) highlights that higher education is today far more critical for the U.S. economy and competitiveness than ever and this carries serious strategic concerns—among others, is whether the U.S. higher education system is preparing a sufficient number of graduates to meet the demands of an increasingly competitive global economy. Concerns are aggravated with literature suggesting that the number of graduates is not nearly enough to keep up with workforce demands as knowledge based and technology jobs expand at an increasingly faster pace.

Economist Michael Spence (2018) discusses in a McKinsey & Company video the role that public and private sectors need to play to help people prepare for changes in the workforce. He forecasts that automation will continue to have an impact on jobs across all industries, and the best way for companies, governments, and individuals to address the challenge is to work together. This integration is essential to reduce the high level of anxiety associated with expectations of jobs disappearing and more concrete steps to take, optimizing human talent and efforts and minimizing capital investments to retrain, reskill, and overall empower employees for the future.

The Industrial Revolution created a lot of middle income jobs but with a big lag, a lot of pain and suffering that brought about a substantial amount of urbanization. Then the transition to the service economy left behind many people, who still feel stranded, because they thought they could contribute productively in the manufacturing sector. However, in employment terms, this sector has shrunk due to the postwar period and globalization and, recently, due to automation and the power of digital technology. Spence (2018) thinks that this revolution is going to impact jobs everywhere across the spectrum. Not just middle income jobs but also high-paying jobs will be affected. He advises individuals to take the initiative and get ready before someone or something else makes decisions for you.

Spence supports my argument that one of the strongest debates for fairness in the distribution of income is deployment of quality standards in the services people need the most, with education at the forefront, as I propose. He sees retraining a critical need and notes that some Nordic European countries are advancing in this direction. He emphasized that not one person nor one sector has all the answers, and highlights the importance of not considering that people of all ages feel discouraged by disruptions and wonder about an uncertain future, not knowing what jobs are going to exist. Instead, all sectors, productive, education, government, and think tanks must synchronize efforts to find realistic solutions. All have to make investments, discover talents, and develop functional partnerships to inform people how this evolution is going, and even when forecasts are imperfect, people increase options to make informed investment decisions.

The Demand Side: A Ride on the Education-to-Employment Highway

In 2013, the social sector division of McKinsey, one of the largest global consultancy companies in business and management, produced a comprehensive report based on a global study on the intersection between education and the workforce affecting young people. The following points summarize outstanding aspects of the study titled *Education to Employment: Designing a System That Works* (Barton, Farrell, & Mouresh, 2013).

The Problem[15]

- 75 million youth are unemployed in the 25 countries surveyed.
- 50% of the youth are not sure if postsecondary education improved their chances of finding a job.
- 40% of employers across the 25 countries said they had vacancies but are unable to find graduates with the right knowledge and skills.

The study reports that around the world, governments and businesses face a conundrum of high youth unemployment and a shortage of job seekers with critical skills. Solutions will come from the national capacity to harmonize how to successfully move young people from education to employment, identifying what interventions have worked and which ones have failed, and how the successful interventions can be scaled up.

Table 7.3 presents the McKinsey's framework of analysis for the education-to-employment system from young students' perspective. It presents

TABLE 7.3 Education to Employment Framework

Enrollment	Building skills	Finding a job
Are enough youth being trained for the job market?	*Is training giving students the right skills?*	*Can graduates find open job positions?*
• **Enrollment:** Number of youth who have access.	• **Accountability:** ensuring quality education at the institutional level	• **Matchmaking:** Connecting graduates with appropriate jobs
• **Completion:** Percentage of youth who graduate.	• **Delivery:** Teaching methods and instructors	• **Credentials:** Skill validation and recognition
• **Student decisions:** How youth choose a path.	• **Curriculum:** Contents and useful learning	• **Coordination:** Sector and system level collaboration

Source: McKinsey (2013), p. 26.

the scope of the demand side of education from three dimensions—school enrollment, building skills, and finding a job—that affect students and graduates and are highly correlated with their employment potential to have a desirable job in their fields of study. Each dimension spells out a set of specific needs.

The Challenge

Think of the transition from education-to-employment as a highway where three drivers—educators, employers, and young people—all want to go to the same destination. But there are three critical intersections—when young people *enroll* in postsecondary education, when they build skills, and when they seek work. At every point, each driver needs to take account of the other two to keep moving safely and efficiently. But research shows that this does not usually happen. Instead, the three drivers do not take one another into account, proceeding obliviously in their own lanes, or colliding, and frequently leaving everyone worse off than when they started.

In such an environment, drivers in stalled segments have the most to gain, if they change the way they navigate in the education-to-employment highway. The main challenge for advancement is that although they are lost, they persistently fail to recognize it or are unwilling or often are unable to take action to improve direction.

The Supply Side: Changing Leadership Model in Higher Education

In his book *Higher Calling: The Rise of Nontraditional Leaders in Academia,* Scott Beardsley (2017) acknowledges a revolution coming from the ranks of higher education. He argues that college and university presidents, who used to be invariably the products of traditional academic scholarship in tenure-track career paths are changing. Instead, a highly diverse group of professionals are being hired to lead higher education institutions, bringing in a wealth of diverse skills and backgrounds, not only as presidents but also as deans and administrative leaders.

Beardsley, now dean of the University of Virginia's Darden School of Business offers a new vision of leadership for higher education. His experience is grounded on his personal story after leaving McKinsey & Company in pursuit of a new source of meaning to his professional life. His book collects the research gathered from search executives who today lead presidential and dean searches. He also explores U.S. liberal arts colleges that many consider the drivers of change in order to find out what institutions of higher education need in a 21st century leader.

Supporting previous discussions in this chapter, Beardsley (2018) highlights in his article "Shaking Up the Leadership Model in Higher Education," as he does in his book, that economic pressures and digital disruptions, raising the job complexity, are prompting academic institutions to overpass traditional hiring practices of tenured-track scholars and to seek leaders outside for top jobs.

The time has come. Higher education has grown exponentially in the last decades and today it is a big industry. In the United States, it accrues over $500 billion in annual expenditures. The industry is under increased scrutiny and pressure because colleges and universities are clasped by rising costs, rocked by increasingly activist stakeholders, and struggling to deal with the effects of technology and digitalization applied to educational models that haven't changed much since the Industrial Age. For brick and mortar institutions, with huge investments in heavy asset/resources, to compete with light digitalized business models and platforms like MOOCs, the new environment is a new and excruciating experience.

Competition for students has become so intense that increasing numbers of institutions and many universities are heavily relying on student aid and student loans to fill in classrooms and optimize the use of costly facilities and infrastructure. But relentless local and global disruptions and changes in demographics require continuous assessment of demands and significantly higher levels of agility to adjust to an increasingly diversified student population.

Although the amount and incidence of disruptions are all too familiar for people in the business sector and private industry, for higher education in general and particularly for universities—accustomed to ruling the world from their academic echelons—the global VUCA environment presents exponential challenges that traditional academic leaders have more difficulty facing. So the industry is seeking non-traditional leaders outside the education industry who pose different sets of skills and can provide new approaches to solve emerging problems. It is evident that nonprofit organizations can use for-profit leaders to repair businesses and make them competitive in the new economy.

Beardsley (2017) explains that the proportion of nontraditional presidents is not uniform and they are less common among top ranking traditional institutions listed in the U.S. News and World Report's Best Colleges. They are more prevalent in institutions that are facing a crisis, with less risk-averse boards, smaller size schools, less well-resourced in endowment per student; these institutions are more common in the East Coast of the United States and in religiously affiliated institutions. Yet, Beardsley's (2017, 2018) study confirms that nontraditional presidents tend to have longer tenures than traditional presidents, median of 6.9 years versus 4.6 years for traditional ones. The reasons for the shift to growing numbers of nontraditional leaders in academia include dramatic increases in size and complexity of the institutions paralleled with drastic decline in the number of tenure-track professors willing to take management positions in the United States. Academic executive jobs have changed substantially. The new leaders are required to undertake more public relations and community participation equivalent to business' corporate social responsibility (CSR), which extend beyond fundraising activities and community peers. Although knowledge of academic culture and rules of the trade remain essential, there is surmounting public scrutiny brought about by 24/7 social media, changing government regulations, declining state funding for public institutions that require better and more agile management, attainment of continuous process improvement, and constant monitoring of quality standards required to comply with increasing number of accrediting agencies that overwhelm academic scholars.

Beardsley (2017, 2018) reports that his research reveals discord on the definition of a nontraditional leader, but regardless of the definition, the number of nontraditional leaders is high and it is growing. He defines nontraditional leaders as those who do not reach their positions through the traditional full-time tenured-faculty track. They represent 33% of the presidents and have potential to become the majority of leaders of liberal-arts colleges within a decade or so if the trends continue. This is a perception I share after observing the economics and social evolution of higher education in the United States and from a global dimension for the last 3 decades. In 1987, I wrote economic thesis on the impact of higher education on economic growth[16] at a time when hardly anybody was aware of the pending challenges that the intersection of education and the productive sector would bring about.

The Agile Economy and Wellbeing in the Workplace

Up to now, I have discussed some of the most critical disruptions that are affecting the transition from the industrial to the digital economy jeopardizing growth potential and sustainable inclusive development largely based on relationship between the productive sector and education. In McKinsey's (Barton et al., 2013) *Education to Employment* highway analysis about joblessness, young people NEETs represent one side of the coin. The following analysis based on a survey of wellbeing in the global workplace conducted by the Gallup organization in 155 countries reveals the other side. This study is based on a global assessment of attitudes and perceptions of workers in the labor force. These results confirm the doubts of young jobless people whether postsecondary education improves chances of finding a job, and still more important, for the Millennial generation, if a job can bring happiness and wellbeing that increases life satisfaction.

Investment in education, time plus money, implies significant commitment for every person who makes the effort to attain a better life. From the organizational dimension, performance, productivity, and competitiveness depend on the commitment and engagement of workers who for years went through the educational system. Studies on wellbeing in the workforce demonstrate that workers' performance has direct relation with the level of wellbeing in organizations. But the study of wellbeing in the workplace, not as a psychological pathology but as a management challenge and responsibility, is a new field that requires special attention (Ochoa et al., 2018). In the next chapter on the quality economy based on human centered management, I discuss implications and efforts that lead to continuous improvement in organizational climate for employees to feel engaged at work and committed with the mission of the organization where they work *in* and *for* (Lepeley, 2017a). This subject is particularly important because for the majority of workers worldwide this is not the case. Gallup reports that 85% of employees worldwide are not engaged or are actively disengaged in their work.[17] Employees' wellbeing in organizations and the workforce has critical implications on sustainable development of nations and the topic is just starting to attract public attention.

Gallup, is of the largest world surveyors tracking employees' attitudes and perceptions continuously on the belief that in any society, employees develop or deplete the stock of human capital that is essential for a society to progress. Gallup's (2017) *State of the Global Workplace*[18] reports the results of surveys from 155 countries to assess how effectively employers and countries around the world are cultivating the human capital of their workforces. Gallup observes that a decade after the recession, the world economy continues to be sluggish. Since 2012, growth of global gross domestic product (GDP) has been below 3%, and this is well below historical record.

Gallup infers that widespread joblessness, particularly among young people, has led to social and political unrest in many regions of the world and frustrations are pressing social unrest and a rise in nationalism and growing resentment towards the establishment. Although Gallup sees this as a problem that affects mainly the United States and Europe, for those of us who travel the world, we see that the same problems affect developing countries that are in better economic condition and offer work opportunities to nationals of deprived nations. It is well reported that the majority of people leave behind their native land and emigrate pressed by economic reasons. Migrations are a global problem, although not new and actually very old, the solutions today will come from very different approaches to sustainable development.

The *State of the Global Workplace* (Gallup, 2017) is a timely report. It assesess structures and strategies that reveal regional workforce metrics and country specific features collected by Gallup's workforce consultants who partner with leading organizations around the world. All these areas reiterate concerns previously discussed in this chapter about workplaces experiencing changes at unprecedented speed, rise of digitalization and automation, increased access to information, and globalization of markets. And, confirm emerging trends that challenge traditional organizational approaches, work environments, management leadership and practices, and sustainability prospects of organizations and nations.

The global record of 85% of employees worldwide not engaged or actively disengaged in their work from any dimension and for all professions, and especially from economics and management, is an astonishing number that deserves deep and immediate scrutiny.

Table 7.4 shows that, worldwide, less than one-third of full time workers, 25% men and 29% women, feel they are thriving, engaged with their daily work, satisfied with their job and the level of wellbeing they desire. But the majority of employees feel they are struggling with conditions at work (61% men and 60% women), and a considerable proportion reports they are suffering with the work they perform on a daily basis (13% men and 11% women).

TABLE 7.4 Percentage of Global Work Wellbeing Evaluation by Employment Status

	Global Total		Full-time Employment		Unemployed		Out of work	
	Men	Women	Men	Women	Men	Women	Men	Women
Thriving	*22*	*24*	*25*	*29*	*14*	*19*	*21*	22
Struggling	64	61	62	60	70	68	64	61
Suffering	14	15	13	11	16	13	15	17

Source: Gallup, 2017.

Gallup (2017) found that a few patterns of global employee engagement are consistent worldwide. For instance, employee engagement tends to be lower in industries with more routinized jobs, such as manufacturing and productions. This coincides with resource heavy work patterns anchored in structures and management strategies of the industrial past that lack employee centered management that is essential for continuous performance improvement based on people's wellbeing as a condition to improve processes and attain sustainability.

Across regions, differences in level of employee engagement cannot be attributed to different job types. Gallup (2017) highlights that the most surprising difference in work engagement found was in Western Europe. In spite of the fact that this is one of the most developed world regions, the level of employee engagement is lower than the global average. Ten percent of the employees in Western European countries are engaged at work. This is one-third of the 33% employee engagement in the United States.[19] Gallup suggests that the disparity between Western Europe and the United States is based on American management practices deployed by companies in the ongoing productivity edge. My studies and experience comparing market economies and centralized systems confirms that macroeconomic policies in free market economies, imposing higher responsibility for improvement on producers and the productive system, result in better working conditions for employees than stringent government controls, laws, and a large amount of labor regulations and bureaucratic practices. And, the same applies to developing countries.

Gallup (2017) explains that there many possible reasons for the alarming results of employee disengagement. Constant struggle to keep up with the pace of social and technological change, is one of the most commonly cited. Also, lagging organizations slow to adapt to change and are hurting to survive in rapidly changing markets. Global results reveal outstanding levels of misuse, waste of human capital, and squandering of talent that weaken the potential of national workforces. And as previously discussed, educational systems, instead of helping, are hindering the productive sector with unprepared graduates.

From the human dimension, Gallup's (2017) results show the difficult and dreadful conditions workers face in the workforce and when they are unemployed and either searching and not finding a job or out of work and not searching for a job. From the organizational dimension, these results reveal heavy burdens imposed by macroeconomic policies harming productivity and competitiveness with growing challenges for sustainability. All this confirms the need to consider wellbeing at work at micro and macroeconomic levels as an urgent matter in management and organization development. The high proportion of people in full-time employment who feel disengaged and dissatisfied with working conditions is a high priority that concerns employers, economists, educators, policy makers, and governments of nations worldwide who are all responsible for choosing and deploying policies aimed to constantly increase human wellbeing optimizing productivity at work and economic growth to realistically build inclusive societies.

Agilizing the Economy to Strengthen the Educonomy

Given that one of the highest levels of employee disengagement with work—and also unemployment rates—is among low skilled workers, this discussion on the agile economy cannot exclude observing the relation of the lower education level on economic growth and inclusive social development.

One of the most evident and stubborn misalignments between education and the workforce is observed in basic and secondary education and the problem affects the largest portion of the labor force in all countries, but it is critical in developing countries with underperforming educational systems highly regulated by central government control.

It is no surprise that countries with the lowest rates of unemployment have the best alignment between education and work. Germany is recognized by the quality standards of its vocational education and apprenticeships that contrast deeply with countries that undervalue the importance of vocational education or the urgency to improve quality standards in all educational levels. In most countries, secondary school students have no opportunity to gain experience working and familiarizing with the challenges that organizations in the productive sector have to face. And all countries with centralized government systems train students to fill in civil service bureaucratic jobs, disregarding demands of companies complaining about shortage of technical skills to fill vacancies in a productive sector facing constant disruptions and changes in the local and global economy.

But vocational training and apprenticeships is not enough, continuous program improvement and updates are essential. Some countries are considering to transform unemployment systems from safety nets into springboards based on retraining and job placement, and expediting liberalization of labor markets. This is particularly the case in developed countries burdened with labor regulations and inflexibility. In most cases, labor market inflexibility costs an important percentage of GDP. And politics matters too. To protect employment with laws, regulations, and organized cartels curtails chances of unemployed people of all ages—and women and young people in particular—to gain access to paid work.

At the organizational level, the most competitive companies have tried to bridge the education shortcoming gap by investing in training either creating corporate universities or diminishing the amount of expensive training. To a large extent, because disruptions in the workplace are so common and change is so fast that training can hardly keep up with levels of investments and required infrastructure. Besides, light business models used in online education are growing and evolving significantly faster than programs in heavy brick and mortar institutions. And this is a fact at all levels of skills.

Entrepreneurship: Critical Element of the Agile Economy

Growing numbers of countries are seeking consolidation of market economies worldwide to promote development of entrepreneurship as an economic activity to foster growth. Entrepreneurial education is expanding in tandem and applicable to all the professions. The imperative is to prepare graduates for a fast changing workplace on one hand, and on the other, to increase options to secure new sources of employment to more people. There are plenty of successful examples to guide policymakers to activate sluggish economies and ignite growth, breaking down monopolistic cartels, and building bridges between education and work.

The support of technology provides one of the most powerful tools to advance entrepreneurship. Countries that follow investment choices to strengthen entrepreneurial ecosystems[20] to consolidate emerging markets are seeing substantial improvement by decreasing unemployment and opening new opportunities for growth.

At global levels, entrepreneurial ecosystems of incubators and accelerators are establishing and expanding networks of outreach that compete in sophistication and coverage including Endeavor's Ecosystems Insights,[21] INBIA,[22] and Global Start Up Ecosystem.[23] Their impact is far reaching around the world, supporting the creation and expansion of national ecosystems.

At the macro level, countries are creating and supporting development of national infrastructure to unleash and consolidate local entrepreneurial ecosystems. Figure 7.1. shows Daniel Isenberg's model of the six domains of entrepreneurial ecosystem with details of its components.[24]

At the micro level, one of the most outstanding entrepreneurial developments is to see how technology and platforms allow people to take advantage of growing opportunities, and to use personal talent and responsibility to assume risks necessary to harvest gains. The following are some examples where people can exploit a growing number of entrepreneurial opportunities. The Danish *Serious Games* project provides opportunity to gain substantial virtual experience at minimal cost.[25] *Firebox* created by Mozilla is a web browser of open badges that allow recognition of programming skills.[26] Amazon's *Mechanical Turk* or MTurk operates a marketplace enabling access to a diverse on-demand workforce. While traditionally, tasks have been accomplished hiring a large temporary workforce that is time consuming, expensive, and difficult to scale, Mturk claims to provide access to human intelligence simply, scalably, and cost-effectively. Mturk enables business acumen to achieve goals faster and at lower cost based on: an on demand workplace, elastic workforce, low cost structure, quality management, and enabling new businesses.[27]

Entrepreneurial Education

For the last 20 years, I have conducted research, designed and taught entrepreneurial programs in general, with special emphasis to support women (Lepeley, 2018b, Lepeley et al., 2019). The aim has been to provide women with the knowledge and skills required to increase work opportunities to earn an income and increase the quality of life and wellbeing (Kuschel & Lepeley, 2016a, 2016b, 2017, Lepeley et al., 2019). I created the first program for women entrepreneurship in Chile in 1998 when I was president of an entrepreneurial college in Santiago. And in Dubai, while I was director of international management programs at the University of Connecticut, I developed a global forum for women in entrepreneurship. In 2003, Dubai's then emerging Knowledge Village,[28] which is by all standards one of the most visionary educational projects, invited me to teach a course in entrepreneurship for women to inaugurate the field. It was a most valuable professional and human experience.

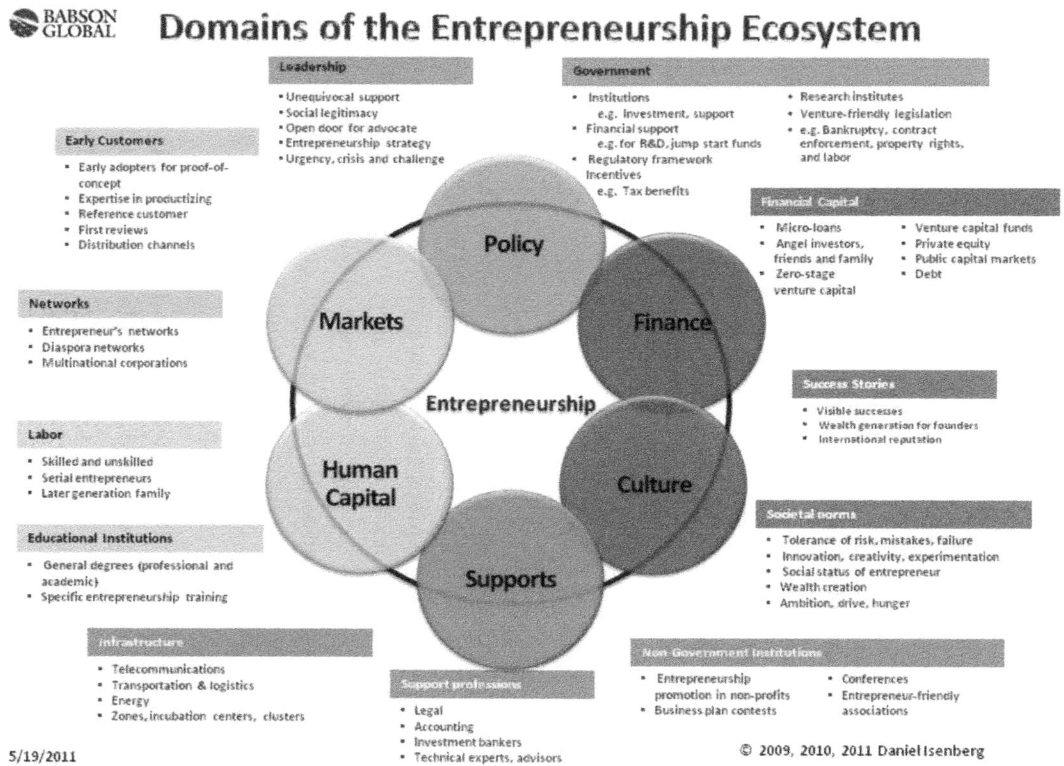

Figure 7.1 Daniel Isenberg's model of the six domains of entrepreneurial ecosystem. *Source:* Babson Entrepreneurial Ecosystem Project (2011).

In general, entrepreneurial education is more common at higher education levels in developed countries but it is becoming an important field of study also at a secondary level in developing countries. I recently conducted a study on Bhutan, a developing country in Asia placing special attention on the quality of education to increase development based on human well-being in addition to economic growth. One outstanding feature is the link Bhutan is establishing to integrate the education system and the productive sector strengthened with the government developing job fairs and entrepreneurial training programs at secondary school levels (Lepeley, 2017b).

Schumpeter and Christensen: Fathers of the Agile Economy

Education in entrepreneurship prepares students better than other disciplines. At all educational levels, entrepreneurship helps to face continuous changes and increasing threats that today not only affect business but organizations in all sectors. Some of the common global disruptions and threats of our times are those related to Schumpeter's *creative destruction* and Clayton Christensen's *disruptive innovation.*

The Austrian political economist Joseph Schumpeter (1883–1950) who became a Harvard scholar, once said that "the entrepreneurs would save the world" (1934). At the Austrian School of Economics he articulated that the world was living in a complex and dynamic phase where innovation and entrepreneurship occupied a decisive role in economic development. In the 1950s his concept of *creative destruction* described the process of industrial changes that was constantly revolutionizing economic structures destroying the old and creating new ones. His ideas on entrepreneurship and innovation seem even more appropriate nowadays. Creative destruction is one of the core principles of the agile economy.

Disruptive Innovation[29] was coined in the early 1990s by Harvard Business School professor Clayton Christensen. His model became common use from Wall Street to Silicon Valley and around the world. Like many concepts that become fashionable and vox populi, its core is often misunderstood or misused in business and economic lexicon. Disruptive innovation refers not to breakthrough technologies that make good products better; but are all kinds of innovations that emerge at the bottom of a competitive market and make products and services more accessible and affordable to everyone and available to a much larger population. *Disruptive innovation* is another core principle of the agile economy (Christensen, 1997, Christensen et al., 2015).

Disruptive innovation forces sluggish firms to rethink operations from the ground up. It coerces companies to constantly redesign and improve work, products, and services to remain competitive. It identifies routine tasks that can be automated or outsourced, and it is constantly identifying skilled jobs that emerge as essential to support central operations. It is constantly compelling organizations to *upsize, downsize, or to outsource.* All these functions are consistent, unavoidable, and increasingly the rule in the global VUCA environment where business chief executives and public policymakers struggle daily to adapt to labor markets fast enough to manage change and benefit from these drives of the agile economy.

Agility Uses Talent to Deploy Quality

The forces behind *creative destruction* and *disruptive innovation* are here to stay and will be increasingly common. The changing environment presents surmounting challenges for organizations of all sizes and in all sectors. It often happens that organizations get so preoccupied with the external disruptions they overlook the importance of maintaining a strong internal structure built on supporting strategies that can hinder sustainability.

As examiner and adviser of the National Award Programs in the United States and Latin American countries including Chile, Brazil, Colombia, Peru, and Ecuador, on a few occasions, I observed organizations that had deployed the quality management criteria and won the quality award but years later lost quality standards and failed. This event is unusual, because it takes substantial human effort, resources, and investment to train quality teams and networks responsible to build the culture of quality for the organization to merit a national award for performance excellence. But when it happens, it is either due to change in leadership and new executives who consider quality a cost instead of a responsibility to attain sustainability; or in a few instances, the organization became convoluted with external disruptions and overlooked the continuous improvement of people and processes essential to attain quality standards that the organization has systematized as its modus operandi.

Creative Destruction, Disruptive Innovation, and Quality Standards

There are important differences between the forces that prod creative destruction and disruptive innovation and quality standards. While creative destruction and disruptive innovation arise from external forces that compel organizations in specific competitive markets to change business models, structures, and strategies to survive shocks, quality management is an option organizations in all sectors and markets have available to them to *adopt* and *adapt* specific methods to modify structures and strategies systematizing continuous improvement across the organization as a necessary condition to attain quality standards.

While creative destruction and disruptive innovation imply changes in business models, efforts to manage organizations to attain quality standards start and are conducted by people who work *in* and *for* the organization. Quality implies changing people to commit to quality standards. Business models require change in processes.

I assign so much importance to the role of people in organizations that this reason led me to establish a book series with Routledge titled *Human Centered Management*. All the authors and editors in the series think on people first, on their wellbeing and the challenges it takes leaders and managers to continuously improve wellbeing as an essential condition to improve organizational performance, productivity, and competitiveness to attain sustainability. The same human centered principles apply to the economy. When economics gets distracted from people, in theory or practice, solutions are obstructed. This book shows the principles of human centered economics emphasizing the need to start deploying quality standards at the micro level in organizations, as a necessary condition to achieve continuous improvement and sustainable inclusive development at the macro and global level. Resources and processes can only optimize results when people have that intent in mind and are responsible for results.

In my book *Human Centered Management: 5 Pillars of Organizational Quality and Global Sustainability* (Lepeley, 2017a), I present the five pillars of management with people at the center. The model is illustrated in Figure 7.2. Agility is one of the pillars. The five pillars to hold together the organizational structure supported in agile sets of strategies are: (a) human capital, (b) disruption resilience, (c) talent, (d) agility, and (e) quality. Where *structure* is the core that carries on the vision, values, identity, and plans deployed by teams responsible for results and long-term projects. S*trategies* follow change and innovation operationalized by networks

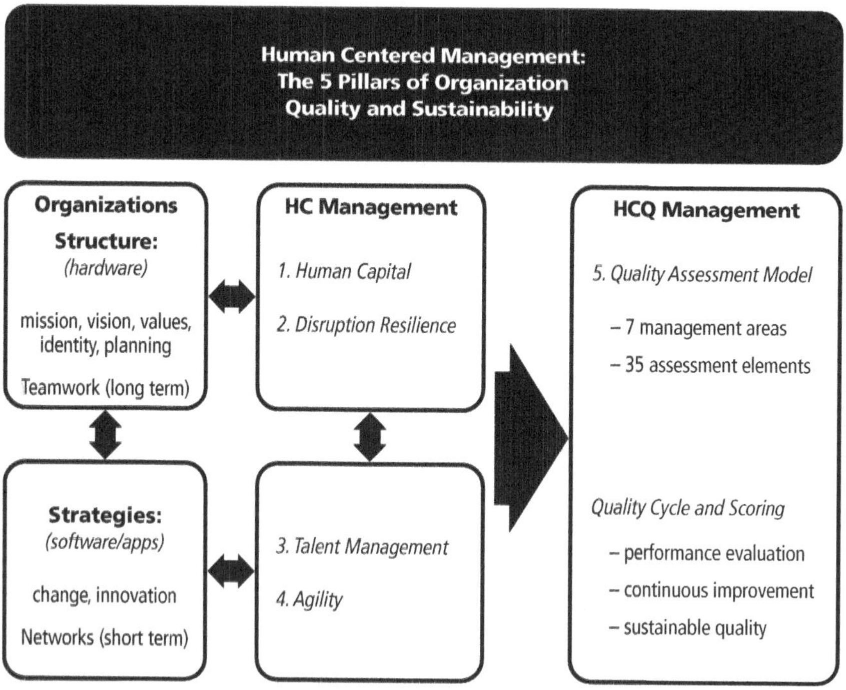

Figure 7.2 Human Centered Management: The 5 Pillars of Organization Quality and Sustainability. *Source:* Lepeley (2017a)

meeting short-term projects and objectives. Structure is founded and consolidated in *human capital* and organizational resilience to manage disruptions (internal and external), strategies expedite *talent* and *agility* and the people and the organization are synchronized with the ultimate goal to attain continuous improvement and *quality* standards to serve as a model of excellence for the community and society.

Agility is an essential factor for people, organizations and national economies in the Knowledge Economy. Agility is also a development imperative to attain sustainability optimizing benefits and minimizing the costs of disruptions of the Forth Industrial Revolution and change in the global VUCA environment.

Why the Agile Economy?

Agility in people, organizations, sectors, and ecosystems has exponential impact in survival rate and sustainability. In the VUCA environment organizations are constantly exposed to disruptions that decision makers and workers have to manage effectively in order to adapt to new circumstances and to adopt innovation to recuperate from economic shocks and setbacks.

In the increasingly complex work environments, people have a natural propensity to get overwhelmed with the speed of change. Change can have negative impacts on people, performance, and productivity (the 3 Ps) when it is not properly managed. During unavoidable transitions, organizations that lack capacity to adapt fast enough or lack guidelines to take advantage of change, have higher potential to get hurt as a result of collapse.

Externally, better informed customers are pressing organizations for products and services, faster delivery, and demanding quality standards. Competition is increasingly driven by innovation and quality as norms of the marketplace.

Internally, old organizational structures and strategies fail to solve new challenges. Diverse demands and impositions, including external laws and regulations are constantly shaking the status quo, while demand for products and services grows faster. Organizations confronting challenges using traditional means of production hinder operations and growth potential.

To adjust and respond effectively to change, organizations need talent, agility, and quality standards. Strategies leading to continuous improvement avoid segmented efforts that increase costs and postpone attainment of quality objectives. Piecemeal interventions to develop agility have low potential of success and induce higher costs than comprehensive efforts to deploy a broad base and integral agility strategy.

Given that nations are shaped by the character and development of their institutions the same goes on for countries. Nations that lack capacity to absorb and respond to the speed of change, internally or externally generated, make their people go through much more difficult, hazardous, and painful conditions than countries with flexible open markets and economies that adjust faster to optimize the benefits of change and globalizations and minimize the inherent costs of transitions. The degree of agility of an economy is directly related with the degree of national understanding of the needs of their people and the capacity of governments and organizations to buffer harmful effects that impact their wellbeing and economic sustainability.

Forces Driving Transition From the Industrial to the Agile Economy

The industrial age was driven by capital assets to help business growth achieve economies of scale adjusting means of production such as plant, equipment, and inventories. In the industrial age, the aim was *bigger is better* in order to gain competitive advantages. Large scale organizations were more efficient concentrating production in or close to headquarters to reduce costs transportation, information, and transaction. But technology, digitalization, artificial intelligence and robotics now allow organizations to significantly reduce size and costs associated with large size. Production processes that in the past took many workers to achieve in dedicated facilities, today, one person with a good idea has potential to do by gaining easy access to helpful online programs to design a product, improve a service, manufacture an invention, or hire freelancers who thrive and abound in the agile economy, as I previously discussed.

Agile Organizations Move on From Central Control to Decentralization: So Do Nations and Economies

The prototype organization of the industrial age was entrenched on Max Weber's model of bureaucracies in Europe and Frederick Taylor's scientific management in the United States. These were highly controlled structures that at that time helped to optimize standardized mass production in large factories managed by central hierarchies and authoritative control of decision-making. Progressive advances in technology, education, and human capital are dwarfing large systems, voluntarily or involuntarily, pressing them to become more agile to survive in totally different ecosystems built on talent networks and cyber platforms where old heavy structures can lead to peril and entropy.

Often technology, more often than human decisions, is driving change from hierarchical to flat organizations structures leading to necessary and extensive decentralization. The same is going on with countries, as I discussed in previous chapters, related to the significant amount of countries whose population enjoy considerable higher degrees of freedom than in previous decades and lower levels of corruption that hinders systems and harms the population leading to social unrest.

There is substantial evidence that the shift from brick and mortar to cyber platforms and access to ecosystems of talent, human capital, and information are drastically changing ways to produce and compete. The old command and control operations are displaced by information and knowledge growth.

Change is exacerbated by a shift in economies worldwide from the manufacturing pattern that prevailed in the industrial age to service economies that flourish today.

The social and economic success of market economies in developed and developing economies worldwide is increasingly the preferred system of nations that value freedom and the wellbeing of their people over regimes of high controls on people and low performance industries.

Although market economies range from minimal to moderate regulated systems where the government plays a lower or more active role interventing the prices system, correcting markets, and promoting welfare, growing evidence shows that the more interventionist governments are, the lower the rate of growth and development. Increasing evidence of populism in nations around the world is the effect controlling central administrations that mistrust the will of people and an educated population. Hence, the importance of agile economies and the Educonomy.

Economic history demonstrates that since mid-20th century, developed and particularly developing countries that have been successful in establishing open market economies trading with the rest of the world, have advanced faster and fared better in terms of economic growth, social progress, and human wellbeing than countries with centralized regimes. In the 70s and 80s when Singapore and Hong Kong in Asia and Chile in Latin America went through deep economic transformations from highly regulated socialist regimens to market economies, their progress was globally recognized as *the Asian tigers* and the *Chilean economic miracle*, respectively. In 2018, Singapore and Hong Kong continue among the highest performing market economies in the world. And Chile, my native country, that by the end of the 20th century had become the most stable economy in the region, between 2013 and 2017 took a significant plunge, socially and economically, as a result of a regime that intended to regress back to the socialist regime Chile had rejected in 1973, after 40 years of successful deployment of a market economy. In 2018, Chile is back on track with a new government trying to invigorate a lethargic economy. Since then, the IMF has increased Chile's growth prospect for 2018–2019 after 4 years of declining forecasts (Edwards, 2018). For more information, review Chile analysis in Chapter 3.

High Returns to Agility

I conclude this chapter showing evidence that agility pays back organizations in terms of higher performance, higher revenues, competitiveness, and sustainability. In other words, this study shows the type of organizations that any economy needs to attain continuous growth and develop inclusive societies. Furthermore, it provides realistic examples of why we need to pay special attention to the agile economy.

McKinsey identifies four types of organizations according to structure, stability, speed, and agility of strategies. As depicted in my graph, my model shows organizational structure anchored on the mission, vision, values, and identity organizations need to strengthen and project in or to provide stability inside and outside the institution—while organizational strategies must be focused on innovation and therefore needs to be agile to adopt and adapt to change and disruptions as fast as possible.

The four kinds of organizations the McKinsey study conducted by Bazigo et al. (2015) identifies are: (a) trapped (low stability, low agility); (b) bureaucratic (strong structure, low agility; (c) start-up (low structure, high agility); and (d) agile (strong structure, high agility). In 70% of the cases, agile organizations reached the best results. The 10 management practices that differentiate the most from the least agile organizations are shown in Table 7.5.

The evidence comes from a longitudinal international study about the impact and benefits of agility in organizations conducted by McKinsey. The article titled *Why Agility Pays* shows results of a decade long analysis based on a survey of two million respondents from 1,000 companies (Bazigo, De Smet, & Gagnon, 2015). The findings of this study converge with the critical drivers of organizational performance embedded in my *Human Centered Management: 5 Pillars of Organizational Quality and Global Sustainability* (Lepeley, 2017a).

TABLE 7.5 The 10 Management Practices That Differentiate the Most From the Least Agile Organizations

#	Management Practice
1	Inspirational leaders
2	Innovation
3	Strong culture of knowledge sharing
4	Meaningful shared values
5	Capture external ideas
6	Role clarity
7	Internally competitive
8	Process-based capability
9	People performance review (instead of function performance review)
10	Operationally disciplined

Source: Bazigo et al., 2015

Notes

1. https://www.accenture.com/t20160823T222808Z__w__/us-en/_acnmedia/Accenture/Omobono/TechnologyVision/pdf/Platform-Economy-Technology-Vision-2016.pdfla=en#zoom=50
2. https://www.accenture.com/us-en/insight-digital-platform-economy
3. Ibid.
4. https://en.wikipedia.org/wiki/Retail_apocalypse
5. Accenture Report, p. 4.
6. The 80-year-old Millennial. Prudential 2017 (https://www.80yearoldmillennial.pru/)
7. Pew Research. Social and Demographic Trends. December 11, 2013 (http://www.pewsocialtrends.org/2013/12/11/chapter-5-balancing-work-and-family/)
8. *The Economist.* April 27, 2013 (https://www.economist.com/news/international/21576657-around-world-almost-300m-15-24-year-olds-are-not-working-what-has-caused)
9. As a comparison youth unemployment in the U.S. in March 2018 is 8.5% (https://www.statista.com/statistics/217448/seasonally-adjusted-monthly-youth-unemployment-rate-in-the-us/)
10. Ibid.
11. Ibid.
12. *The Economist,* April 27, 2013 (https://www.economist.com/news/international/21576657-around-world-almost-300m-15-24-year-olds-are-not-working-what-has-caused)
13. 2015 World Migration Report (https://www.iom.int/world-migration-report-2015)
14. United Nations Migration Report (http://www.un.org/en/development/desa/population/migration/publications/migrationreport/docs/MigrationReport2015_Highlights.pdf)
15. These results correlate highly with analyses discussed in previous chapters and similar surveys conducted by the Gallup organization.
16. Archived in the library of the University of Miami, Florida.
17. Gallup 2017 State of the Global Workforce. Page 1.
18. Gallup's 2017 State of the Global Market Place (http://news.gallup.com/reports/220313/state-global-workplace-2017.aspx?utm_source=2013StateofGlobalWorkplaceReport&utm_medium=2013SOGWReportLandingPage&utm_campaign=2013StateofGlobalReport_Redirectto2017page&utm_content=download2017now_textlink#formheader)
19. State of the Global Workplace 2017. Page 5.
20. Entrepreneurial ecosystem refers to the social and economic environment affecting the local/regional entrepreneurial activities as a development strategy.
21. Endeavor's Ecosystem Insights (http://www.ecosysteminsights.org/everything-you-wanted-to-know-about-accelerators/
22. INBIA (https://inbia.org/)
23. Global Startup Ecosystem (http://globalstartupecosystem.com/)

24. Babson Entrepreneurship Ecosystem Project (http://entrepreneurial-revolution.com/2011/05/08/introducing-the-entrepreneurship-ecosystem-four-defining-characteristics/)
25. Serious Games website (http://www.seriousgames.net/)
26. Firebox website (https://developer.mozilla.org/en-US/Add-ons/Themes/Create_Your_Own_Firefox_Background_Theme)
27. Amazon's MTurk (https://www.mturk.com/)
28. Today Knowledge Park (http://www.dkp.ae/)
29. Disruptive Innovation video. The Christensen Institute (https://www.christenseninstitute.org/disruptive-innovations/?gclid=EAIaIQobChMIwtSrnZvM2gIVwi-BCh1ZJgu5EAAYAiAAEgIXCfD_BwE)

8

The Quality Economy

In the quality transformation the first step is transformation of the individual. This comes from understanding of the system of knowledge. The individual, transformed, will find new meaning of life, events, numbers, and interactions between people. Once the individual understands the system of knowledge, the person has a basis for judgment of own decisions and can apply quality principles in every kind of relationship with other people to foster transformation of the organizations the person belongs to.

—Edwards Deming, *The Father of Quality*

Quality attainment has been a concern across the book because it is a central element and major challenge to attain sustainable development anchored in human wellbeing. I have discussed and correlated the quality imperative at individual, organizational, and national levels. Chapter 4 included extensive discussion of claims that call for the improvement of quality in education coming from all sectors. Claims arise from growing concerns that in spite of increasing investments in programs and policies, and significant increases in enrollment in the last decades and worldwide, the quality of education is lagging stubbornly behind. Targets are unmet

Educonomy, pages 183–220

and evidence of the misallocations of funds is curtailing the potential well-being of generations of students. This is increasingly unfair for people and societies and economically unjustifiable.

This chapter on the quality economy concentrates on quality attainment in education, addressing challenges and presenting options for solutions. This section is based on a sustainable quality (SQ) model I designed to manage for continuous improvement and quality standard. SQ aligns individual commitment with the quality culture and values the projects to customers, suppliers and the community at large. Quality is not an isolated event or results from segmented efforts, but it is the result of multiple synchronized dimensions.

Quality Is Centered on People as a Condition to Improve Processes, Organizations, and Nations

Today there are many management and assessment models aimed at improving quality using systematic approaches that go from International Organization for Standardization (ISO) norms and lean management in organizations applicable to all sectors and industries to national quality awards aimed at recognizing the importance and impact of high performance and productivity on development.

All of the approaches have the potential to be helpful. But the most important decision before embarking on the quality endeavor at the organizational level to deploy the quality culture is to make sure all people in the organization believe in and will align with and support the transformation. Testing the engagement of individual efforts required for continuous improvement and quality standards—from the executive board to cleaning crews—informing unequivocally that in the long run quality standards benefit all, are essential to feel confident, comfortable, and to gain a deeper understanding of the implications of quality and the model or approach chosen. Reaching continuous improvement, which is essential to attaining quality standards, is not an easy undertaking by any means; but a systematic application of a preferred chosen method can benefit people and the organization considerably.

In my experience the most effective quality management models are human centered, instead of resource-based.

The Quality Transformation Starts With Individual Transformation

I confirm what Deming states in the introductory quote—quality starts with personal transformation.

It wasn't until my students came to me and told me how much of what they had learned in my class had been useful to them, that I realized that education was not only about teaching, but it was more about students' learning.

It was not until I wrote my thesis in economics about the impact of higher education on economic growth and development that I understood how critical education at all levels was in advancing growth and development.

It was not until I was captivated by and cultivated in quality management, and later became an examiner of the U.S. Baldrige National Quality Award, that I confirmed that quality standards were essential for sustainable progress and essential for transformation.

It was after two decades, when I designed my first human centered quality management for education model (Lepeley, 2001); after lecturing, training, and certifying educators at all levels and in many nations; and after I was a U.S. Baldrige examiner and adviser to six of the most important National Quality Award programs in Latin America, that I claimed that education and economics were inseparable as two points in the same human development continuum where quality is the common denominator to integrating and optimizing sustainable development anchored in human wellbeing.

All the above led me to contest that the main problem nations worldwide face is not income inequality, but it is education inequality.

After Personal, Organizational Quality Transformation

My experience, and a growing volume of literature on quality, helped me identify and expose the increasing amount of waste accrued when quality standards are missing, and the damage it inflicts on organizations when employees feel disengaged with work. Waste is growing to intolerable limits in an age of technology that induces high connectivity and transparency.

I end the book with this chapter on the quality economy, a most critical pillar of the Educonomy, exposing findings that show detrimental consequences when quality standards do not exist. I end this chapter with a preview of the human centered economic and management principles and practices that underline the sustainable quality model that I have presented in previous books (Lepeley, 2001, 2017a) and is displayed in the complementary book to this one titled, *Eduquality. Human Centered Quality Management in Education. A Model for Deployment, Assessment and Sustainability.* (Lepeley, 2019).

Lack of Quality, Surmounting Yet Avoidable Squander

The *Harvard Business Review* article "Creating a Quality Culture" (Srinivasan & Kurey, 2014) reports results of interviews conducted by the authors to organizational quality leaders in 60 multinational corporations. Findings include survey results of 850 employees in a wide range of functions, industries, and at all levels of seniority. The results showed that many of the strategies that were traditionally assumed to increase quality, such as monetary incentives, training, and sharing best practices, had little effect on improvement. Instead, successful outcomes were observed in companies that had developed quality cultures centered on people. Organizations that are peer-driven and emphasize collaborative approaches show higher levels of engagement with work, employees make fewer mistakes saving companies a significant amount of resources, and they spend less time and money correcting mistakes (Srinivasan & Kurey, 2014).

But the results showed that quality is not deployed in the majority of these multinational companies. Among the 60 companies surveyed, 40% of the employees believed their organization had succeeded in making quality a core value. While 60% said the work environment had not attained a desirable culture of quality, especially in relation to co-workers who are not engaged and supportive. The study emphasizes how much these companies are gaining and missing. Employees who ranked their organization in top quintiles in terms of quality reported making 46% fewer mistakes in their daily work than companies that have not reached quality standards. Considering that it takes 2 hours on average to correct a mistake, and assuming an hourly wage of US$ 42.55, a firm with 26,300 employees would spend nearly US$ 774 million a year resolving preventable errors. Although the authors warn that these figures can vary widely according to industry and company, a rule of thumb is that for an organization with 5,000 employees moving from low performance to quality standards could save US$ 67 million annually.

Given that this research was conducted by business consultants and researchers in companies that were already moving along the quality culture scale—which are commonly more transparent and easier to calculate gain and waste and savings—studies of this kind in business resonate louder on the need to conduct similar studies of gains and waste in education.

Next, I discuss studies in economics of education conducted by specialists in the field. Studies like these are needed and helpful to improve resource allocation, but in general they are based on traditional quality standards associated with education inputs and outputs proxied exclusively by grades and test scores, not associated with quality standards of students' learning, attainment of holistic development and a better life, or access to good jobs or higher contribution to society. Most studies omit to measure effects of economic externalities of education as a public good, which are more difficult to assess but in terms of human capital and development have more significant implications than business on growth and development at individual, organizational, and national levels.

In the study, The Economic Value of Higher Teacher Quality, Stanford University professor, Eric Hanushek (2011), one of the best known specialists, argues that there are ambiguities in policies to assess and improve teacher performance because there are no effective methods to evaluate teacher quality. Although Hanushek claims that lack of information could be eliminated by a set of pay experiments, the current negotiated pay alternatives of teachers do not provide information, in part because data shows that salaries are relatively insensitive to effectiveness or quality. He states that the problem can be solved when teacher salaries are economically justified and reflect teacher effectiveness in terms of students' learning. Without this linkage, low performing teachers and underperforming schools perpetuate, and teacher salaries lag far behind salaries in general labor markets. Transparency in teacher salaries and competitiveness based on realistic quality standards and effectiveness on students' learning beyond traditional methods are key elements to consolidate quality advances in education.

In his article "Economic Growth in Developing Countries: The Role of Human Capital," Hanushek (2016) argues that the focus on human capital as a driver of economic growth in developing countries has led to undue attention on school enrollment and completion. He argues that although developing countries have made considerable progress closing gaps with developed countries in terms of school attainment, the most recent research underscores the importance of students' learning and cognitive skills necessary to foster economic growth, shifting attention away from critical issues of school quality. In terms of quality attainment in education, Hanushek (2016) emphasizes that developing countries have been much less successful in closing the quality gaps than developed countries. He states that, "Without improving school quality, developing countries will find it difficult to improve their long run economic performance" (Hanushek, 2013, p. 207).

A March 2018 article in the *Los Angeles Times* titled "Money Matters in Education, as Long as You Spend It at the Right Time and on the Tight

Students" by David Kirp, a University of California professor at Berkeley, presents contending views of education investments and allocations in California. He claims that half a century ago, when sociologist James Coleman conducted the U.S. Department of Education study on educational inequality, a quality school meant teachers with advanced degrees, a well-stocked library, and state-of-the-art science labs. All assumptions focused on *inputs* as the key to students' success, but Coleman's results of his Equality of Educational Opportunity Survey showed unexpected findings. Families mattered more, schools mattered less, and extra resources did not matter much at all. Since then, Kirp claims, battles about whether the size of school budgets make a difference in school quality has been center stage.

Kirp (2018) argues that advocates of the concept that more money does not improve education, rely on evidence that after five decades of K–12 funding increases, 17-year-olds' reading and math scores on the U.S. National Assessment of Educational Progress (NAEP), the nation's report card, have not changed. He specifically cites professor Hanushek, who in 1989 reviewed 400 studies and found no strong or consistent relationship between bigger school budgets and greater student success, which led him to conclude that the focus on how much school districts spend appears misguided in school financing. Furthermore Kirp believes that the skeptics of booming school budgets without backups of good results are asking the wrong question. He argues that the issue is not whether money matters, but when money matters and for which students.

Kirp (2018) refers to a number of studies that show that increased expenditures in low income students has improved learning scores and has potential to change the trajectory of their lives.

Throughout the book I have emphasized that income inequality is not the problem but it is educational inequality, so I highly commend Kirp's (2018) article for bringing into focus the need to allocate funding to improve learning and opportunity for low income students and schools. But I find serious limitations with the validity and reliability of studies that rely exclusively on traditional methods, such as test scores and school completion rates, but ignore and neglect new quality standards that require transparency of results to allocate resources.

I started the Introduction of this book and will close this last chapter referring to the results of two Gallup studies—the *2016 State of the Global Workplace* (Gallup, 2016)—reporting that 85% of employees worldwide are not engaged or are actively disengaged with their jobs and the 2018 *Global Great Jobs Briefing: 3 Billion Still Looking for Great jobs* (Gallup, n.d.).

The Gallup 2016 report highlights findings from an ongoing research of workplaces in 140 countries with data providing insights into employee engagement and performance of their companies. The results show that less than one-quarter of the world's workers feel engaged with the work they do every day and are thriving in good jobs, while three-quarters feel low engagement or are alienated with daily duties that allow them to earn a living (aside from those unemployed either by personal decision or unable to find a paid job).

These results are appalling, not only for work providers of organizations affected by amazing amounts of waste, as reported in the Gallop study above (2016), and for development economists, but for educators, parents, and overall for international development organizations and policy makers. This shows clear evidence of gaps and disconnect between education and the workforce, and ineffective development and growth policies unable to stimulate job creation and activate workforce absorption. To a very large extent these results expose the level of ignorance and neglect of quality standards that have been pervading the global environment for the last 3 decades. This chapter on quality will connect the dots with a proposal to deploy and assess quality standards.

Human Centered Management of Quality

In 2001, I published the first book on quality management in education. In 2015, I created a book series on human centered management with England's Routledge publishing, with all the books addressing the challenges in management and the workforce from a sustainable perspective anchored on quality management principles. This book, *Educonomy: Unleashing Well-being & Human Centered Sustainable Development,* and the complementary book, *Eduquality. Human Centered Quality Management in Education. A Model for Deployment, Assessment and Sustainability,* are part of a new book series on human centered sustainability with Information Age Publishing. The complementary purpose of these two books is to bridge the stubborn gaps I discussed in the previous paragraphs with quality management as a common denominator in education and the workforce—or quality as a necessary condition to align, articulate, and integrate education with labor markets as complements in a human development continuum.

Education and Labor Market Inequality

In previous chapters on the Educonomy, the talent economy, and the agile economy, I discussed the complexity of the links between education and labor markets as well as the challenges that barricade wellbeing attainment at the personal, organizational, national development, and societal levels. To a large extent, this happens because education and labor markets are deeply fractured. They function as segmented, segregated sectors, not parts of a continuum. But the central problem is that given the pace of change and connectivity in the Knowledge Economy and the global VUCA environment in the 21st century, these gaps will increasingly hamper development, sustainability, and wellbeing unless effective measures are implemented to avoid waste of human capital and resources.

The above discussions have confirmed with sufficient evidences and clarity the need for the quality economy. In this chapter, I discuss the underlying quality principle of my model aimed to improve education and bridge gaps between education and the workplace.

Putting the Pieces Together With Quality Standards

The quality principles that support the Educonomy, and in turn the balanced sustainable development (BSD) of the economic, social, technology, environment (ESTE) strategy, are anchored in personal responsibility, self-cultivation, and life-long learning as conditions for every person to make better contributions to improve organizations and the economy and to attain inclusive societies. The axiom is that the economy, society, technology, and the environment must combine and be balanced to serve people and increase their wellbeing, not the inverse. In this model, people are at the center, not marginal as frequently happens in some economic, social, technological, and environmental approaches.

At the national level (macro-economy), nations deploying policies and programs striving for ESTE HC BSD (economic, social, technology, environment, in this order) have higher chances to progress and benefit from change and disruptions than nations that deploy segmented approaches with higher potential to interfere in sustainability. Although some short-term imbalances are natural in rapidly changing environments, pronounced and long-term imbalances hurt the economy, the society, and people's wellbeing.

Progress in the Knowledge Economy implies that the four components of ESTE HC BSD are articulated with the *Educonomy* to strengthen education quality as leverage and a driver of development.

The Educonomy is responsible to move national development forward gaining strength from the complement of its three fundamental pillars—the talent economy, the agile economy, and the quality economy. The talent economy is responsible for the identification of talent to increase the stock of human capital embedded in all the students to help them attain a better life and make a significant contribution to society. The agile economy aims to maximize benefits of change and minimize costs of unavoidable disruptions, ensuring that education bridges gaps and keeps pace with demands in the workforce and society. The quality economy monitors systematic assessment of performance and keeps records of continuous improvement at individual, organizational, and national levels to secure quality standards essential for sustainability in the 21st century.

The Educonomy is deployed to increase income parity and diminish inequality stimulated by quality standards in education for all students, with particular attention in the most vulnerable groups, schools, and nations where quality improvement attempts have been more elusive and unsuccessful.

Income inequality is a stubborn problem that societies must address to advance from the erroneous perceptions of the causes of inequality. Confusing effect (income inequality) with the cause (deficient and inadequate education) is the most significant obstacle for progress.

Figure 8.1 displays the people's wellbeing analytical framework embedded in the ESTE HC BSD model with the Educonomy at the top and the

Figure 8.1 Balanced Sustainable Development ESTE and the Educonomy.

talent, agile, and quality economies as integral components of human centered development.

Balance between economic, social, technological, environmental dimensions of development.

Wellbeing: a sustainable human condition embedded in the Aristotelian eudaimonic philosophical principle of personal responsibility for the cultivation of self-improvement as a necessary condition to make better contributions to help others and improve society.

Nations unable to provide quality education for all are wasting talent and human capital, required to optimize change, and are restricted to achieve sustainability in the global VUCA environment.

Figure 8.2 shows the hypothetical stages of entropy of economies that ignore the pursuit of people's wellbeing as a central development strategy in the Knowledge Economy.

In the global VUCA environment, the Educonomy is a critical component of development to unleash the talent and the human capital necessary to avoid stagnation. The Educonomy is strengthened by the agile economy (optimizing benefits and minimizing cost of change and disruptions) and the quality economy (responsible for fostering high performance, productivity, and competitiveness at the individual, organizational, and national levels).

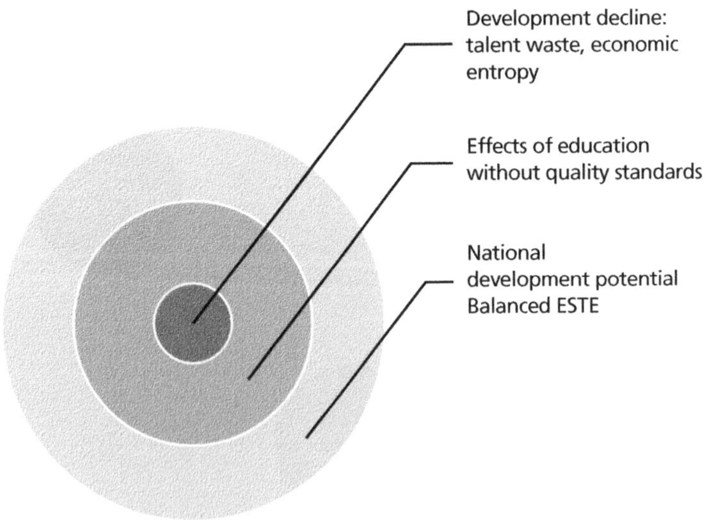

Figure 8.2 Impaired development.

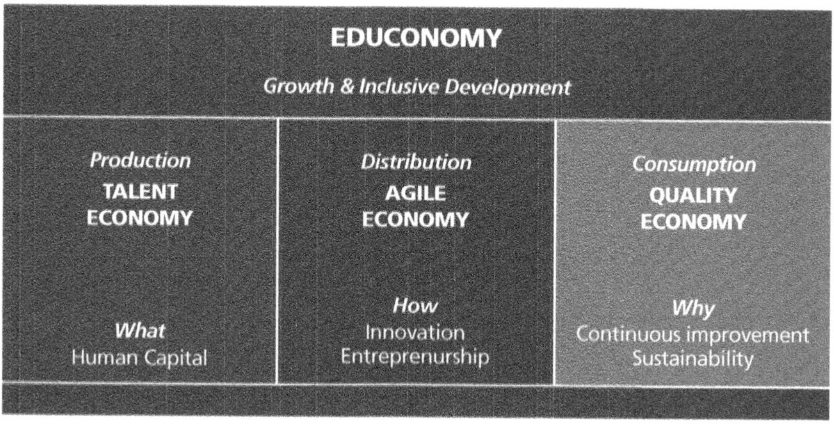

Figure 8.3 The Educonomy.

Figure 8.3 presents the composition of the Educonomy built on the talent, agility, and quality economies facilitating the production, distribution, and consumption functions of the gross domestic product (GDP) growth, balanced with progress in human wellbeing. Each pillar strengthens the Educonomy to provide the knowledge base to advance sustainability.

Like any economic system seeking optimization in the use of limited resources, the Educonomy is not static. It is constantly pressed and driven by the continuous improvement imperative and the interactions of talent, agility, and quality support systems. These interactions can take different shapes and orders as demonstrated in Figure 8.4, but they always align and integrate to attain human centered development and sustainable wellbeing.

Deployment of the Quality Economy

The sustainable quality model I developed integrated economic utility theory and quality management principles. It is anchored in the utility and satisfaction of the needs of people and future expectations. The quality economy is a customer-demand-driven economy where producers of educational products and services innovate, align, and synchronize production and distribution to meet the utility and needs of students, as *direct consumers of education*, and also the needs of parents and demands of the workforce as *indirect consumers of education.* This direct and indirect identification of consumers of education is one of the most significant differences between my quality management model and others in the market. Failing to understand the extensions of the quality outreach impairs results and curtails options of success in quality deployment.

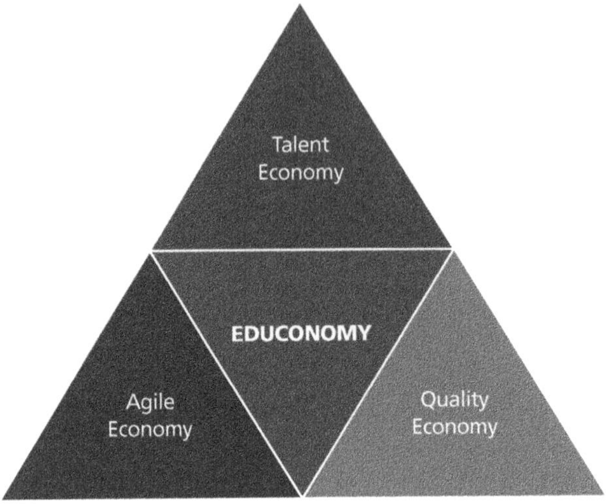

Figure 8.4 Strategic changes in the Educonomy.

The following economic assumptions strengthen effective deployment and functioning of the quality economy:

- fair, functional, transparent markets
- customers' freedom to choose among multiple alternatives
- producers' freedom to decide what to produce and how much
- *constructive competition*[1] as a fundamental instrument to display and compare quality standards that people, organizations, and nations recognize, value, and can share
- constructive competition is the strongest deterrent of monopolistic power

Figure 8.5 Quality focus: the core of the Quality Economy.

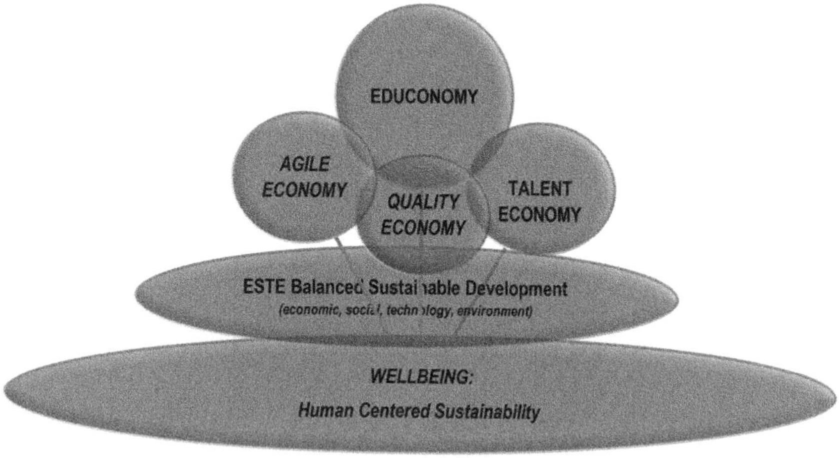

Figure 8.6 Interactions and Integration. Framework of the Balanced Sustainable Development ESTE (economic, social, technology, environment).

Figure 8.6 displays the interactions and integration of the four economic subsystems of BSD ESTE that contribute to the growth of wellbeing and human centered sustainability.

Sustainable Quality Development

Continuous GDP growth is essential for nations to progress and continuously improve the wellbeing of people. I have discussed before the surmounting evidence and scientific studies that support the need for continuous GDP growth that have derailed Easterlin's (1974) paradox that GDP and income is irrelevant for people's wellbeing. The peculiar Easterlin paradox evolved from data misinterpretation collected in some of the richest countries that ignored fundamental economic development principles that people are better off when their income level increases and worse off when human needs go unsatisfied for lack of income. The Easterlin theory of no need for GDP or income growth is valid exclusively for the very wealthy, with all needs satisfied and marginal utility of income diminishing significantly when income grows faster than human needs. Except for the very rich and very wealthy who have all their needs satisfied, GDP growth is essential to increase income of households and critically important for human wellbeing. Wrong assumptions like this have significant potential to harm nations and households. Ignoring the implications of uneven development can lead to serious errors of interpretation with harmful effects on human wellbeing. Erroneous misconceptions like this are growing among elite groups in high-income developed nations with serious implications on lower income groups and nations.

GDP growth in developed and developing countries is a fundamental condition to increase the demand for labor. To increase the size of the workforce and decrease unemployment. To optimize the use of talent required to increase returns to human capital. And in turn to increase national income to distribute among all citizens. With high awareness that income and equal opportunity are only achievable with quality education and systematic high performance of educational systems. Otherwise economic history shows that there is no better solution to deter poverty. And any argument to the contrary have proven reiteratively wrong across developed and developing countries.

For economies to grow, markets, decision-making, and policies need to be closely aligned to a cycle of continuous improvement that facilitates effective assessment of quality standards along the following stages of progress: (a) innovation, (b) planning and design, (c) production, (d) continuous evaluation aimed to attain, and (e) continuous improvement required for sustainable development in Figure 8.7.

Principles of continuous economic growth are core to the consolidation of quality standards and they apply to management and organizations that are required to reach high performance, productivity, and excellence through competitiveness to meet the needs of customers and free trading in self-regulated markets moved by ethical values and free from corruptive motives.

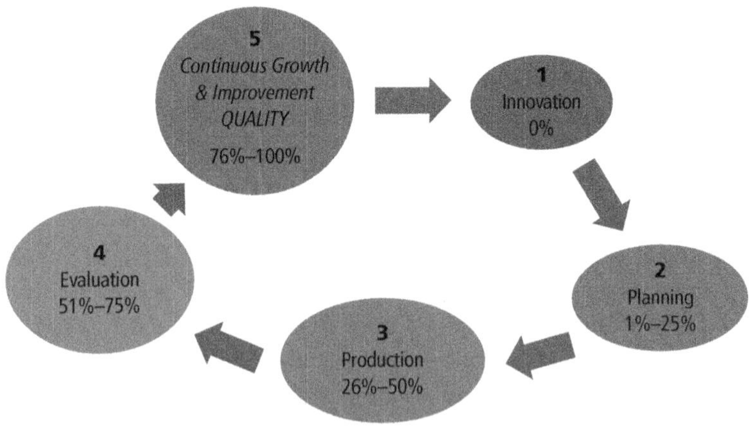

Figure 8.7 The Sustainable Quality and Development Circle.

Wellbeing and the Balanced Sustainable Development ESTE Model

The model of ESTE cannot be defined without explaining the meaning of wellbeing—and clarifying the difference that exists between happiness (transient, short term, pleasure seeking, absence of pain) and wellbeing (long term, assuming responsibility, and capacity in cultivation and continuous improvement of self as a necessary condition to make a better contribution to improve society).

In contrast with happiness, the concept of wellbeing in sustainable development implies individual responsibility for self-improvement as a necessary condition to help others and society. In the wellbeing framework, the mantra is "help yourself first, to help others well," not the inverse.

Table 8.1 shows the human wellbeing framework that is at the core of the BSD ESTE model. The framework aligns and articulates the principles behind Maslow's hierarchy of needs, Rath and Harper's (2010) wellbeing approach used by Gallup to assess wellbeing globally, and an educational

TABLE 8.1 Framework of Human Wellbeing: Lepeley's Construct

Maslow's Hierarchy of Human Needs	Gallup Wellbeing Dimensions	*Wellbeing in the Educonomy*
Theoretical bases	*Desirable outcome*	*Learner-centered education*
5th. Spiritual	Spiritual growth and inner peace	*Wellbeing pursuits in human development, creativity, talent*
4th. Intellectual	Intellectual curiosity Lifelong learning	*Learner-centered disciplines subject to continuous evaluation, improvement, and quality standards*
3rd. Economic	Economic & financial literacy	*Investing in people* *Human centered economic education* *Principles and practices of lifelong financial management and planning*
2nd. Love, affection, respect	Social needs. Psychological Mental fitness	*Soft Skills, empathy* *Value of diversity* *Value added of unification and integration*
1st. Food, shelter	Good health Physical needs and fitness	*Nutrition* *Pysical fitness* *Environment care*

version of students' wellbeing, developed by the Organisation for Economic Cooperation and Development (OECD) and recently introduced as a variable in the Program for International Student Assessment (PISA) standardized global test. Each one of these approaches adds value to an integral conception of wellbeing that I compound in the right column as wellbeing in the Educonomy supporting the model to attain sustainability.

The model is the result of the integration of the following narratives: Figure 8.8 represents a personal interpretation of the original Maslow's hierarchy of needs, but instead of the original triangular hierarchical shape more pertinent to the Knowledge Economy of the 21st century, I use a circular representation that enhances interactions of needs as more realistic assumptions.

Figure 8.9. shows Raph and Harper's (2010) theories presented in their book *Wellbeing: The Five Essential Elements.* This model is extensively used by the Gallup organization to conduct global surveys. Given the influence of Gallup in the global workforce environment, these wellbeing parameters are increasingly associated with global standards of wellbeing.

Following closely on the expanding wellbeing revolution in the productive sector, Figure 8.10 shows that the OECD approach to students'

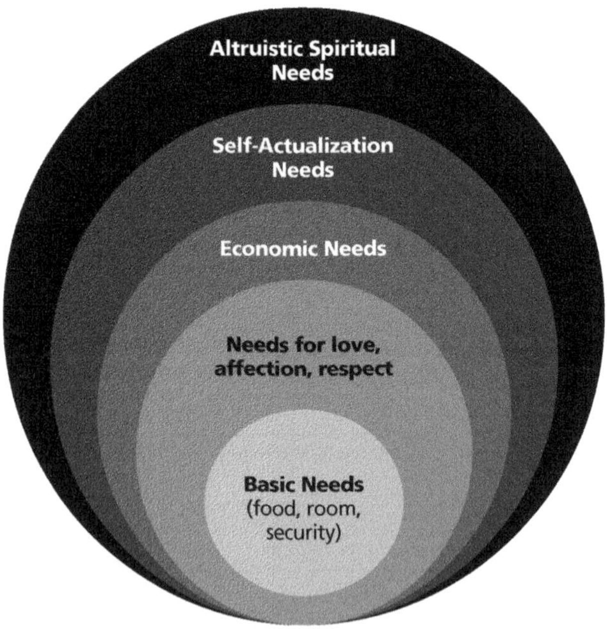

Figure 8.8 Circular adaptation of Maslow's Hierarchy of Needs.

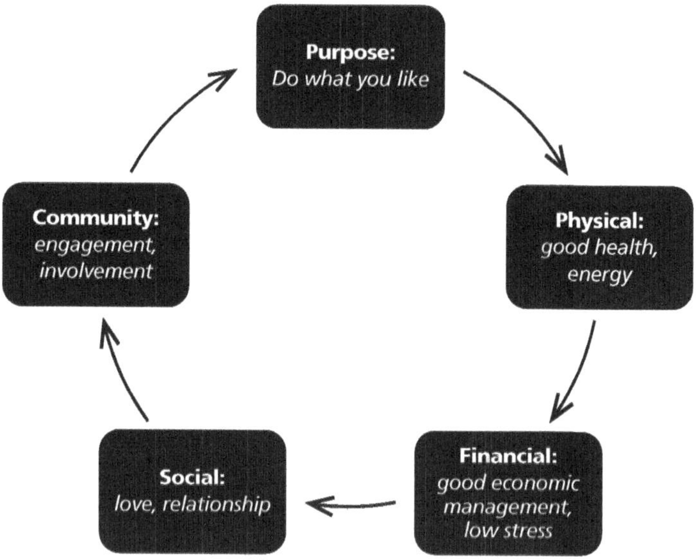

Figure 8.9 Gallup's What Does a "Great Life" Look Like. The Wellbeing Cycle. Source: Rath & Harper, 2010.

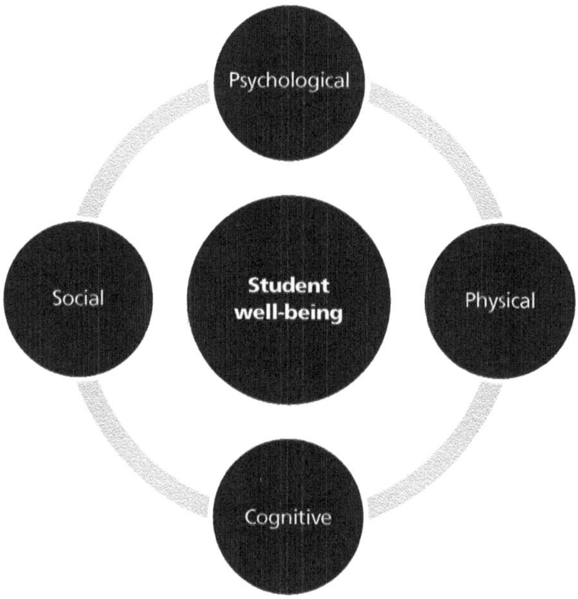

Figure 8.10 OECD's PISA Contributors to Student's Wellbeing. Source: Source: OECD. PISA 2015. https://www.oecd.org/pisa/Well-being-Infographics.pdf

wellbeing since 2015 is included as a variable to assess additional aspects of educational performance. Although students' wellbeing is one of the latest trends in education, it is drawing increasing attention supporting the development of the Educonomy.

The OECD effort to enhance students' wellbeing uncovers a critical need that education should not focus exclusively on the cognitive dimension, but must have balance with the psychological, physical, and social dimensions.

Composite of Human Centered Wellbeing

Figure 8.11 presents wellbeing as the base for human centered sustainability which is operationalized through the BSD ESTE model supported by the Educonomy and its three pillars. In this chapter, the quality economy is highlighted as the common denominator designed to continuously increase wellbeing and sustainability. Success in the Educonomy depends on the progress of the talent and agile economies in reaching world recognized standards of quality that I call *sustainable quality* (SQ).

Origin of the Quality Economy

Deming's quote at the beginning of this chapter points out that the essence of quality is the human being. I chose this quote carefully.

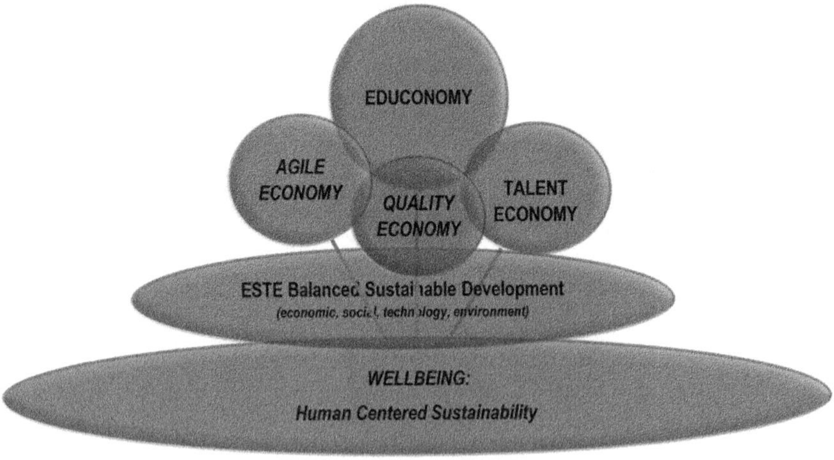

Figure 8.11 Composite of Human Centered Wellbeing and elements of sustainable development.

In the model I propose to strengthen the Educonomy, the development of the talent economy and the agile economy are external and unavoidable forces. Then at the personal level will be increasingly difficult to advance and attain wellbeing avoiding self improvement and education. Given that continuous talent development and agility will help optimize benefits and minimize costs of disruptions in the VUCA (volatile, uncertain, complex, ambiguous) environment. The same effects apply to organizations with respect to talent and agility. Organizations will not become sustainable if they lack the people with talent and agility required to manage disruptions of the 21st century. But the quality economy is propelled by forces internal to people and organizations. Quality is optional. It cannot be imposed. The individual and the organizations make the decision for transformation to adopt quality and the efforts and responsibilities that quality implies.

In spite of the benefits associated with the attainment of quality standards, quality achievements require deep understanding of human nature and economic processes leading to efficiency embedded in the continuous improvement to optimize the use of resourses that are limited.

Quality achievements that benefit all people link individual and collective efforts to systematically transform institutions. In spite of the optional or discretionary preference, it needs to be recognized that quality standards are increasingly important to determine success and sustainability.

The Quality Economy: Markets as Wellbeing Optimizers

The quality economy and quality standards are better deployed in free markets where the price system—or the *invisible hand* according to Adam Smith—is the most effective mechanism to synchronize and balance customer's demands with the producer's supply of products and services (Smith, 1759, 1776).

Freedom to choose among different alternatives offered, and transparency of the price system that activates markets, deters monopolies or oligopoly power in developed and developing countries worldwide, making a significant contribution to sustainable development. After World War II, Deming fostered the quality transformation, and the demand side and human wellbeing concepts were integrated as the priority development targets.

Quality systems introduced consumers' needs and wellbeing as fundamental elements that organizations use to attain high performance, productivity, and sustainability. Quality systems shift the supply-driven markets and economies that prevailed in the industrial age to demand-oriented organizations and economies that are propelled by better informed and educated consumers, aligned with advances and priorities of the Knowledge Economy.

In addition to the information provided by the price system, better informed customers use knowledge to demand quality in products and services. Freedom to choose allows consumers to press producers to continuously improve products and quality standards. In the quality economy, price continues to be an important signal but the quality of products and services is the highest pitch for customers to choose and make a decision to buy or accept a product or service.

Supply Driven Versus Demand Oriented Economy

In a supply-driven economy, price transparency is the only mechanism that can regulate what is produced and sold in the market, if there is no collusion or monopolistic power. Suppliers command what and how much to produce, and what price to sell contingent on market power. Powerful supplies of products or services that control a large part of a specific market acquire monopolistic or oligopolistic power that can control prices and hurt consumers.

The lower the amount of producers (concentration) and the larger the demand of consumers for their products or services, the higher the potential to control prices and to take advantage of and abuse consumers by suppressing competition.

In demand oriented economies, price continues to be an important part of the information for customers and users, but decisions are made based on additional information about quality standards, merit, and excellence of the producers of products and services that provide the best options to maximize the wellbeing of customers and users.

Quality Standards Deter Power Concentration and Price Controls

Quality standards provide incentive and promote high performance and constructive competition essential in deterring monopoly controls and oligopoly forces that obstruct the market efficiency that protects customers and users.

For practical purposes the concepts of consumer, customer, and client refer to people who pay merchants and organizations for products and services. User and recipient refer to people who may pay or receive products and services free of charge provided by agencies in the government sector. Both sectors are subject to the same consumer quality standards.

Fundamental Quality Economy Concepts

1. *Customers, consumers, clients.* Organizations exist because there are consumers or users who demand their products or services. Otherwise organizations do not have a reason to exist. Quality principles apply equally to the business and government sectors. Organizations exist to meet the needs and expectations of consumers and users in order to increase their wellbeing as a fundamental element to attain sustainability. Categories within this group are also called *external consumers.*
2. *Workers, employees,* also called *internal customers,* are essential in the production of products or services that organizations sell or deliver to meet the needs and demands of external consumers. Humanly speaking, workers and employees cannot meet the needs and expectations of external customers unless the organization first meets their needs. This is a fundamental principle that underlines the culture of quality in organizations and converges highly with the Aristotelian eudaimonic philosophy of wellbeing discussed at the beginning of the book, where an individual must self-cultivate first in order to better help others next.

The principles and practices of this people-centered quality model come from my book *Human Centered Management: The 5 Pillars of Organizational Quality and Global Sustainability* (Lepeley, 2017a). Quality principles and values were first applied to management in organizations within the productive sector as the base of economies and society. I am here adopting quality management principles and practices and adapting them to the economy. In 2001, I wrote the book *Management and Quality in Education. A Model for Evaluation* (Lepeley, 2001). It is included in the references. This is to demonstrate that quality standards apply to all scientific and professional fields that intend to increase wellbeing.

Quality and Fairness

I will show how the pursuit of continuous improvement and quality standards improve fairness and efficiency in market economies where people are free to choose among many alternatives. I have emphasized that achievement of quality standards is an option: quality it is a choice, it cannot be imposed. Quality efforts fail when there is no trust among people commonly in hierarchical organizations and where high controls and lack of trust are the norm.

While I was writing this chapter I received an update on organizational innovation from McKinsey, the global business consulting company I consult with frequently as a pioneer in change, agility, and innovation.[2] I copy the link for readers interested in learning details of how the quality principles and practices I have discussed are deployed by an outstanding U.S. organization. Greg Kalicker, the visionary CEO of an energy company, explains how a human centered management model applies to organizations in all sectors of the economy. Kalicker highlights the impact and effect of organizational simplicity, clear accountabilities, and agile planning processes that distinguish innovative companies. He also discusses the steps to achieve transformation starting with people, just as Deming did in relation to quality management (Deming, 1982a, 1994). Kalicker clarifies that *innovative organizations* come in all shapes and all sizes. His company was founded in 1989 and now has more than 1,800 employees in the United States. For the last 6 years his company, Hilcorp, has been among the top 100 best places to work in *Fortune* magazine and the Great Place to Work Institute, and it is the highest ranked company in its sector on both lists. Kalicker remarks his company began embracing agile practices long before these were buzzwords. He notes an important feature in innovation—his company is comfortable that only half of the goals emerging from the planning process are met. This provides evidence that the company accepts talent to test and fail as a necessary step for improvement.

A Human Centered Sustainable Quality Model

I studied economics and learned how to optimize and make the best use of scarce resources. But every person *lives economics on a daily* basis. The thing is that we are not aware that we are all constantly optimizing utility. But it was not until I was well advanced in my quality transformation that I realized the critical importance of understanding economic principles. I would not say that an economic background is essential to become a quality specialist, by any means—I have trained thousands of educators without economic or mathematical backgrounds that have achieved total quality transformation—but to teach quality management, an economic background helps significantly.

Everybody Likes Quality

Most people and organizations that fail to pursue quality standards and optimization, do not do so for lack of interest. It is for lack of understanding of the conditions, level of responsibility, commitment, and engagement with the specific methodology that leads to quality standards that hinders their pursuit. Some consultants project quality management and assessment models as very complex, analytical, and convoluted. Indeed, advancing the quality transformation is not a very easy task, but it is possible, efforts are worthwhile, and the benefits are outstanding.

When I conduct knowledge and attitude assessment sessions, prior to training people in organizations that will deploy my sustainable quality model, applicable to all industries, from business to education and from government to nonprofits to facilitate cross fertilizations, I train everybody in the organization, from top executives to cleaning personnel. Success of the quality transformation correlates highly the capacity of each person, with an organizational culture that promotes and shares values, knowledge and commitment with the quality transformation. All the people who work *in* and *for* the organization are invited to participate in all or parts of the quality training. The purpose is so that all share the same quality language, values, and assume the same level of responsibility for outcome to advance continuous improvement. Regardless of the job each one does, quality standards are the ultimate goal to optimize workers' wellbeing, leading to high performance, productivity, and competitiveness. Although an individual can learn quality principles and practices in a course to start the quality transformation, segmented efforts in organizations are discouraged because the participation of the organizational leaders is essential.

Quality Parity

In spite of the fact that National Quality Awards are in reality for top organizations with well advanced deployment of quality criteria, quality standards are not exclusively for elites of privileged people or organizations. Every person, regardless of the type of work, who is committed to personal improvement, has the potential to be successful. And who doesn't want to succeed?

The quality revolution starts with the transformation of the individual. I use the word revolution because the quality transformation is so deep and broad that any other adjective is deceptive. Once the individual can apply quality principles and practices to self-improvement, the transformed person perceives the world from a more positive dimension that applies to the meaning of life and interactions between people. When the individual understands the quality system, its application has no limit.

Be Aware of Fake Quality!

It often happens that when something becomes prominent and prestigious, useful and valuable, imitations escalate. Quality standards are no exception.

Quality sells well, so many unscrupulous parties abuse the term as a bite to catch a fish. Quality abuses abound among people unable to distinguish between quality as a systematic approach to continuous improvement and quality as a qualifying adjective.

How to distinguish fake from legitimate quality? We all have the opportunity to test it with simple examples. For example, if you call an organization and get a recorded message announcing that your conversation may be recorded for quality purposes, you have the optimal environment to test. Many callers ignore the fact that if you hear this announcement the customer has the right to have any problem solved by the agent during the course of that call to their entire satisfaction. If the representative is unable to solve it, or does not have the required soft skills—customer service skills—to help you, a supervisor should be called to duty to provide the promised quality service. Just mentioning quality standards implies that an immediate solution is an imperative.

But the quality culture has been anchored largely in organizations, so unless a person works in an organization deploying quality management, or has read about quality, not too many customers are aware of their responsibility for quality. Quality standards mean optimal customer service and immediate solution. Besides, people sometimes believe that complaining about an undesirable product or service may not be the best solution. Indeed, to promote quality standards, complaints are the way to go to improve standards. It may take time and effort, but it is a learning experience that pays high returns to customers and organizations.

From the point of view of promoting the quality culture, a central theme is the consumer's responsibility. Customers/consumers/users are as responsible for quality standards as are the producers, retailers, sellers, or service organizations. To show the importance of consumers' responsibility for quality standards I developed the consumer code of quality responsibility, shown in Table 8.2. Quality is a culture and it has benefits and costs. Those of us who are quality advocates need to work for it and demand quality when it is offered, but not provided.

Consumers Are Responsible for Quality Standards

The responsibility of consumers for quality is important because the benefits of quality are substantial not only for the individual but for organizations, the economy, and society at large. If Japan was able to assume responsibility and deploy a quality system that transformed its national culture, then why can't other nations achieve the same? This is the reason why countries

TABLE 8.2 Consumer Code of Quality Responsibility
Consumer's responsibility for quality standards
When you buy or receive a product or service that you are not satisfied with, do you take time and effort to inform the person/organization that sold you the product or provided you the service?
If you do not receive a satisfactory explanation for the lack of quality standards from the attendant, do you politely request to talk to a supervisor? At this point are you aware that you are investing your time to help the organization improve by providing your feedback?
Do you customarily assume your responsibility for quality to help improve organizations and the economy? Not only for your wellbeing, but for the wellbeing of customers who will come after you?
Do you take the time and make the effort to clearly inform the salesperson or clerk of your concerns conveying that your purpose is to help and you are doing a favor by identifying areas of needed improvement? Can you be sympathetic to an untrained salesperson who gets upset as a natural reaction of evidence of a lack of quality standards?

around the world have established national quality programs and awards to promote the national culture of quality.

Quality Economy Standards and High Performance

At the center stage of the quality economy is people's wellbeing. Wellbeing is unattainable unless some conditions are met and synchronized at the personal, organizational (micro), and the economical (macro) level. Among them are high levels of performance and productivity. Performance and productivity are commonly associated with organizational imperatives of profitability, but a less discussed side of high performance and profitability is the wellbeing people accrue from high performance and productivity.

At the personal level, performance refers to the completion of a task using the application of talent, knowledge, skills, and abilities. In the workplace, performance refers to meeting specific requirements to accomplish a task that contributes to the advancement of the mission of the organization. The level of performance is determined by the level of competency, skill, and knowledge necessary to accomplish the task. Performance can be low, medium, or high according to the level of achievement.

In April 2018, McKinsey and Company published two articles—"6 Elements to Create High Performing Cultures" (Dewar & Doucette, 2018) and "The 2 Cs of Management Excellence" (Gagnon, 2018)—that emphasized the importance of human centered quality standards in global organizations pursuing increases in performance, productivity, and competitiveness. These practical examples converge with the imperatives and help to understand implications of the talent, agile, and quality economies. They demonstrate dimensions of management that consolidate quality standards in organizations like McKinsey consulting with extensive experience among global customers.

In the article, "6 Elements to Create High Performing Cultures," Dewar & Doucette (2018) argue that organizational culture is the feature that most deeply differentiates high-performing organizations from the rest. Culture is defined as the cumulative effect of *what* people do and *how* they do it because people are the key that ultimately determines organizational performance. The study shares concerns and a query: If culture is so critical, then what do organizations need to do to attain a high-performing culture? The authors assess, accurately, that there is *no one-size-fits-all formula to success*. Based on their research and experience, they highlight six elements that organizations have to pay attention to in order to improve organizational culture. The six elements are shown in Table 8.3.

McKinsey (Dewar & Doucette, 2018) concludes that organizations need to treat culture as a top priority from the structural and strategic dimensions because it is an essential driver of performance. Organizations that successfully transform culture triple the returns for shareholders and wellbeing of people who work in the organization.

To complement the culture dimension of high performing organizations, McKinsey's Chris Gagnon (2018), focuses on three essential strategies organizations undertake to face challenges and opportunities to thrive in a fast-changing world. First, organizations need to integrate their culture around talent and agility with high-impact constructive leadership. Second, organizations use analytic methodologies to advance decisions faster. Last, high-performing organizations align people with consistent and personally significant principles that stimulate them to get engaged in creating stable processes, tasks, and roles that facilitate successful decision-making.

In his presentation, of "The 2 Cs of Management Excellence, "Gagnon (2018) highlights the importance of complementing consistency[3] and coherence[4] as a top characteristic of high performance management. When people in the organization know what they can expect from their leaders they look and trust them for guidance and direction. There are five reasons why the complement of consistency and coherence proves to be important to achieve quality standards.

1. Facilitates performance assessment and attracts people willing to thrive in the system. The clearer a leader can be the better at helping people to develop and thrive.

TABLE 8.3 6 Elements of High-Performing Organizational Culture

#	Element	Description
1	Identify necessary changes in people's behavior that enhance organizational performance	These behaviors need to be specially tailored to the organization needs and context because no two organizations are the same. Communicate these behaviors clearly so everyone understands what they look like in practice. This experience advances a shared vocabulary to mobilize for change and facilitates to monitor progress and improvement in a shifting organizational culture.
2	Uncover strong attitudes that obstruct change and propose agile approaches that foster a new culture	Attitudes people have about what they can and should do drive workplace behaviors. Often these attitudes originate away from work but the workplace has profound effect shaping beliefs and values that impact how people approach their work. All these clues—from how performance reviews are conducted to how meetings are run—are constantly sending signals to all about the "right organizational way" to think and behave. To successfully shift to a new set of behaviors, organization leaders at all levels need to identify old clues the organization sends that antagonize change and reframe them to improve agility and achieve behaviors.
3	Design and deploy major organizational initiatives to role model and reinforce the desired culture	People take their clues of organizational values from the signals leaders send. For a successful culture shift to take hold, the organization needs to spotlight leaders' behaviors and attitudes that deliver the most agile organization value and male it self-reinforcing. When desired behaviors and attitudes deliver value, they generate a magnetic pull within the organization that support leaders accelerating momentum about what and how is continuously improving.
4	Adjust work to create a coherent and valuable employee experience	Four energies shift attitudes and behaviors: articulating a compelling change story; leadership role modeling; skill building; and organizational changes to processes, systems, and incentives. The organization should execute a plan where each source of energy works in harmony shaping a coherent experience for all employees that minimizes confusion and accelerates the transition to a new culture.
5	Produce opportunities for individuals to overcome personal barriers to change	For organizations to change, people must change first. But this is challenging because everyone possesses a different level of willingness, ability and agility to change. Design an approach that help individuals recognize what propels their attitudes so they can make conscious choices about how to change attitudes associated with benefit of agility and the cost of the status quo for the individual and the organization.
6	Lead the journey in rigorous and employee-centric ways	Often a call for culture change tends to move from the top down through the ranks. But successful experiences take an "employee-back" view from the start when designing the change efforts. Culture change cannot be treated as a marginal project but must be an integral organizational collective endeavor.

Source: Dewar & Doucette (2018). McKinsey and Company

2. Sends a predictable message to others. Workers and customers prefer dependable responses rather than inconsistent jargon.
3. Avoids unpredictable management behavior with potential to breed disaffection and alienation which may lead to damaged trust and leadership ability.
4. Consolidates organizational clarity and drive productivity of employees who benefit from a well-defined management style.
5. Expedites assessment and measurement of effectiveness of organizational structures, strategies, and processes—from capital investment to talent development and from selection of personnel to financial sustainability.

Gagnon (2018) argues that not all recipes for leadership and not all leaders are equal. And, he is right. We have all seen in the course of our careers and in different industries, sectors, and countries, bosses (I don't call them leaders, review material where I differentiate between leaders and bosses) whose management styles suffocate instead of stimulate people and progress. To show a sample, Gagnon calls attention to a 2016 issue of *Fortune* magazine, where editors identified the world's "19 Most Disappointing Leaders,"[5] men and women from different industries, companies, and government sectors and countries. The common denominators are rigid command-and-control style and significant inconsistent management approaches. Gagnon's advice for leaders is to focus on the development of a people centered management philosophy that can be applied across the organization and to apply this philosophy consistently.

High Productivity and Human Wellbeing

Naturally, every human being prefers to attain high levels of performance and productivity with the limited resources that are available. Human beings unable to attain high performance and high productivity do not accomplish these objectives, not because they lack the human capacity to do so, but because they do not have the necessary level of knowledge and information. This argument is at the core of this book and is central to the debate that the main problem is not income inequality, but lack of quality in education for all. Quality education is required to help people discover their talents and optimize their chances for thriving and building inclusive societies.

Quality in Education

The following assumptions facilitate understanding of the core values embedded in quality education and the need for integration of different dimensions.

Quality Education From the Demand—Consumer Dimension

Students

Quality education is the tutoring and coaching students of all grades receive to help them discover and maximize innate talents, become self-sufficient, and develop a passion for continuous learning and the accumulation of knowledge, skills, and human capital necessary to attain a better life, a good job, and engaging work in a fast-changing world and workplace. The fundamental principle is based on Aristotelian eudaimonic philosophy of the need for self-cultivation and personal improvement as a precondition to make a better contribution to help others and improve society. *Students are direct consumers of education.*

Parents

Quality education is the outcome of schooling their children receive that will allow them to become self-sufficient persons maximizing their talent, knowledge, and skills to get a good job and make a meaningful contribution to improve society. Quality education is the multiplier that increases the rate of return (ROR) to investment in education. *Parents are indirect consumers of education.*

Workforce

Workforce is the talent, knowledge, skills, ingenuity, creativity, agility, and human capital that workers accrue from schooling that allows them to participate in agile organizations and contribute to increased performance, productivity, and competitiveness in a workforce with rapidly changing demands and facing surmounting disruptions. *The workforce is an indirect consumer of education.*

Society

Society gets the benefits from quality education through the behaviors and actions of learners and graduates, but also pays the costs for lack of quality in education generated from income inequality, poverty, and social and economic problems. The term used in economics is positive or negative externalities of education. *Society is an indirect consumer of education.*

Quality Education From the Supply–Producer Dimension

Educators are the most important professionals in a nation. They are responsible to develop present and future generations of students who will lead the society and the economy; to prepare students to face the challenges of today; and must be visionaries to anticipate and train students to be competent in the future, in a fast-changing world, workforce, increasingly competitive economies, and inclusive societies that must offer equal opportunities to all human talent. Educators should be compensated based on the education quality they give to students in relation to (a) professional responsibility compared with other professions impacting the present and future of many human beings, and (b) based on students' performance in discussions, respectful debates, soft skills, tolerance, leadership, and team building that contribute to education and institutional improvement, beyond memorizing data or standardized tests scores.

Educational leaders are major representatives and promoters of quality standards in education. They are responsible to position education as a crucial factor of sustainable social and economic development. Educators perform the most important profession of all. Are responsible to help all students build a better future. Educators need to be examples of excellence, high performance, productivity, team players. To fulfill such important responsibility educators need to be empathetic, possess strong Soft Skills, ethical principles and share the values and social responsibility embedded in such noble profession. Educators committed to quality standards seek continuous improvement of all their students who in turn project quality standards to the economy and help to shape inclusive societies.

Educational institutions: Human centered and agile management and leaders in social responsibility aiming to optimize the present and future wellbeing of learners of all ages; accountable for the impact graduates have in organizations where they work and participate, in the workforce, the economy, and society; and dependable to hire the most qualified and visionary educators and liable to challenge them to provide the best support to optimize students' talent and continuous learning in order to face the challenges of a fast-changing world, subject to continuous disruptions.

Educational systems: Decentralize decision-making on educational matters; increase schools' responsibility and agile capacity to solve local problems with focal solutions; collect information, manage databases, and offer reliable sources of data for schools to consult; monitor optimal alignment of education at all levels with changing demands in labor markets; inform schools and the workforce of gaps and misalignments; keep record of quality standards in education based on students' wellbeing beyond standardized testing; reward schools accordingly; use quality schools as examples and promote collaboration and cooperation to share and expand quality standards in the system; and voice recognition of educators as the profession with the highest level of responsibility and promote at all levels for quality education to become a national and unparalleled bastion.

Sustainable Quality Management in Education SQME

At the core of quality in education and the quality economy is the sustainable quality management for education (SQME) model. SQME is a human centered management model designed to facilitate the deployment and assessment of continuous improvement that is required to attain quality standards and sustainability of the Educonomy.

SQME is embedded in the critical impact that educators and educational institutions have on economic growth and inclusive societies, through the education students receive in their constant wellbeing pursuit in the Knowledge Economy. SQME supports educators and institutions in the discovery and enhancement of the talent and human capital of present and future generations. SQME is an agile mechanism to consolidate systematic efforts to achieve high performance and productivity, creating a virtuous cycle of continuous improvement and constructive competition, and expediting diffusion of quality standards and affiliation to a national culture of quality in education.

From the economic dimension, SQME is a demand-drive/supply-following model aimed to meet demands of the Knowledge Economy, maximizing the wellbeing of people, and minimizing cost of unavoidable disruptions in the VUCA environment.

From the management dimension, SQME is a knowledge-based system that educational institutions deploy to integrate planning, deployment, and assessment strategies to attain quality standards using the management model anchored in seven distinctive and complementary areas evaluating performance with the IPIEI sustainable quality cycle.

SQME's seven management areas are (a) consumers of education, (b) producers of education, (c) leadership for quality in education, (d) planning for institutional quality, (e) data management and technology, (f) quality management in supporting process, and (g) vertical and horizontal integration, benchmarking and environment care.

Table 8.4 shows the seven management areas and details of the elements that influence each area. The scores assigned to each management area represent the level of importance of each area within the model. These scores are used to measure improvement when the model is deployed and allow to differentiate performance from quality standards.

The SQME model is normative, it is not restrictive or regulatory. Aside from the seven management areas it does not impose variables, because each institution is different and no one schedule can fit all institutions. The leaders of each institution are responsible for identifying institutional and division

TABLE 8.4 Sustainable Quality Management in Education Model

	Management Area	Elements	Score in SQME
1	Education consumers: meeting demands and wellbeing	• Direct consumers of education: students • Indirect consumers of education: parents, the workforce	190
2	Education producers: refines, recognition, wellbeing	• Educators: qualification, Soft Skills, continuous training, performance evaluation, recognition • Educational support agents: quality pursuit	180
3	Leadership for quality	• Constructive leadership • Internal quality model • External quality guide • Institutional quality culture	170
4	Planning quality structure and strategies	• Design quality standards for principal and supportive educational processes • Identify quality standards for institutional structure: Mission and Vision • Set agile strategic planning to optimize use of talent and human capital aiming as sustainable quality	160
5	Data management and technology	• Knowledge management covering all institutional levels • Systematic data collection to support institutional performance, monitor results and secure continuous improvement • Big data management • Technology use, awareness of benefits & costs of automatization, Artificial Intelligence AI, robotic on agility and continuous improvement • Cyber security	100
6	Quality in supporting process	• Economic and financial structure and strategies • Talent and people management: recruitment, hiring, merit recognition promotion, firing principles & practices	100
7	Vertical and horizontal integration, benchmarking and environment care	• Vertical integration of the institutional with educational institutions that supply students and organizations in the workforce that hire graduates • Horizontal integration and benchmarking with similar institutions to share and propagate quality standards in the system to benefit all • Comprehensive care of the internal and external institutional environment. Awareness of benefits and individual responsibility for environment care to improve human wellbeing	100

quality leaders who identify the most relevant variables the institution consider relevant and optimal to assess progress in each management area.

SQME is designed for self-implementation. The book *Sustainable Quality in Education: A Model for Deployment, Assessment, and Sustainability* (Lepeley, 2019) contains necessary guidelines and information for assessment and scoring.

The SQME model uses the IPIEI Sustainable Quality Cycle to assess improvement in the elements of the seven management areas and to identify areas of improvement that require special attention. IPIEI has a central role in quality management as an evaluation mechanism that differentiates between performance and quality standards.

Figure 8.12 illustrates the five stages of progress of the IPIEI Sustainable Quality Cycle. IPIEI allows progress assessment of individual, process, and institutional performance. The % in each stage represents proportional advance of the variables selected ranging from an idea to continuous improvement. Where Stage 1: "New Idea" represents the basic creation and essential element for innovation, but it contributes 0% of the score because ideas are useful only when they advance to Stage 2: "A Plan" that is Stage 3: "Implemented," and Stage 4: "Evaluated" to secure Stage 5: "Continuous Improvement" which is fundamental to demonstrating quality standards.

The maximum score attainable in the SQME is 1,000 points. Table 8.5. shows a summary of the scores that represent performance, quality, and excellence (Lepeley, 2001, 2017a, 2018).

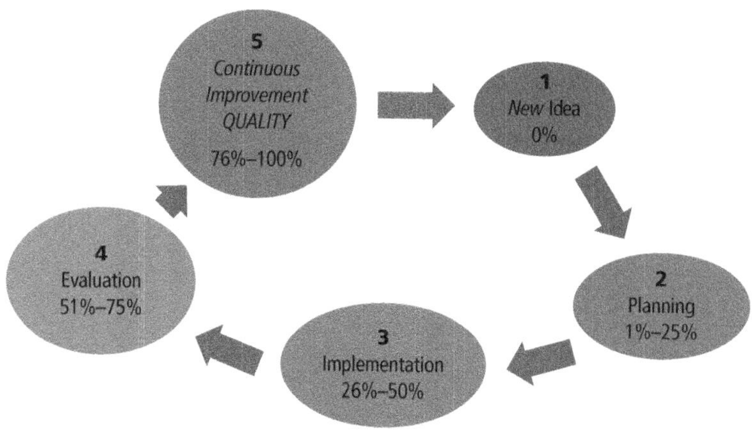

Figure 8.12 The five advance stages of the IPIEI Sustainable Quality Management Cycle

TABLE 8.5 Scoring Performance and Differentiating Quality Standards

SQM Model requirements	Score	Standard
Maximum	800–1.000 points	Excellence—Sustainable Quality
Over	+600	Minimum for quality standard
Below	600	*Performance. NOT QUALITY*

Table 8.5 clarifies the difference between performance and quality which is emphasized throughout the book. It shows the lowest score an organization needs in order to demonstrate it is advancing quality standards towards performance excellence after reaching objective score points based on the systematic evaluation of improvement in all the elements that represent the seven management areas of the SQME model. Continued efforts and assessment help educators, individuals involved in educational processes, and institutions align and integrate all of the elements in order to reach the highest score closer to the maximum 1,000 points. Although not all persons or institutions reach the maximum score, the implementation of quality, based on the systematical assessment of progress, significantly reduces the workload and enhances wellbeing at personal and work levels.

A Crucial Point to Remember: Quality Is a Road, *Not* a Destiny

The moment a person, institution, or nation believes quality has been reached and stops seeking continuous improvement, quality is impaired. Quality is continuous improvement.

Quality Standards in Education and High Workforce Performance: Paramount Features for Sustainable Development and Human Wellbeing

One of the biggest investments that human beings make in life is education. Whether a person pays directly for educational services or is subsidized by the government, the amount of time and personal effort are significant. These investments are worthwhile when the individual receives an education that helps to optimize potential wellbeing for a better life and a better job. But, when these basic human needs go unmet, education is nothing more than schooling that fails to fulfill its most salient responsibility.

If any organization or system produces faulty products or services that squander consumers' trust, the organization declines and eventually closes. Why should education be any different? On the contrary, education, as the most important industry in all nations, must provide quality standards so that all of its citizens can secure their wellbeing in synch with progress, inclusiveness, and sustainable development.

But, education has not always been considered a national bastion. To a large extent, this stems from quality objectives that are frequently ignored and commonly unmet, as I have highlighted throughout this book. The time has come to assume full responsibility for quality education.

Quality standards are required to ensure competence of present and future generations of students and graduates, to avoid misalignments that curtail workforce performance and productivity, and to reverse endemic income inequality. Lack of quality education is the main cause of the inequality drama. It is time to acknowledge this and take realistic corrective actions.

To date, education has not been a solution for the majority of people. Instead, education has become a burden for many. There are surmounting problems, gaps, shortcomings, deceptions, and disruptions. Societies worldwide are lagging behind in the *unfulfilled promises of education*, as the World Bank is now calling the lack of quality standards for all.

Gaps and problems have always existed in educational systems. Education is a large, complex industry that serves more people than any other industry in virtually every nation. Problems in education were less noticeable and even acceptable in the industrial era, when the education sector was considered the universal master in knowledge creation and transmission. Such authority gave the education sector an unprecedented monopoly of a supply-leading, demand-subdued industry. But things have changed drastically in the 21st century. Technology, connectivity, and globalization have unleashed the Knowledge Economy, thereby displacing education from its podium as primary knowledge producer and transmitter. Changes are propelling the voices of consumers, turning education into a demand-led enterprise.

Consumers of education, namely students, parents, the workforce, the economy, and society, are all pressing for change, demanding the development of talent and human capital, agility, and quality standards required to bridge persistent quality gaps.

Education quality is a stubborn problem that affects primarily low-income groups and countries worldwide and low income developing countries. But today, as never before, there is a consensus about the urgency to improve educational quality in all nations, sectors, industries, and among all constituencies. This includes compelling efforts underway by all of the international development organizations. The efforts I observe today are closely aligned with the quality education imperatives that I set in motion in 2002. At that time, the World Bank invited me to present my quality management in education model, and I did the same at the Inter-American Development Bank. However, the world was not ready then for a revolutionary educational shift. But now the claims for quality in education are louder and clearer. These voices cannot be ignored. Quality in education is no longer an option, it is an imperative.

Still, problems will continue, even increase, unless all constituencies recognize the need for change and assume responsibility for acknowledging the critical difference that exists between quality as a superficial and innocuous qualifying adjective, and the systematic human centered wellbeing focused on a multidisciplinary economic, management, and assessment methodology. These orderly efforts lead to the continuous improvement formula I unveiled in my presentations at the World Bank, the Inter-American Development Bank, and the Organization of American States (OAE) in Washington, DC. I then advised them of the importance of moving education quality to the top of the inclusive sustainable development agenda.

To solve quality problems in education, I propose the creation of the Educonomy supported by three fundamental and complementary pillars—the talent economy, the agile economy, and the quality economy. Strengthening of these pillars will propel nations to undertake results-oriented initiatives to restore education to its rightful place as the most essential, critical, and important national industry.

But education can only become the most important national industry by attracting the most highly qualified professionals. To educate with quality standards requires highly effective, human centered educators, whose merit, recognition, and rewards are unparalleled in comparison with other professions. Top educators should be measured by their success in inspiring students to become better persons first, and ultimately by how much they help improve society. (The inverse is impossible!) This shows explicitly that quality education is anchored in the Aristotelian eudaimonic philosophy of personal responsibility for self-cultivation, as I have emphasized throughout the book (Ryff, 2008). Let us highlight examples of our best teachers—at all levels—who inspired us to change our lives for the better. Nothing less is acceptable to attain quality standards for all in education. Educators unable to meet these difficult, yet most rewarding professional challenges, are better off in other fields and other professions.

Schools of education need to be national bastions of excellence in talent formation, agility, and quality training. Schools at all levels must hire the best to teach. Educators must be given full freedom and responsibility to use their knowledge, skills, and ingenuity to help students succeed in life; not exclusively in memorizing facts. Educational evaluation must move beyond memorization, getting passing grades, or achieving high scores on standardized tests. We now know that these outcomes are poor predictors of a better life and future wellbeing.

Decentralize educational systems make educators and institutions responsible for the continuous improvement of processes and programs and providing unequivocal evidence of achievement, helping students, the workforce, and societies overall. In the Knowledge Economy ethical nations, transparent governments and political systems, cannot allow underperforming educators or institutions continue hurting and harming students, economies, and societies.

Education is one of the largest national expenditures for most countries. It is financed mostly using public funds that belong to all citizens. This compels the education sector to be subject to the highest standards of transparency, accountability, and optimal use of limited resources. Nothing less is acceptable.

It is time to abandon and avoid dubious quality promises that have recurrently failed. Let us all, as a united global society, undertake personal and collective responsibility to attain quality education for all and begin now!

Notes

1. Constructive competition is the opposite of destructive competition. Quality standards are promoted through constructive competition—being the best and showing off quality standards to help others, individuals or organizations,

and nations to improve to secure sustainability. Quality people, teachers, organizations are fully aware that only if others assume and share responsibility for quality, will quality be sustainable. Otherwise disruptions may jeopardize good examples.

2. McKinsey interview with Greg Kalicker, CEO of Hilcorp Energy. "Digging Deep for Organizational Innovation." Retrieved from https://www.mckinsey.com/business-functions/organization/our-insights/digging-deep-for-organizational-innovation?cid=other-eml-alt-mkq-mck-oth-1804&hlkid=7e2f2da6c1cd4311a1d2c149d3a805ca&hctky=2823006&hdpid=7a46958e-e879-4514-8bd6-56926f9394f1
3. Consistency: conformity of an application based on logic, accuracy, or fairness.
4. Coherence: capacity of designing and presenting a unified whole.
5. http://fortune.com/2016/03/30/most-disappointing-leaders/

References

Argyris. (1957). *Personality and organizations: The conflict between system and the individual.* New York, NY: Harper & Row.

Aristotle. (350 BC). *Politics* (B. Jowett, Trans). Retrieved from http://classics.mit.edu/Aristotle/politics.1.one.html

Baldrige National Quality Award. (n.d.). Retrieved from https://www.nist.gov/baldrige/publications/baldrige-excellence-framework/education

Baldrige National Quality and Excellence Program in education. (n.d.). Retrieved from https://www.nist.gov/baldrige/self-assessing/baldrige-sector/education

Bardy, R. (2018). *Rethinking leadership: A human centered approach to management ethics.* Abington, England: Routledge.

Bardy, R., & Massaro, M. (2013). Stakeholder dialogues in transition economies: Educating and training leaders to build relations between investors and local communities. In I. Alon, V. Jones, & J. McIntyre (Eds.), *Innovation in Business Education in Emerging Markets* (pp. 162–178). Basingstoke, England: Palgrave Macmillan.

Barret, L. (2017). *How emotions are made: The secret life of the brain.* Boston, MA: Mariners Books.

Barriere, M., Owens, M., & Pobereskin, S. (2018). Linking talent to value. *McKinsey Quarterly.* April. https://www.mckinsey.com/business-functions/organization/our-insights/linking-talent-to-value

Barton, D., Carey, D., & Charan, R. (2018, March). An agenda for the talent-first CEO. *@McKinsey Quarterly.* Retrieved from https://www.mckinsey.com/business-functions/organization/our-insights/an-agenda-for-the-talent-first-ceo

Educonomy, pages 221–231

Barton, D., Farrell, D., & Mouresh, M. (2013, January). *Education to employment: Designing a system that works.* Retrieved from https://www.mckinsey.com/industries/social-sector/our-insights/education-to-employment-designing-a-system-that-works.

Batter, L. F. (2017). *You aren't at the mercy of your emotions: Your brain creates them.* TED@IBM. Retrieved from https://www.ted.com/talks/lisa_feldman_barrett_you_aren_t_at_the_mercy_of_your_emotions_your_brain_creates_them

Bazigo, M., De Smet, A., & Gagnon. C. (2015, December). *Why agility pays. McKinsey Quarterly.* Retrieved from https://www.mckinsey.com/business-functions/organization/our-insights/why-agility-pays

Beardsley, S. C. (2017). *Higher calling: The rise of nontraditional leaders in academia.* Charlottesville: University of Virginia Press.

Beardsley, S. C. (2018, February). Shaking up the leadership model in higher education. *McKinsey Quarterly.* Retrieved from https://www.mckinsey.com/business-functions/strategy-and-corporate-finance/our-insights/shaking-up-the-leadership-model-in-higher-education?cid=other-eml-alt-mkq-mck-oth-1802&hlkid=538065b444e24f4fbcb3e1457a3bebe1&hctky=2823006&hdpid=74f8582d-c665-4642-a44c-0a092312e3b7

Becker, G. (1964). *Human capital: A theoretical and empirical analysis, with special reference to education* (3rd ed.). Chicago, IL: The University of Chicago Press.

Becker, G. (1965). A theory of the allocation of time. *The Economic Journal, 75*(299), 493–517.

Becker, G. (1971). *The economics of discrimination.* Chicago, IL: University of Chicago Press.

Becker, G. (1974). A theory of social interactions. *Journal of Political Economy, 82*(6), 1063–1093.

Becker, G. (1976). *The economic approach to human behavior.* Chicago, IL: University of Chicago Press.

Becker, G. (1985, January). Human capital, effort, and the sexual division of labor. *Journal of Labor Economics, 3*(1), Part 2: Trends in Women's Work, Education, and Family Building, S33–S58.

Becker, G. (1991). *A treatise on the family.* Cambridge, MA: Harvard University Press.

Becker, G. (1992). *The economic way of looking at life* [Nobel Prize lecture]. https://www.nobelprize.org/uploads/2018/06/becker-lecture.pdf

Becker, G., & Ghez, G. (1975). *The allocation of time and goods over the life cycle.* New York, NY: NBER.

Becker, G., & Murphy, K. (2000). *Social economics. Market behavior in a social environment.* Boston, MA: Harvard University Press.

Beutell, N. J. (2013). The value of a college degree in relation to career, occupation, and organizational metamorphosis. In S. M. Natale & A. F. Libertella (Eds.), *Higher education: Economic and social mobility.* New York, NY: Global Scholarly.

Bill & Melinda Gates Foundation. (n.d.). *Who we are: Foundation fact sheet.* Retrieved from https://www.gatesfoundation.org/Who-We-Are/General-Information/Foundation-Factsheet

Boccia, R. (2015, July 29). *Social security: $39 billion deficit in 2014, insolvent by 2035.* Retrieved from https://www.heritage.org/social-security/report/social-security-39-billion-deficit-2014-insolvent-2035

Brooks, D. (2005, October 6). The Pillars of Cultural Capital. *The New York Times.* Retrieved from https://www.nytimes.com/2005/10/06/opinion/pillars-of-cultural-capital.html

Bush, G. W. (2001). *The 2001 President's Commission to strengthen Social Security.* https://www.ssa.gov/history/reports/pcsss/potus.html

Busteed, B. (2014a, July 2). It's the educonomy, stupid. *@Gallup News.* Retrieved from http://news.gallup.com/opinion/gallup/173954/educonomy-stupid.aspx

Busteed, B. (2014b, August 19). The education economy: America's next big thing. *Gallup Business Journal.* Retrieved from https://news.gallup.com/businessjournal/174275/education-economy-america-next-big-thing.aspx

Cadieux, S., & Heyn, M. (2018, April 18). *The journey to an agile organization at Zalando. @McKinsey & Company.* Retrieved from https://www.mckinsey.com/business-functions/organization/our-insights/the-journey-to-an-agile-organization-at-zalando?cid=other-eml-alt-mip-mck-oth-1804&hlkid=f44f036022584c7f96a7e6f5b270c7fa&hctky=2823006&hdpid=f84e8fae-4e89-4b4a-84a1-39b17653d791

Charan, R., Barton, D., & Carey, D. (2018). Talent wins: The new playbook for putting people first. Boston, MA: Harvard Review Press.

Chile Happiest Country in South America, Says UN Report. (2018, March 17). Retrieved from the Santiago Times website: https://santiagotimes.cl/2018/03/17/chile-happiest-country-in-south-america-says-un-report/

Christensen, C. (1997). *The innovator's dilemma. The revolutionary book that will change the way to do business.* Boston, MA: Harvard Business School Press.

Christensen, C., Raynor, M., & McDonald, R. (2015). What is disruptive innovation? *Harvard Business Review.* December Issue.

Clemens, M., Kenney, C., & Moss, T. (2007). The trouble with the MDGs: Confronting expectations of aid and development success. *World Development, 35*(5), 735–751.

Coleman, J. (1968). The concept of equality of educational opportunity. *Harvard Educational Review, 38*(1), 7–22.

Corrigan, G. (2017, April 12). *Lessons from Norway, the world's most inclusive economy.* Retrieved from https://www.weforum.org/agenda/2017/04/lessons-from-norway-the-world-s-most-inclusive-economy/

David, S. (2017). The gift and power of emotional courage (TEDWomen 2017). Retrieved from https://www.ted.com/talks/susan_david_the_gift_and_power_of_emotional_courage

David, S., & Congleton, C. (2013, November 1). Emotional agility. *Harvard Business Review.* Retrieved from https://hbr.org/product/emotional-agility/R1311L-PDF-ENG

Delsol, J. P., Lecausin, N., & Martin, E. (Eds.). (2017). *Anti-piketty: Capital for the 21st century.* Washington, DC: CATO Institute.

Deming, E. (1982a). *Out of the crisis.* Cambridge, MA: MIT Press.

Deming, E. (1982b). *Quality, productivity, and competitive position.* Cambridge, MA: MIT Press.

Deming, E. (1994). *The new economics for industry, government, and education.* Cambridge, MA: MIT Press.

Denison, E. (1985). *Trends in American economic growth, 1929–1982.* Washington, DC: The Brookings Institution.

DeSilver, D. (2016a, June 20). *More older Americans are working, and working more, than they used to.* Retrieved from http://www.pewresearch.org/fact-tank/2016/06/20/more-older-americans-are-working-and-working-more-than-they-used-to/

DeSilver, D. (2016b, September 1). *10 facts about American workers.* Retreived from http://www.pewresearch.org/fact-tank/2016/09/01/8-facts-about-american-workers/

Diener, E., Tay, L., & Oishi, S. (2013). Rising Income and the Subjective Well-Being of Nations. *Journal of Personality and Social Psychology. 104*(2), 267–276.

Dobbs, R., Manyika, J. & Woetzel, G. (2015). *No ordinary disruption: The four global forces breaking all the trends.* Philadelphia, PA: Perseus Books Group.

Drucker, P. (1954). *The practice of management.* New York, NY: Harper Business.

Drucker, P. (1959). *The landmarks of tomorrow.* New York, NY: Harper & Row.

Drucker, P. (1967). *The effective executive: The definitive guide to getting the right things done.* New York, NY: HarperCollins.

Easterlin, R. (1974). Does economic growth improve the human lot? Some empirical evidence. In R. David & R. Reder (Eds.), *Nations and households in economic growth: Essays in honor of Moses Abramovitz.* New York, NY: Academic Press.

Easterlin, R. (2004). The economics of happiness. *Daedalus, 133*(2), 26–33.

Easterlin, R., & Angelescu, L. (2009). *Happiness and growth the world over: Time series evidence of the happiness–income paradox.* IZA Working Paper #4060. Institute for Study of Labor (IZA). Bonn.

Eatock, D. (2015). *European Union pension systems: Adequate and sustainable?* (Briefing November 2015). European Parliamentary Research Service. Retrieved from http://www.europarl.europa.eu/RegData/etudes/BRIE/2015/571327/EPRS_BRI(2015)571327_EN.pdf

Edwards, S. (2018, April 21). Chile, un país destronado [Chile, a country out of a throne]. *@El Mercurio.* Retrieved from http://www.elmercurio.com/blogs/2018/04/21/59640/Chile-un-pais-destronado.aspx

Essens, P., & Lepeley, M. T. (2018). From stress to wellbeing: Is buffering stress enough? In P. Ochoa, M. T. Lepeley, & P. Essens, P. (Eds.), *Wellbeing for sustainability in the global workplace* (pp. 76–84). Abington, England: Routledge.

European Commission (2000). *Early School Leavers. Pag.1.* https://ec.europa.eu/info/sites/info/files/european-semester_thematic-factsheet_early-school-leavers_en_0.pdf

European Commission (2009). *Sustainability Report 9.* European Economy 9. 2009. http://ec.europa.eu/economy_finance/publications/pages/publication15998_en.pdf

European Foundation of Quality Management EFQM. (n.d.). EFQM award history. Retrieved from http://www.efqm.org/what-we-do/recognition/efqm-award-history

Freedom House. (2018). *Freedom in the world 2018.* https://freedomhouse.org/report/freedom-world/freedom-world-2018

Frey, B. (2010). *Happiness: A revolution in economics.* Cambridge, MA: MIT Press.

Frey, B., & Stutzer, A. (2007). *Economics and psychology: A promising new cross disciplinary field.* Cambridge, MA: MIT Press.

Gallup. (n.d.). 2018 *global great jobs briefing: 3 billion still looking for great jobs.* Available at https://news.gallup.com/reports/233375/gallup-global-great-jobs-report-2018.aspx?g_source=link_NEWSV9&g_medium=SIDETOP&g_campaign=item_233459&g_content=2018%2520Global%2520Great%2520Jobs%2520Briefing

Gallup Report. (2015). *Lack of teacher engagement linked to 2.3 million missed workdays.* http://news.gallup.com/poll/180455/lack-teacher-engagement-linked-million-missed-workdays.aspx

Gallup. (2017). State of the global workplace. Retrieved from https://www.gallup.com/workplace/238079/state-global-workplace-2017.aspx?utm_source=2013StateofGlobalWorkplaceReport&utm_medium=2013SOGWReportLandingPage&utm_campaign=2013StateofGlobalReport_Redirectto2017page&utm_content=download2017now_textlink

Gagnon, C. (2018, April 5). *The 2 Cs of management excellence.* Retrieved from https://www.mckinsey.com/business-functions/organization/our-insights/the-organization-blog/the-2-cs-of-management-excellence

Global Competitive Index. (2018). World Economic Forum.

Greenhouse J., & Beutell, N. (1985). *Sources of conflict between work and family roles.* The Academy of Management Review, 10(1), 76–88. Retrieved form https://www.researchgate.net/publication/259309989_Source_of_Conflict_Between_Work_and_Family_Roles

Hahneman, D., & Tversky, A. (1979). Prospect theory. An analysis of decision making under risk. *Econometrica, 47*(2), 263–291.

Hanushek, E. (2011). The economic value of higher teacher quality. *Economics of Education Review, 30,* 466–479.

Hanushek, E. (2013). Economic growth in developing countries: The role of human capital. *Economic Education Review, 37,* 204–212. Helliwell, J., Layard, R., & Sachs, J. (2017). *World Happiness Report.* Retrieved from http://worldhappiness.report/ed/2017/

Heritage Foundation. (2018). *2018 index of economic freedom.* https://www.heritage.org/index/

Illanes, P., Lund, S., Mourshed, M., Rutherford, S., & Tyreman, M. (2018, January). *Rethinking and reskilling workers in the age of automation.* McKinsey Global Institute. https://www.mckinsey.com/featured-insights/future-of-work/retraining-and-reskilling-workers-in-the-age-of-automation

Ingersoll, R., Merrill, L., & May, H. (2014, July). *What are the effects of teacher education and preparation on beginning teacher attrition?* (Research Report 82). Retrieved from http://www.cpre.org/sites/default/files/researchreport/2018_prepeffects2014.pdf

International Monetary Fund. (2018). *World economic outlook, April 2018 cyclical upswing, structural change.* Retrieved from https://www.imf.org/en/Publications/WEO/Issues/2018/03/20/world-economic-outlook-april-2018

Isenberg, D. (2010). A big idea. How to start an entrepreneurial revolution. *Harvard Business Review.*

Isenberg, D. (2011). *The entrepreneurship ecosystem strategy as a new paradigm for economic policy principles for cultivating entrepreneurship.* Babson Entrepreneurship Ecosystem Project. Babson College. MA. http://www.innovationamerica.us/images/stories/2011/The-entrepreneurship-ecosystem-strategy-for-economic-growth-policy-20110620183915.pdf

Isenberg, D. (2014). What an entrepreneurship ecosystem actually is. *Harvard Business Review.* May.

Kaufman, S. B. (2013). *Ungifted: Intelligence redefined: The truth to talent, practice, creativity and the many paths to greatness.* New York, NY: Basic Books.

Kirp, D. (2018, March 22). Money matters in education, as long as you spend it at the right time and on the right students. *Los Angeles Times.* Retreived from http://www.latimes.com/opinion/op-ed/la-oe-kirp-money-in-education-20180322-story.html

Klein, D., & Daza, R. (2013). Gary S. Becker. Ideological profiles of economic laurates. *Econ Journal Watch, 10*(3), 285–291.

Kritzer, B. E. (2005). Individual accounts in other countries. *Social Security Bulletin, 66*(1). Retrieved from https://www.ssa.gov/policy/docs/ssb/v66n1/v66n1p31.html

Kumar, R. (2017, January 30). Critics of the sustainable development goals were wrong. Here's why. *@World Economic Forum.* Retrieved from https://www.weforum.org/agenda/2017/01/turns-out-sdg-critics-were-wrong/

Kuschel, K., & Lepeley, M. T. (2016a). Women start-ups in technology: Literature review and research agenda to improve participation. *Int. J. Entrepreneurship and Small Business, 27*(2/3), 333–346.

Kuschel, K., & Lepeley, M. T. (2016b). Copreneurial women in start-ups: Growth-oriented or lifestyle? An aid for technology industry investors. *Academia Revista Latinoamericana de Administración, 29*(2), 1–19.

Lepeley, M. T. (1996). *Challenges for universities in the new millennium in the new role of universities: An initial inquiry.* Foundation for the Advancement of Higher Education. Chile.

Lepeley, M. T. (1987). *Higher education and economic development: The case of Chile.* Mimeograph. Miami, FL: University of Miami Archives.

Lepeley, M. T., (2001). *Management and Quality in Education. A Model for Evaluation.* McGraw-Hill Latin America. In Spanish. Gestión y Calidad en Educación. Un Modelo de Evaluación.

Lepeley, M. T. (2002, December). Quality management in higher education: A condition to maximize the benefits of globalization. *Journal of Education.* Catholic University of Chile.

Lepeley, M. T. (2017a). *Human centered management: 5 pillars of organization quality and sustainability.* Abington, England: Routledge.

Lepeley, M. T. (2017b). Bhutan's gross national happiness: An approach to human centred sustainable development. *South Asian Journal of Human Resource Management, 4*(2), 174–184.

Lepeley, M. T. (2018). Wellbeing and gender parity in the workforce: Need for a new global approach. In P. Ochoa, M. T. Lepeley, & P. Essens (Eds.), *Wellbeing for Sustainability in the Workforce* (pp. 15–31). Abington, England: Routledge.

Lepeley, M. T. (2019). *Eduquality. Human Centered Management in Education. A Model for Deployment, Assessment and Sustainability.* Charlotte, NC: Information Age.

Lepeley, M. T., & Albornoz, C. (2013). *Advancing people skills in business education in Chile.* In I. Alon, V. Jones, & J. R. McIntyre (Eds.), Innovation in business education in emerging markets (pp. 27–42). Basingstoke, England: Palgrave Macmillan.

Lepeley, M. T., Kuschel. K., Neubell, N., Pouw, N., & Eijdenberg, E. (Eds.). (2019). *Wellbeing of women in entrepreneurship. A global perspective.* London, England: Routledge.

Lepeley, M. T., von Kimakovitz, E., & Bardy, R. (Eds). (2016). *Human centered management in executive education.* Basingstoke, England: Palgrave Macmillan.

Majluf, N. (2016). Teaching human centered management to engineering students: A personal account. In M. T. Lepeley, E. von Kimakowitz, R. Bardy (Eds.), *Human Centered Management in Executive Education* (pp. 156–170). Abington, England: Routledge.

Malthus, T. (1798). *An essay on the principle of population.* Oxford, England: Oxford University Press.

Martin, R. (2014, October). *The rise (and likely fall) of the talent economy. Harvard Business Review.* Retrieved from https://hbr.org/2014/10/the-rise-and-likely-fall-of-the-talent-economy

Maslow, A. H. (1943). A theory of human motivation. *Psychological Review, 50,* 370–396.

Maslow, A. H. (1954). *Motivation and personality.* Oxford, England: Harpers.

Mauldin, J. (2017, October 3). *The pension storm is coming to Europe: It may be the end of Europe as we know it.* Retrieved from https://www.forbes.com/sites/johnmauldin/2017/10/03/the-pension-storm-is-coming-to-europe-it-may-be-the-end-of-europe-as-we-know-it/#566308a71a5c

Mayo, E. (1933). *The human problems of an industrial civilization.* London, England: Routledge.

McDonald, M. (2018, January 3). Do your measures make employees mad? Or motivate them? *Gallup Blog.* http://news.gallup.com/opinion/gallup/224342/performance-measures-motivate-madden-mployees.aspx?g_source=Gallup+Blog&g_medium=sidebottom&g_campaign=tiles

McGregor, D. (1960). *The human side of the enterprise.* New York, NY: McGraw-Hill.

McKinsey & Company (2018). *Winning with talent management strategy.* August. https://www.mckinsey.com/business-functions/organization/our-insights/winning-with-your-talent-management-strategy

Michaels, E., Handfield-Jones, H., & Axelrod, B. (2001). *The war for talent.* New York, NY: McKinsey & Company.

Ochoa, P., Lepeley, M.T., & Essens, P. (Eds.). (2018). *Wellbeing for sustainability in the global workplace.* London, England: Routledge.

OECD's Better Life Index. (n.d.). Work–life balance. Retrieved from http://www.oecdbetterlifeindex.org/topics/work-life-balance/

Organization for Economic Cooperation and Development OECD. (2013). *Education at a glance.* http://www.oecd.org/education/eag2013%20(eng)-FINAL%2020%20June%202013.pdf

Organization for Economic Cooperation and Development OECD. (2015) *PISA. Volume III. Students' Well-Being.* http://www.oecd.org/education/pisa-2015-results-volume-iii-9789264273856-en.htm

Organization for Economic Cooperation and Development OECD. (2018). *Education at a glance.* https://read.oecd-ilibrary.org/education/education-at-a-glance-2018_eag-2018-en#page3

Passy, J. (2018, February 14). Why Americas teacher shortage is going to get worse. *New York Post.* Retrieved from https://nypost.com/2018/02/14/why-americas-teacher-shortage-is-going-to-get-worse/

Pew Research Center (2015). *Raising kids and running a household: How working parents share the load. In close to half of two-parent families, both mom and dad work full time.* http://www.pewsocialtrends.org/2015/11/04/raising-kids-and-running-a-household-how-working-parents-share-the-load/

Petroff, A. (2017, April 13). Europe's lost generation: Young, educated, and unemployed. *@CNN Business.* Money. Retrieved from http://money.cnn.com/2017/04/13/news/economy/europe-youth-unemployment-france/index.html

Pew Research Center. (2013, December 11). Chapter 5: Balancing work and family. Retrieved from http://www.pewsocialtrends.org/2013/12/11/chapter-5-balancing-work-and-family/

Pfeffer, J. (2018). *Dying for a paycheck: How modern management harms employee health and company performance—and what we can do about it.* New York, NY: Harper Collins.

Piketty, T. (2013). *Capital in the 21st century.* Cambridge, MA: Harvard University Press.

Pinker, S. (2018). *Enlightenment now: The case for reason, science, humanism, and progress.* New York, NY: Penguin Random House.

Powell, W., & Snellman, K. (2004). The knowledge economy: Annual review of sociology, 30, 199–220. Retrieved from https://web.stanford.edu/group/song/papers/powell_snellman.pdf

Psacharopulos, G. (Ed.). (1987). *Economics of education: Research and studies.* Oxford, England: Pergamon.

Psacharopoulus, G. (2015). *Benefits and cost of education targets for the post-2015 consensus.* Copenhagen Consensus Center for Education Assessments Papers. Retrieved from https://www.copenhagenconsensus.com/sites/default/files/education_assessment_-_psacharopoulos_0.pdf

Psacharopoulos, G., & Sanyal, B. (1981). *Higher education and employment: The Iiep experience in five less developed countries* (Fundamentals of Educational Planning). Washington, DC: United Nations Educational Division.

Psacharopulos, G., & Tzannatos, Z. (1992). *Women's employment and pay in Latin America: Overview and methodology* (World Bank Regional and Sectoral Studies). World Bank.

Psacharopoulos, G. & Woodhall, M. (1986). Education for development: An analysis of investment choices. Washington, DC: Oxford University Press.

Rath, T., & Harper, J. (2010). *Wellbeing: The five essential elements.* New York, NY: Gallup Press.

Ryff, C. (2008). Knowing thyself and become more you: An eudaimonic approach to psychological wellbeing. *Journal of Happiness Studies, 9,* 13–39.

Ryff, C., & Keyes, C. (1995). The structure of psychological wellbeing revisited. *Journal of Personality and Social Psychology, 69*(4), 719–727.

Samuel, J. (2016, March 6). *Europe faces pension predicament: Mismatch of lifespans and birthrates means too few workers are paying into state pension plans.* Retrieved from https://www.wsj.com/articles/europe-faces-pension-predicament-1457287588?utm_campaign=JM-305&utm_medium=ED&utm_source=for

Samuelson, P. (1980). *Samuelson economics (11th edition).* New York, NY: McGraw-Hill.

Schultz, T. W. (1960). Capital formation by education. Journal of Political Economy, 68(6), 571–583.

Schultz, T. (1961). Investment in human capital. *The American Economic Review, 51(1), 1–17.*

Schultz, T. (1962). *Investment in human beings.* Chicago, IL: University of Chicago Press.

Schultz, T. (1963). *The economic value of education.* New York, NY: Columbia University Press.

Schultz, T. (1971). *Investment in human capital: The role of education and of research.* New York, NY: Free Press.

Schultz, T. (1972). *Investment in education: Equity-efficiency quandary.* Chicago, IL: University of Chicago Press.

Schultz, T. (1974). *Economics of the family: Marriage, children, and human capital.* Chicago, IL: University of Chicago Press.

Schumpeter, J. (1934). *The theory of economic development. And inquiries into profits, capital, credit, interest and business cycle.* London, England: Routledge.

Schwab, K. (2016, January 14). *The fourth industrial revolution: What it means, how to respond.* World Economic Forum. Retrieved from https://www.weforum.org/agenda/2016/01/the-fourth-industrial-revolution-what-it-means-and-how-to-respond/

Simon. H. (1947) *Administrative behavior: A study of decision-making processes in administrative organizations.* New York, NY: The Free Press.

Smith, A. (1759). *The theory of moral sentiment.* Printed by Millar, A. London & Kincaid, A., Bell, J. Edinburg.

Smith, A. (1776). *The wealth of nations.* Batman Classics.

Smith, R. (2018, February 9). The Dutch have the best work–life balance. Here's why. Retrieved from https://www.weforum.org/agenda/2018/02/the-dutch-have-the-best-work-life-balance-here-s-why/

Spence, M. (2018, April). *Retraining and reskilling to ease the strain of automation.* McKinsey Global Institute. https://www.mckinsey.com/featured-insights/future-of-work/retraining-and-reskilling-to-ease-the-strain-of-automation

Srinivasan, A., & Kurey, B. (2014, April 1). Creating a quality culture. *Harvard Business Review.* Retrieved from https://hbr.org/product/creating-a-culture-of-quality/F1404A-PDF-ENG

Stevenson, B., & Wolfers, J. (2008). *Economic growth and subjective well-being: Reassessing the Easterlin Paradox.* National Bureau of Economic Research NBER. Working paper # 14282. August.

Steverman, B. (2018, May 4). *This Facebook co-founder wants to tax the rich: Chris Hughes thinks $290 billion a year is small price to pay for equality.* Retrieved from https://www.bloomberg.com/news/features/2018-05-04/facebook-co-founder-chris-hughes-wants-universal-basic-income

Suri, R. (2017). *Who we are.* Retrieved from https://www.nokia.com/en_int/about-nokia/who-we-are/group-leadership-team/rajeev-suri-president-and-chief-executive-officer-ceo

Tarr, R., & Weeks, J. (2016). Soft skills: Demands and challenges in the United States workplace. In M. T. Lepeley, E. von Kimakowitz, R. Bardy, (Eds.), *Human Centered Management in Executive Education* (pp. 49–60). London, England: Routledge.

Todd, P., Gigerenzer, G. (2000). Précis of Simple Heuristics that makes us smart. *Behavioral and Brain Sciences. 23,* 727–780.

Torkington, S. (2016, October 13). *Everything you need to know about neuroeconomics.* Retrieved from https://www.weforum.org/agenda/2016/10/everything-you-need-to-know-about-neuroeconomics/

Townsend, M., Surane, J., Orr, E., & Cannon, C. (2017, November 8). America's 'retail apocalypse' is really just beginning. *@Bloomberg*. Retrieved from https://www.bloomberg.com/graphics/2017-retail-debt/

United Nations. Population Division. (2015). *World population prospects 2015 Revision*.

United Nations (2015). *17 sustainable development goals*. https://sustainable development.un.org/?menu=1300

UNESCO Institute for Statistics. (2016). *Who pays for what in education: The real costs revealed through national education accounts*. Retrieved from http://uis.unesco.org/sites/default/files/documents/who-pays-for-what-in-education-national-revealed-through-accounts-2016-en_0.pdf

UNESCO Institute for Statistics. (2017, September). *More than one-half of children and adolescents are not learning worldwide* (Fact sheet no. 46). Retrieved from http://uis.unesco.org/sites/default/files/documents/fs46-more-than-half-children-not-learning-en-2017.pdf

Vartiainen, J. (2017). The future of the European welfare state: The intriguing role of demographics. *European View, 16*(1), 131–139. Retrieved from https://link.springer.com/article/10.1007/s12290-017-0428-8

Veenhoven, R. and F. Vergunst (2014). The Easterlin illusion: Economic growth does go with greater happiness. *International Journal of Happiness and Development, 1*(4), 311–343.

World Bank. (2018). *Learning to realize education's promise*. Washington, DC: Author. Retrieved from http://www.worldbank.org/en/publication/wdr2018

World Economic Forum. (2017). *Global agenda: World economic forum annual meeting 2017: Responsive and responsible leadership*. Retrieved from http://www3.weforum.org/docs/WEF_AM17_Report.pdf

Printed and bound by CPI Group (UK) Ltd, Croydon, CR0 4YY

15/09/2026

14962335-0002